Xmas 1995

Mother,
love from
Ann

The
Generous
Garden

Louise Odier and Painted Lady
Wood engraving by Yvonne Skargon
commissioned for the cover of HORTUS 6 (Summer, 1988)

The
Generous
Garden

A Second Anthology of Garden Writing
from
HORTUS

Edited by David Wheeler

ALAN SUTTON

1991

This anthology first published in 1991 by
Alan Sutton Publishing · Phoenix Mill
Far Thrupp · Stroud · Gloucestershire

British Library Cataloguing in Publication Data

The generous garden.
I. Wheeler, David   II. Hortus
712.6
ISBN 0–86299–997–9

Typeset by Gloucester Typesetting Services and Ronset
in Monotype (hot metal) Van Dijck (203).
Printed in Great Britain by
The Bath Press, Avon.

Foreword

RONALD BLYTHE

If any one single conclusion is to be drawn from this welcome second collection of HORTUS essays it is that those of us who garden also have a most varied plant-linked further cultivation in common. *En passant* though we may have acquired it, many of us do eventually find ourselves in possession of a garden universe, a realm of shared talk and understanding. But where, one has to ask, could all this plant-based recollection, history and philosophy find expression if there was no HORTUS? Which is why in such a short time this unique magazine has become a necessary pleasure for 'like minds'. It has established itself as a forum for a special kind of garden talk and a particular kind of garden learning, and there is nothing quite like it. Horticulture – even its flights of fantasy – must be the sanest of human activities. One of my favourite images is of the great Stuart gardener John Tradescant collecting species in the midst of a battle. Somewhere in this anthology Mirabel Osler observes, 'The word "species" has immense power', and she is right. But as this book's title insists, it is a giving power and these twenty-seven contributions are a revelation of the generosity of gardens. Toil we may, but what repayments!

The biographical contribution to this book is outstanding. It reveals that what these devoted plantsmen and women gave to their gardens and received from them amounted to a quid pro quo in generosity, and that what they gave to posterity was something which is wonderfully open-handed. Take Audrey le Lièvre's scholarly account of the life of Max Leichtlin, an amiable bachelor who gradually forsook the prosperous family business to search for plants, at first for Kew and other national collections, but soon for his own two acres on the edge of Baden-Baden. To many of us before this enthralling little biography of some twenty-six pages, Leichtlin's was not much more than an academic-sounding name in a botanical history; thus to meet him full-faced, as we do here, has the effect of completely altering our perception of the nineteenth-century plant-hunter-cum-nurseryman. Like Graham Thomas, who also gets a thought-provoking study here, Leichtlin was something of a loner, and with a loner's strength of purpose. We are reminded that extraordinary

gardeners must, in the nature of things, be unusual individuals, the
pattern of whose lives give us pause, as they used to say. Leichtlin's
discipline was to look at his plants several times a day. Such information is disturbing and accusative. Do not we all spend most of our day
gardening and not looking? To toil without contemplation – not to
actually watch the daily progress of some species – this he would have
found a negative activity.

The Leichtlin and Thomas biographies are balanced by Beth
Chatto's 'thank you' to her formidable and unconscious mentor Mrs
Desmond Underwood. Known in the proto flower-arrangement world
as 'the Silver Queen', Mrs Underwood could not have guessed where
her influence would lead the girl next door. Mrs Chatto describes her
first teacher, a grand, rather sad woman towards whom life had not
been at all generous, but who yet was able to give her what a twenty-
year old needs most, the right direction. The anthology is full of
homage and gratitude but this is the most moving. Comedy and an
affectionate kind of tartness are used by John Francis to sum up
Beverley Nichols (a once bestselling garden writer), and by Cavan
O'Brien to evoke the garden designer John Fowler's way with his
weekend guests, which was immediately to set them to work. Staying with Fowler in his restored Hampshire hunting lodge meant
endless chores and good meals. The subject of work and how to deal
with it seems to find its way on to every page of this book. Gardening
is about the most work-generous of all human activities, and nowhere
is there any more upsetting a man-made creation than a garden denied
its basic requirement of continual attention. Gardens are made for
leisure, but not the gardener's leisure. 'Why garden?' asks Mirabel
Osler. Looking around at an England crammed with gardens, countless numbers of which are unknown to the garden writer, yet glorious,
she sees a nation possessed. Certainly, we are all more generously
inclined towards our garden, be it only a patch, than to almost anything else. And so, since nobody does anything for nothing, there
must be great rewards. The writers make various stabs at trying to
define these but soon give up, the rewarding nature of gardens being
obvious. And it is true, as one reads on, that gardening, whilst devour-
ing so much of our energy, knows no limits when it comes to feeding
our senses. The hardest lesson for the gardener to learn is inactivity.
How to be still. How to walk through what we have created, looking,
listening and smelling, beginning as with prayer for just a minute or

two, and then stepping-up the idleness. People become oppressed by gardening because they do not use their gardens as observatories – even oratories. The HORTUS writers all possess an intuitive understanding of the 'watching' factor. Maybe we should have a text over our favourite flower bed – 'Remember Max Leichtlin'. Dig, but also drift.

The plant essays in this volume are unusual and a delight. Tulips in wild grass, day-lilies (*Hemerocallis*), homely beauties in this country, but with sensuous Asian antecedents; orchids, of course, and cushion saxifrages. The latter allows Nigel Colborn to pay homage to Valerie Finnis, a distinguished gardener by inheritance, as it were, as she is a third-generation plantswoman in her family, and a celebrated plant photographer. Illustrating species has been an essential part of the botanist's and gardener's business from the earliest times, and HORTUS itself recognises this in printing a fine range of the work of flower and garden artists, and has become closely identified with drawings by Simon Dorrell and wood-engravings by Yvonne Skargon. One of the most famous portraits of a gardener, that of 'Mr Rose, the royal Gardener presenting to King Charles II the first pineapple raised in England', is witily analysed by Hermia Oliver. Could Rose have raised the pineapple? That has long been the question. Yes, he could, is the answer – discovered via much detective work.

Some of the contributors are traveller-gardeners, an ancient race. We follow them on an intellectual and lyrical excursion to Ninfa, Fontevraud Abbey, the Alhambra, and, poignantly, to that England in India, the cool hill stations, especially Simla. Gardens almost everywhere in the twentieth century are the evidence of vast journeys and are a vegetable social history. As at Ninfa and Fontevraud, they are ideal living continuities for places which, without them, would be scenes of abandonment and death. But, as we know, fortunate is anyone whose garden includes a bit of ruin for a rose to cling to. Ninfa was an entire ruined town just waiting to be gardened. The role of architecture in regulating and inspiring gardens, or simply dramatising them, has always been enormous, and the HORTUS writers are clearly enthralled by it; also by re-creating medieval gardens in medieval courts and cloisters, and Raj gardens where the memsahibs dreamed of Surrey.

Finally, praise has to go to those writers who guide us through the plotted gardens of novels and stories. Such scenes are notorious for horticultural fictions, though not those described by Jane Austen, Elizabeth Bowen, M. R. James and Lewis Carroll. Nancy-Mary Goodall examines 'the unattainable garden' of so much children's literature, and the preoccupying theme of the walled garden in so many classics. There can be little doubt that the intense garden privacy so beloved by the British is rooted in tales by Frances Hodgson Burnett, E. Nesbitt and Philippa Pearce. Jane Austen, of course, carries gardens into 'grounds' and utilises them correctly for sudden revelations, escape, exercise and social calamities. Also for love. Also for funny snobbery. And Elizabeth Bowen remains an exquisitely accurate authority on the beauties and subtleties, human and floral, of London gardens.

The HORTUS anthologies are an imaginative development of the scientific and aesthetic traditions of garden-writing, and this second volume is purely for instruction and pleasure.

RONALD BLYTHE

Editor's Introduction

This second collection from HORTUS emanates from Wales. The first anthology – *By Pen & By Spade* – celebrated the journal's first year of life. This volume delves into the second year, 1988. In 1987 HORTUS was published from a small, brick cottage on the outskirts of Farnham on the Hampshire/Surrey border. Its quarter-acre garden was made entirely on a south-facing sandy slope where Mediterranean plants thrived in free-draining soil. Around the terrace I grew irises whose rhizomes baked assuredly in the summer sun, and there were clouds of grey-leaved artemisias and many herbs handy to the kitchen door. Old gage trees offered welcome summer shade, and throughout the winter months the apple trees maintained an evergreen appearance – so full were their branches of glistening mistletoe. I built a large pond into the grassy bank and on warm afternoons slothful goldfish barely stirred among the reeds and deeply-planted water-lilies. In the principal border, twenty feet wide in places and backed by a high glossy laurel hedge, I grew tall campanulas, achilleas, acanthus and centaureas. There was no separate kitchen garden but a few valuable sorrel plants and lettuces co-existed happily among their more flowery companions. In a damper, shadier spot I established a colony of fritillaries between camellias whose springtime blossoms were shielded from scorching sun.

I sketch this outline of my old Farnham garden because it played no small part in my setting up a publishing business to produce a quarterly gardening journal. With a lifelong interest in gardens I found myself with the perfect opportunity to make them, and their literature, my livelihood. How HORTUS actually came to be born is told in the Introduction to *By Pen & By Spade*, but it's worth mentioning here that my garden served me as a budding garden publisher as a library serves a scholar. I was able to grow many of the plants that appeared in the printed pages of HORTUS and I was able, continually, to learn how to garden better, how to propagate more of the plants I grew and how to deal with the sometimes tricky business of tending to plant sicknesses – in short, all good working experience.

When I moved to Wales just before Christmas 1987 I left behind me a garden full of memories associated with many plants I felt I could not uproot. There was the spreading clump of dark blue *Iris sibirica* given by friends who by the time I moved had both died. There was a 'hedge' of alchemilla started from one seedling kindly brought by a weekend guest, and there were literally hundreds of plants bought on many garden visiting excursions all round the country. Such is the gardener's lot when he moves from one location to another. It never occurred to me to dig the irises thinking they would soon sulk and die in heavy wet Welsh clay (fortunately that turns out not to be the case and irises play important roles in the new garden), and many of the shrubs and small trees had grown too large to move.

The main reasons for packing up were to find a larger house from which to run the publishing business and to have a large garden while I was young enough to handle it. Although my father was Welsh I did not come here to discover lost family roots. I could just as easily have gone to Cornwall (where I spent many happy but frustrating weeks house hunting), Shropshire or Suffolk. I had no geographic ties and I was prepared to sail off in almost any direction.

Gardeners do not often willingly exchange their existing part of the world for one whose reputation is for heavier rainfall coupled with the threat of later and earlier frosts. But when I first saw The Neuadd garden I knew immediately it was exactly what I had been looking for; the components were as varied as they were numerous. Within four acres I had *two* streams, a pond, stone terraces, formal lawns and old runs of yew and box hedging sprouting bits of topiary that I knew could be revitalised and made to flourish. In addition there were two pieces of woodland, an old orchard and bits of former paddock that could easily be brought into cultivation.

My immediate task, of course, was to set up the office. HORTUS was then run single-handed and the quarterly deadlines loomed up dramatically. At the same time I had all this new terrain to examine each day for signs of emerging plants where one or two neglected borders might be expected, at the very least, to yield a couple of interesting perennials or some welcome bulbs. As the new year grew, so did the grass and weeds. While snowdrops appeared everywhere and one of the lawns seemed to sink beneath the sheer profligacy of daffodils (an appropriate Welsh-seeming house-warming present), the garden offered little else in terms of good plants. But as most gardeners do, I waited a full year to see what might yet appear. Could there be autumn-flowering bulbs, late Michaelmas daisies and other sorts of treats? There was much to do outside by tackling just the grass and hedges, and indoors I could beaver away at my publishing programme to occupy those days when any work in the garden was impossible.

In the four years that have passed I have been joined by Simon Dorrell whose role as art editor for HORTUS has brought fresh ideas as well as a constant stream of fine illustrations. His own painting career has taken a strong curve towards garden-minded projects and our combined interest in horticulture led us to explore that wonderful crop of Cotswold gardens for our book, *Over the Hills from Broadway* (Alan Sutton, 1991) in which I described, and Simon painted and drew, nearly fifty remarkable places.

Despite our other ventures we manage somehow to spend part of almost every day in the garden. Simon has discovered an extraordinary talent for designing further parts which leaves me the enviable, though expensive, task of planting in his wake. With full regard for the manner in which this garden was laid out in Edwardian times we have planted over eight hundred beech, yew and box trees in hedges to divide the space into a series of intimate garden 'rooms' and we have created a few grand gestures. A pair of crinkle-crankle beech hedges lead from the orchard to high woodland, a lavender parterre glows deep purple through most of July and August (with lily-flowered tulips playing their own tune in May), and a large formal vegetable garden in the French *potager* style keeps the kitchen well supplied.

Regular readers of HORTUS will have followed The Neuadd's transition from a sleepy and slightly down-at-heel time capsule to a garden which stimulates its owners in all they do, and provides, I hope, some pleasure for the visitors who have discovered that we open our gates shyly to the public a couple of days a year under the National Gardens Scheme.

By moving to Wales I thought I would see less of friends. It has not turned out that way. Old ones have learnt their way here, and con-tributors to HORTUS as well as other writers and artists have found the valley track which leads to our door. People have come from all over Britain, from Europe, from Australia, New Zealand and the United States. I hope they have found their journeys worthwhile; we have gained immeasurably from their visits and from the ideas (and plants) they sometimes bring. Technology allows us to publish in the hills, and a rather too-often-used telephone answering machine allows me to indulge myself in the garden during hours which might otherwise be wasted in fruitless meetings or mind-crippling traffic jams.

By Pen & By Spade introduced many new readers to HORTUS; I have no doubt that *The Generous Garden* will do the same. Both these anthologies have taken only half the contents from the issues in their respective year. Each issue of HORTUS has 128 pages devoted entirely to the art of gardening. It will not tell you how to bud a rose, treat the blackspot or tend your hanging baskets, but I guar-antee it will mulch your spirit, cause you to laugh occasionally and feed your appetite for ever more good garden writing.

DAVID WHEELER, *Editor*
The Neuadd, Rhayader
October, 1991

Drawing of THE NEUADD *by Simon Dorrell*

Contents

Why Garden?

MIRABEL OSLER

I think I may know. The reason creeps up on you slowly. Like a childhood memory of gardens its origins may begin with a mild hankering, a non-thinking conformity, or just an erosion of your peace of mind by writers and photographers. Whichever way you succumbed there is no going back. Gardens are as compulsive as hunger and warmth.

Each gardener must have begun from a different incentive and perhaps the most common reason is merely physical – just by having a piece of land, a space, an area of debris or a thicket of weeds outside the window. And yet it isn't that simple. Look at a row of back gardens in a city and you see a variety of responses. Some are cultivated, some are totally neglected. So where is the germ? Where is the seed which lies dormant in some of us and doesn't even exist in others?

For years my mind was closed to gardening. I wanted none of it. Children and animals had held us down for so many years it seemed sense that once through them, then there would be freedom. And when we were living in Greece, when we had sea, mountains and wild flowers to offer, too many friends being invited to stay had said, 'We can't both come – the garden can't be left', or 'I couldn't possibly be away then, the day lilies are at their best'. The *what*?

And yet I can almost remember a day when sitting in a chair on a warm Mediterranean spring noon, when the asphodels (said to thrive on neglected land) were so prolific around us, the view at eye level was a pinkish glaucoma. Sitting in total idleness, slack and vacant, my hand dangled on the damp earth and I suddenly thought if I weren't careful my fingers would take root in such fecund ground. From that moment something shifted. A small grain of impulsion, curiosity or awareness – a small Why Not? germinated.

So why do gardeners garden? What is the attraction? Look around and the answer is so obvious that supposedly no one has asked the question. The whole of England flourishes with gardens and it happens from something more than boredom or convention; it is subtler than the mere appreciation of flowers. The scope for creativeness is infinite. With each of us our eyes are different; our intake of colours so varied; our response and alignment so individual. Give several people the same space and dimensions to cultivate and think what a variety of solutions you would end-up with. Not just because of the part of the country you live in or the type of soil or the altitude you may have, of course these count, but gardens are comprised of so much more than flowers, shrubs and trees.

There is another element. Forceful and invisible; it is as if a garden once started by you with care and forethought becomes a growing entity well outside your own life. Gardens grow. They go on growing; they may even take over. They do. In fact in the end you can have a love-hate feeling for this great yeasty creature – this thing that keeps 'working'.

It is then that what each of us decides to do with this culture will make the contrast of gardens we see everywhere. It depends on how restrictively we control and contain that ferment. How much we allow it to spread or alternatively restrain its momentum; how we see colours, arrange shapes or understand the inherent value of each plant. And something else too. So much depends on how ruthless we are with failures. We each at one time or another have walked round our garden looking at a grossly overgrown shrub or an overpowering patch of saxifrage and said, 'Oh I must do something about that!' when obviously we haven't and won't. A coward lives with his mistakes – hoping for a change of attitude towards it next year or that by planting something nearby the mistake will be filtered. The brave man does it with a sword. And it is then that you discover one of the many unexpected pleasures of gardening – the relief when finally with decision and courage you do remove that hideous forsythia you had hoped you would come to love.

Pleasures? Oh, yes, for gardeners there are many. Not only achievement, which is obvious and surely will happen sometime to even the most acid-fingered of us. But unexpected pleasures. For instance one of mine is to go round the garden untwining an uncompliant clematis scrambling into the wrong rose. With infinite patience I must delicately unpick a tendril that holds the stem with the tenacity of a baby's finger. To make it grow the way I want and not in the arbitrary direction the wind has taken it requires the precision of unpicking Victorian hem-stitching. That's a pleasure I had not imagined.

But there is the other side too. That burgeoning flora outside the

window is a creature you cannot shut out, even when you are dead-
beat in the summer days when you cannot possibly draw the curtains
against all that flowering. There it is, pulling at you, calling,
needing you. Waiting to be noticed or waiting for water – either
way it gets you. And although it can be calming to consider the
liquid manure it takes to make a peach – it is not necessarily something you want crammed down your throat every time you turn
towards the light.

Why garden? Some of us know. For so many reasons; once begun,
the reasons proliferate. We, for instance, grow shrub roses which
are often criticized for their short flowering season and yet we don't
expect daffodils to reappear in summer or buddleias to bloom for
Easter. Imagine the tedium if roses bloomed all the year – what
anticipation we would miss looking at the black sticks in winter
which we know, but hardly believe, contain next summer's garden.
And it is that swing of season that partly answers the question. The
bleak melancholy of a winter garden full of debris not tidied-up in
time before the frost and snow arrive, the sight of that desolation
and bareness, that is the reason; to be confounded one day when there
really will be summer again, when we will have to believe our eyes.

So roses for many of us are certainly responsible. They do answer
the question – Why Garden? There is 'Belle de Crécy' whose strange
colour forms contusions on the ageing petals; or 'Mme. Hardy' with
her surprising viridian eye; 'Ricardii', whose hundreds of single
blossoms are as transitory as dew; and 'Souvenir de la Malmaison'
with its quartered delicacy. But there is a further intrinsic reason
for gardening – not just for the plants themselves which are forever
carrying us along – but because a garden is always on the move.
You have never, never arrived. Next year will be different from this
one – nothing will be concluded, nothing will be static, however hard
we have tried, and we all at some time have wanted to do this, to
hold back the growth just as it is. To keep the perfect days so that
what we have laboured over and nourished, petted or protected,
can be held at its zenith; when everything somehow has come off
right and the colour, blooming and survival have all happened at
once – then how badly we would like to hold it just so. Just to be
able to prevent those petals from opening further; to stop the sun
or rain from destroying such perfection. The moments are rare
enough indeed, but what joy it would be to be able to petrify the

whole fulfilment for just a few days more. It never happens. On, on, that uncontrollable force is pushing us so that inevitably we are already planning for this moment to happen again next year. Only then, naturally, it will be even more perfect. And there is the flaw. What gardener isn't of two minds? Even as you are sighing with satisfaction with what you have at last pulled off after three, five or ten years of endeavour – the other ambitious mind is already making greedy notes for what must be done next year.

It's not like that with cooking! You cook a meal; either it is a success or it is all right; or uneatable. But at the time, in the proper Zen mentality, you are concentrating on making that meal. But not a gardener. That split mind; those compelling lists. Those bullying little notes to yourself for even further perfection. All to be faced again in a year's time.

But wait, this is the very essence of gardening. This is the very incentive that keeps us going; the implicit fact that a garden is always on the move keeps up our pace. It is not us forcing it on-wards, but long ago, unnoticed the onus shifted and now – a garden started – it is the garden forcing us. We are indeed possessed. No wonder non-gardeners sometimes stand aghast and ask Why Garden?

Mrs Desmond Underwood – the Silver Queen

BETH CHATTO

Mrs Desmond Underwood was born Pamela Montgomery Cuninghame, daughter of Sir Thomas Montgomery Cuninghame, Bart. of the Foreign Office, and at one time Military Attache in Vienna. He was also an enthusiastic naturalist, and a tireless mountain walker.

His second marriage found him living in Portofino, in Italy, where he was sometimes joined by his young daughter who delighted in holidays with him, scrambling among the richly-scented, grey-foliaged plants growing on the dry, stony hillsides.

Later as a young woman she did a spell of secretarial work for Sir Eustace Percy MP, where possibly her gift for organization was first encouraged, but her marriage carried her away from that train of thought. The honeymoon involved a trip to New Zealand, but somewhere on the journey, differences between two highly-charged individuals required some respite. On landing Pamela took the initiative and headed for the hills where she ended up cooking over an open fire for a party of gold miners. Search parties were sent out to look for her and eventually the recalcitrant bride was restored, and peace declared.

During the last war we were neighbours. My husband Andrew and I lived then in a house situated on the outskirts of Colchester sheltered beneath the tree-lined ancient ramparts that had once formed its protective boundary. Adjoining our land was Ramparts Nursery growing primarily carnations for the cut flower trade, and outdoor tomatoes for local sale. Since we did not use all our land, we offered some of it to our neighbour who now, re-married, was Mrs Desmond Underwood, mother of two daughters and a baby son. Being myself somewhat raw and twenty, I was rather in awe of this tall and imperious person whose far-reaching voice occasionally floated across my garden. I was drawn by the spell of things growing in her greenhouses so would sometimes seek her there and keep her company as she tied in the carnations, or showed me how to take 'pips' for cuttings. After my two daughters were born her small boy came sometimes at bathtime and stayed to listen to the bedtime story.

After the war times were not easy on the nursery. The cut flower trade suffered from competition, with Dutch flowers flooding the market. The problem was similar to today when many businesses were obliged to diversify. Pamela had already introduced the sale of imperial pinks; her stock plants cushioned with flowers had already replaced the tomatoes and band of Italian prisoners-of-war, employed as land workers, who had entertained us with heart-felt renderings of Sicilian songs.

My husband's study of the ecological homes of garden plants had already encouraged us to build up a large collection of drought-resistant plants, since our average rainfall in Essex is often the lowest in the country. In some years we have many weeks in summer without measurable rain. The sight and scent of our grey-foliaged plants reminded Pamela of those hot hillsides where she had been happily scratched and torn among scrubby bushes of thyme, lavender and artemisia. Why not sell a grey and silver collection to set off her pinks? Why not? We were glad for her to take cuttings, and so began the grey and silver nursery whose reputation became famous nationally and internationally. From other sources more species were introduced until eventually she grew a hundred and sixty five different kinds. Later she was the first person to write an authoritative book on the subject. *Grey and Silver Plants* was published by Collins (1971) and sensitively illustrated by Marjorie Blamey.

However, there was still a hard row to hoe. The gardening public were not yet aware of the value of foliage plants. Flowers large and colourful still fulfilled most gardeners needs. But something was in the air to revise this point of view for many, if not all. The Flower Club movement was about to be born. Flower arrangement clubs and societies flourish today throughout the length and breadth of the land. It was not always so. Some thirty-five years or so ago, the first, in Dorchester was founded by Mrs Mary Pope who herself originally came from a well-known Colchester family. The second, the Colchester Flower Club quickly followed led by Mrs Underwood, its founder and chairman for many years. Repressed and depressed housewives were still struggling with shortages and ration books. There was little sign of the affluent and uninhibited society to come. Driven by infectious enthusiasm and single-minded resolution, Pamela swept me into her new club, where I found myself, like hundreds and eventually thousands of other women, looking at all kinds of things I hadn't properly paid attention to before. Every garden, hedgerow, or waste plot suddenly sprouted delicious shapes, colours and forms that somehow had escaped our attention in the past. As the years have gone by I wonder if some of the spontaneity and simplicity of those early lessons may have become lost, since I remember best those demonstrators who made us see beauty in economy – after all not everyone has large gardens from which to pick basketsful of flowers, while many who live in flats without gardens were shown what could be done with a mere handful, either given, bought, or collected along the roadside.

For several years Mrs Underwood took a leading part in this new movement, encouraging and advising new clubs in their beginnings. One day my telephone rang and I found myself turning faint with dismay as she informed me confidently that she had arranged for me to be the first speaker at a newly formed club some distance away. She was determined to lever me out of my complacent domesticity. (Although I did not realize it at the time she was guiding me into the path that eventually led to my becoming a nurserywoman myself, but that story was many years away.) Suddenly I had much to learn, to drive a car for example, as well as teach myself the art of demonstrating flower arrangement. Turning as always to my garden for support, I based that first talk, and every subsequent one, on foliage and flowers from the garden, and was astounded at the response to plants which were not then commonly seen in gardens.

Over the past thirty or so years the flower club movement has promoted a huge demand in species and foliage plants; nurserymen everywhere have benefitted by the surge of interest in gardening, which does not abate. The garden has for many people become far more than an attractive addition to the home. It is often a form of therapy. The dedication and devotion needed, and the response from plants, provides both solace and inspiration, supportive through many crises that inevitably come in the course of life.

It could not be said of Pamela that she was a conventional mother. On her shoulders lay much of the responsibility of providing for her family which was enlarged by two young half-brothers who could always find a home with her. Holding the domestic life of the household together in very capable hands was Mrs Eichhorn, known and loved by everyone as Nanny. She also was a remarkable woman. As the children grew up she became personal assistant, secretary, and devoted friend to Pamela. Together they weathered fierce storms which cemented their friendship.

While not obviously involved in the running of the nursery Desmond Underwood was a very necessary moral support when the way seemed lost in a fog of petty details. I remember an incident at a committee meeting of the Colchester Flower Club where, having sat silent all evening, he suddenly raised his head and cut through the useless debate on what should or should not have been done with a short gruff bark of well-aimed common sense.

Visitors to flower shows both in London, or up and down the country, will remember the slightly stooping figure, with ash gently drifting down the front of her London suit from the inevitable cigarette held between her lips, her fine eyes half closed against the smoke. Away from the shows, few can know the lengths to which she drove herself to maintain her business. For years she supplied cut flowers to London and other main markets, often driving her van herself to arrive at day break. When I was young and inexperienced I listened to her tales of adventure, and sometimes fiasco, as she drove to exhibit all over the country, and I came to have great admiration for her courage and endurance. As I grew older I recognized the brave spirit hiding a vulnerable woman constantly buffeted by the strains and stresses of life, but who could reply, when someone asked if she were not afraid of the future, 'Yes of course I am, perpetually frightened, but that is what keeps me going'.

She had physical courage too. In 1956, in Edinburgh, which had been cut off for twelve hours after severe flooding Pamela, with her son and a load of flowers, somehow got through only to be stopped by a policeman. Her brakes failed of course, but the arm of the law was not steam rollered. No one else got through for another forty eight hours.

She was without doubt, a character. Well-known on Colchester station, pressed and dressed to city standards by Nanny, she regularly caught the train to be in time for the opening of the fortnightly shows. Harassed often by last minute matters at home, she arrived one morning just as the train was departing. Horrified, she turned for assistance. It came. The train was halted, reversed, and arrived to take her on board. For who else I wonder, would this happen?

In some ways she was born, as country people say, 'afore her time'. She was always interested in politics, and peripherally involved, but perhaps today women are more easily accepted into public walks of life. Her cousin, Reggie Paget, now elevated to the House of Lords, stood as a socialist and successfully contested the seat held by his Conservative father, Major Guy Paget, in their Northamptonshire constituency. For five years from 1955–60 Pamela sat on the Essex County Council, and later served on the Colchester Town Council. On one occasion, chairing a meeting, she came to apologies from members not present. From the list she read the name of a certain individual who, on some previous occasion, had displeased the lady chairman. Despite his frantic efforts to draw attention to his presence, she studiously looked in the opposite direction. For her, he remained absent for the rest of the meeting.

In 1970 the Royal Horticultural Society awarded Mrs Underwood the Veitch Memorial Medal for the unfailing high standard and regular appearance of her plants at the fortnightly shows held in Westminster. Here she was surrounded by admirers and would-be buyers of her well-grown plants, to whom she gave vehement decisions on the suitability, or not, of almost any area in the country where they might be grown. She was quite capable of refusing a good order, as she did once to an astonished American, because she felt convinced the plants would die in the conditions he had to offer. She was concerned for her plants, but also for her customers' pockets – and her own reputation. Dead plants are no recommendation. Flourishing ones may inspire the question, 'Where did you find them?'

For the Queen's Silver Wedding anniversary in 1977 the RHS proposed planting a silver foliage garden in the grounds of Buckingham Palace. Pamela provided the plants and planted them.

During the later years of her travelling career she was rarely seen separated from Skiffles, a totally loyal but uncertain-tempered Jack Russell. He was her companion on many lonely assignments. He had even been known to keep guard, unofficially of course, beneath her Chelsea exhibit. On this one occasion when the Queen approached the stand, with its elegant bowls of pinks arranged above a sea of grey and silver leafed plants, Skiffles emerged and was presented. The Queen asked if she might stroke him. 'Yes,' came the reply, 'but he might bite you Ma'am!'

'Ah, perhaps that would cause an embarassment for us both,' was Her Majesty's reply.

The last years of Pamela's life were clouded as she struggled valiantly to over-come ill-health. Desmond had died several years previously, the zest for life was never the same without him.

In 1977 she was awarded the highest accolade in horticulture, the Victoria Medal of Honour in Horticulture. Only 63 can be held at any one time, each representing one year of the reign of Queen Victoria. It was a well-deserved reward for her courage, and un-quenchable enthusiasm in her fight to introduce her 'weeds' as they were called in the early days of her showing. She had travelled far, had done more than most to introduce foliage plants to the gardening public. Not for nothing did she become affectionately titled 'The Silver Queen'. She died on 5 May 1978 aged 68. There are not many like her about these days.

The Wrinkle-leaved Rose

HAZEL LE ROUGETEL

Among species roses, *Rosa rugosa* is one of the most stalwart; flourishing in poor, sandy soil, braving the elements, resisting disease, pest and predator. Large flowers of five petals (deep pink in *R. rugosa typica* and pure white in *R. r. alba*) are followed by magnificent hips and the deep-veined (rugose), dark green leaves turn gold in autumn. Yet these attributes did not lead to ready acceptance, and interest in the species dates from the introduction of the first hybrids, when breeders began to appreciate that a robust quality might be introduced to other roses of more delicate constitution, and appealingly resilient offspring of great diversity began to appear.

This rose originated in the Far East, thriving on the coastlands of Japan, Korea, eastern Siberia and northern China but, although it was grown in Chinese gardens a thousand years ago, introduced into Europe from Japan by Thunberg, a Swedist botanist, in 1784 and offered in England by Lee and Kennedy of Hammersmith in 1796, scant evidence can be found of its use in the west until the last two decades of the nineteenth century. Henry Hammond, nurseryman of Bagshot, Surrey, listed 'Hedge Hog' amongst his roses for 1827/28* and this was most likely a Rugosa because of its abundance of spines. The unwelcome characteristic may have prevented consideration at a time when attention was directed towards producing bigger and better blooms for the shows and handling was a necessity. In any case, it was not a good cut flower.

In the United States *R. rugosa* was described as 'Wrinkle-leaved Rose' by Bernard M'Mahon in *The American Gardeners Calendar*, published in Philadelphia in 1806; but Robert Buist, who had emigrated from Edinburgh to that city, made no mention of it in *The Rose Manual* of 1844, a comprehensive account of roses to that date. By 1889, however, B. A. Elliott, plantsman of Pittsburgh, issued a directive: 'We desire to call attention to the Japanese Rugosa Roses, almost strangers to this country, but of the hardiest constitution

---

* Manuscript quoted by permission of the Trustees of the Wedgwood Museum, Barlèston, Stoke-on-Trent, and Keele University Library, where it is deposited.

and free from pests and diseases, showing scarlet fruit and handsome glossy foliage – one of the most desirable plants for embellishment of Lawn, Flower Garden or Shrubbery.' (*A Few Flowers Worthy of General Culture*, 6th ed. 1889).

Records of the Adelaide Botanic Garden show that Rugosas had reached South Australia by 1874, when a variety named 'Regeliana' was received from a Belgian grower named J. Linden, and in the following year five shillings was paid for another from William Bull of King's Road, Chelsea, London. This was *R. rugosa typica* and the name 'Regeliana' is still sometimes found in Australia today. Both the pink and white were included in nursery lists of G. Brunning and Sons, St Kilda, Melbourne and Nairn and Son of Christchurch, New Zealand, in the 1890s, one charging one shilling and the other one shilling and sixpence.

English authors around the turn of the century stressed certain qualities: William Robinson emphasised strong growth in any soil, resulting in a handsome bush when isolated, but he felt that large gardens should have great groups of *R. rugosa*. Gertrude Jekyll pointed out its great hardiness, enabling its use in exposed places

Species Rugosa hedge, early autumn, in Rosemary Verey's garden, Barnsley House, Gloucestershire.

where other roses would fail, and a 'somewhat ferocious armament of prickles' making it eminently suitable for use as hedges, both ornamental and effective in enclosure and defence. Joseph Pemberton wondered whether there was a rose to be found more handsome in habit, foliage, flower and fruit and, moreover, it was perpetual. Rose Kingsley recalled seeing for the first time, some thirty years before, the large, bright scarlet fruit enrapturing both gardeners and birds and now, having grown some of the new hybrids, she foresaw a great future for the race of Rugosas.

The developments are usually divided into forms and sports close to the species – of which 'Blanc Double de Coubert', 'Fru. Dagmar Hastrup', 'Roseraie de l'Haÿ' and 'Scabrosa' are examples – and the deliberate hybrids, of which there are a great number. The first of these, 'Thusnelda', coming from Germany in 1886, was the result of a union between the white species and 'Gloire de Dijon' and was in turn used to produce 'Conrad Ferdinand Meyer', enthusiastically described by Rose Kingsley. 'Its colour, a warm tender pink, its large size and perfect shape, its more than vigorous growth and its persistence in blooming – I have it in flower here [Eversley, Hampshire] from the middle of May till December – render it one of the most valuable additions to the rose garden of the new century'. By 1908 she listed eighteen Rugosas and included 'Mrs Anthony Waterer', raised in England in 1898, its deep crimson, scented blooms inherited from the Victorian favourite Hybrid Perpetual, 'Général Jacqueminot'.

Tenderness of Tea Roses in northern Europe and the northern United States was a reason for promoting a hardy alliance and in a paper, *Roses since 1860*, read at a National Rose Conference in 1889, George Paul alluded to the advance of Rugosas, quoting 'Madame Georges Bruant' from France as an example. This had resulted from a liaison with the popular white Tea Rose 'Sombreuil' in 1887 and was soon to make an impact in America, appearing on the cover of *The Californian Florist* for August 1888 and described as a new and distinct class of rose. This illustrated monthly publication – then cited as 'the only florists' journal west of Chicago' – also mentioned both species Rugosas as beautiful Japanese shrubs. By 1896 Ellwanger and Barry of Rochester, New York, could recommend 'Madame Georges Bruant' as exceptionally hardy and vigorous and Norton's Premier Nurseries of Pahiatua, New Zealand included this rose in their 1899 list as 'papery white, large and double, produced in clusters; a valuable decorative rose', pricing it at one shilling.

Cochet-Cochet had named the deep crimson-purple 'Roseraie de l'Haÿ' (1901) for the wonderful rose garden of M. Jules Gravereaux on the outskirts of Paris, where its owner was also working on rugosas. He brought out 'Rose à Parfum de l'Haÿ' another rich crimson from 'Général Jacqueminot', and 'Madame Henri Gravereaux', white with a salmon centre -- perhaps from use of a lovely Tea rose of peach and salmon tints, named for his wife 'Madame Jules Gravereaux' by Soupert et Notting of Luxembourg in 1901.

'Blanc Double de Coubert' had come earlier from Cochet-Cochet and Gertrude Jekyll, who seemed to love pale roses above all others, judged this the whitest rose of any known; one to eclipse the duller white of 'Madame Georges Bruant'. She also praised its 'rich deep green foliage, highly polished though heavily reticulated, persisting till late in the year [giving] it that look of perfect health and vigour that the leafage of so many roses lack in late summer'. Rugosas grew well on her light sandy Surrey soil and two others which pleased her were 'Schneelicht', a single white from Hungary with *R. phoenicia* as a parent, and 'Fimbriata', a French hybrid derived from the Noisette,

'Blanc Double de Coubert', pure white favourite of Gertrude Jekyll, but not a good weatherer.

'Madame Alfred Carrière', its small pink-tinged flowers delightfully fringed and frilled.

The rugosa influence spread to prostrate roses. George Paul used it with *R. arvensis,* trailing rose of the English countryside, to introduce *R. paulii* at the beginning of this century; a vigorous rose providing good ground cover of dense dark foliage and large single, fragrant white blooms. There is a pink form, *R. p. rosea,* believed by Graham Thomas to have 'beauty of flower unexcelled by the single pink roses'. Another came from the Arnold Arboretum, Massachusetts in 1900, derived from *R. rugosa* and *R. wichuraiana* (then called 'The Memorial Rose' in America on account of its spread over cemeteries at that time) and was originally known as 'Lady Duncan'. This was lost and later reintroduced as 'Max Graf' by Bowditch in 1919 and, proving unusually fertile for a Rugosa hybrid, was taken up by Herr Kordes in Germany for breeding purposes. Its strong trailing foliage and prominent bright pink flowers have proved valuable for under-planting. Another American breeder, Van Fleet, had produced a double white hybrid, 'Sir Thomas Lipton', in 1900, using yet another type of rose, Polyantha 'Clotilde Soupert'; and from a popular Hybrid Tea, 'My Maryland', came the acclaimed 'Sarah Van Fleet' in 1926, with lilac-pink blooms lasting over a long period on an upright bush.

As well as for underplanting, 'Max Graf' can be used to tumble down a bank or low wall.

One of the most upright of Rugosa hybrids, lilac-pink flowers of
'Sarah Van Fleet' will reach 8 feet.

The Rose Encyclopaedia (1922) by Geoffrey Henslow, with over eighty plans for formal rose gardens in intricate bedding patterns, shows how Rugosas were used in the post-war period. Frequently the whole was surrounded by a hedge of them, in one case alternating with Hybrid Sweet Briars from Lord Penzance. Here ten varieties were listed, most previously mentioned, but single purplish/crimson 'Calocarpa' and semi-doubles 'Delicata' and 'Souvenir de Pierre Leperdrieux', cerise pink and wine red, were also included.

A recent introduction from Denmark, deep crimson 'Rugspin', here seen in South Island, New Zealand.

Sometimes they were planted on the outside of pergolas, their dark foliage providing good foil for paler climbing roses.

Canada's climate is well suited to Rugosas: two yellow hybrids came from Dr W. Saunders of the Central Experimental Farm, Ottawa. 'Grace' from the Spinosissima 'Harison's Yellow' seems to have disappeared from lists, but 'Agnes', from *R. foetida persiana* in 1922, is still a favourite, with full double rather buff-yellow flowers splendid in dark foliage. The 1986 list of twenty-one Rugosas available from Pickering Nurseries, Ontario, includes seven raised in Canada, some named for Canadian explorers. 'Martin Frobisher', a double soft pink and very fragrant, seems popular in the Antipodes, where Trevor Griffiths of Temuka, South Canterbury, also has an extensive Rugosa collection. Dates of the thirty-nine in his catalogue range over a century; from 'Madame Georges Bruant' to recent introductions, like one I noticed in his display garden: an outstanding deep wine-red single, 'Rugspin', from Denmark.

Rugosas also thrive in Scandinavia and a very good collection may be found in Gothenburg's new Rosarium, in which Göte Haglund played an important part and describes in his book *The Rose, Queen of Flowers* (Gothenburg, 1987). He divides Rugosas into five categories and specifically mentions two yellows: 'Dr Eckener' (Berger of Germany, 1930), from Hybrid Tea 'Golden Emblem', and its sport 'Golden King' (Beckwith, 1935). Holland has also played a part in furthering Rugosa influence through another Polyantha, 'Madame Norbert Levavasseur', with crimson 'F. J. Grootendorst' in 1918 and its rather better pink sport of five years later, from which a white arrived in the United States in 1962. All have small, clustered flowers with fringed petal edges and, unlike most of the hybrids, they last well when cut, although they have little scent. They will make a continuous display in mixed planting, and may be found in the island bed area to the right of the large herbaceous borders at The Royal Horticultural Society's garden at Wisley in Surrey.

There is a comprehensive collection of all types of rugosas planted on the left of the entrance to the National Trust Rose Garden at Mottisfont in Hampshire, designed by Graham Thomas, and a prime example of a 'Scabrosa' hedge lines the lane leading to the Gardens of The Rose near St Albans in Hertfordshire. Rugosas will often be seen planted on road verges and central reservations to form robust barriers and good use of them has been made on a perimeter road in Norwich. Tolerant of salt-laden air, they have become established on many coastal areas of the eastern United States and around Britain and act as an efficient deterrent to sand erosion by wind. I have seen this shore-look echoed in a garden, where gravel was extended from a driveway over a bed in which they were planted, and this seems an eminently suitable way to display roses of Japanese origin.

In kitchen and dispensary Rugosas also play a part. For centuries their petals have been infused for tea in China, the dark pink made into a paste with sugar for sweetening and embellishment, as well as being used in a scented drink known as 'Dew of Roses'. In the

Far East, the medicinal value of the large hips has long been appreciated. Ken Nobbs, one of the founders of the society, Heritage Roses New Zealand, has researched deeply into this valuable source of vitamins (found in the Sweet Briar and *R. moyesii* as well), and thinks hips of 'Scabrosa' and 'Fru. Dagmar Hastrup' the most palatable. His detailed analysis shows that the well-known Vitamin C content is accompanied by an abundance of carotene (pro-vitamin A) as well as several others. (*New Zealand Rose Annual*, 1982).

I am sometimes asked to suggest trouble-free rugosas for a moderate-sized garden and so will conclude with a varied half dozen. For bushes of good form and flowering long, perhaps 'Fru. Dagmar Hastrup' comes first, its pale pink single flowers associating with large crimson fruit. Semi-double 'Schneeswerg' is best of the white hybrids and, again, is right with orange-red fruit. Although 'Roseraie de l'Haÿ' bears little fruit, the exquisite scrolled buds and velvety purple loosely formed flowers more than compensate. 'Agnes' is lankier, but this soft yellow Rugosa can well be grown on a pillar, bringing rose height and distinctive foliage to the back of a border. 'Max Graf' is invaluable for low cover in front, especially if encouraged to weave with a prostrate silver plant a mixed foliage carpet beneath bright pink single flowers. Finally, perhaps a hybrid introduced this year could fill a wild corner. 'Corylus' (*R. nitida* x *R. rugosa typica*) will provide colourful interest with deep pink single flowers, bright red hips, warm red/brown bristly stems; but its chief asset is brilliant autumn foliage of fiery tones – my own contribution to the family of wrinkle-leaved roses.

Photographs by the author

The Tower, part of the castle walls built by Pietro Caetani in the
12th century.

NINFA:
A Garden in the ruins of a town

ALVILDE LEES-MILNE

In the ancient ruins of the little town of Ninfa lies the most imaginative and botanically interesting garden. Some fifty miles south of Rome and off the old Appian Way, it nestles at the feet of the 1000 ft. high rocky Lepini mountains with the town of Norma perched precipitously on the ridge.

The history of Ninfa is long and fascinating, its origins lost in the mists of time. The earliest mention of it is by Pliny who went there in the 1st century. He records that in the neighbourhood of the lake, which still exists, and where the spring of the River Nympheus appears to rise, stood a Roman temple sacred to the Nymphs. On the mirror of the crystal-clear waters were to be seen, according to Pliny, floating islands which he calls *saltuares*, and which rotated to the sound of music.

Ninfa and Norma were recorded as two vast possessions given by the Emperor Constantine V Copronimus to Pope Zacharius in about AD 740. It was at this time that beside the lake arose the little town that took the name of Ninfa. Being on the consular road from Rome to Naples (the old via Appia was submerged in marshes), it soon assumed importance as a comfortable stopping place. Ninfa grew and flourished. By 1159, when Alexander III sought asylum and was crowned Pope there, the city was enclosed by a double girdle of walls and embellished with seven churches and a town hall. About a hundred years later it was acquired by Pietro Caetani, Count of Caserta, an ancestor of the late owner. It was he who built the very tall tower which, with part of the castle walls, still stands today. Ninfa prospered until 1382, when during the ravages of civil war it was sacked, burned and destroyed, never to rise again. The population, decimated by war and malaria, dispersed. Many took refuge in the little mountain towns of Norma and Sermoneta nearby. For some time a few churches that had survived were still in use as places of worship, but towards the second half of the 15th century they also fell into ruin. Then for more than five centuries what Gregorovius chose to call the 'Pompeii of the Middle Ages' remained deserted and forgotten. 'Truly this place looks even more charming than Pompeii,' he wrote, 'for there the houses stare like crumbling mummies dragged from the volcanic ashes. But over Ninfa waves a balmy sea of flowers.'

No one has written more poetically about it than Augustus Hare, who visited the place about 1874. 'It is an unspeakably quiet scene of sylvan beauty, and there is something unearthly about it which possesses and absorbs every sense. If fairies exist anywhere surely Ninfa is their capital; Ninfa where Flora holds her court, where the only inhabitants are the roses and the lilies and all the thousands of flowers which grow so abundantly in the deserted streets, where honeysuckle and jessamine fling their garlands through the windows of every house, and where the altars of the churches are thrones for flame-coloured valerian. Outside the walls you would hardly believe it was a town, so encrusted in verdure is every building that the houses look like green mounds rising out of the plain. One tall tower stands near the entrance and watches its reflection in the still waters of a pool white with lilies and fringed with forget-me-nots.' This is the lake mentioned by Pliny. Hare then goes on to say, 'Ninfa can never be rebuilt. Even the shepherds cannot bear to pass the night there. Death garlanded with flowers is death still.'

Another great Victorian traveller and artist who visited Ninfa about this time was Edward Lear. He was a friend of the Duke of Sermoneta of the day, and the family have some of his letters as well as an original drawing of Ninfa and a painting of Sermoneta. The surrounding country looks very much the same today.

The story of the rebirth of Ninfa began in 1922, when the Duchess of Sermoneta and Prince Gelasio Caetani her son, grandmother and uncle of the late owner, who must both have been people of great vision and imagination, decided to create a garden among the ruins. Photographs of the place at that time show that it was still as Gregorovius, Hare and Lear found it in the 19th century, only more so – a tangled mass of ivy and brambles, even the ruins being barely visible.

The walls of the medieval town hall were, however, still intact. The family were able to convert this building into a house, which fits perfectly into the setting. The next task, after clearing away some of the jungle, was to plant trees. Groups of cypresses were

A view of the house from the bridge across the river.

placed in strategic positions, as were various species of pine, ilexes, cedars and planes. The Duchess of Sermoneta was English and particularly fond of roses. Many of those she introduced – such as *R. × odorata* 'Gigantea', 'General Schablikine', *R. laevigata*, *R. bracteata* and 'La Follette', to name a few – still flourish and cascade over ruins and trees. The climate of Ninfa seems to suit most plants, both northern and southern, and everything grows at a speed that many a struggling gardener would envy. From March to October the sun is very strong, and as Ninfa lies on the plain the summer heat is tremendous. Yet because of the place's proximity to the mountains and, above all, because of the abundance of water the nights are cool, and at times there is a heavy dew. Water, in fact, is everywhere, and without it, of course, it would have been impossible to create in southern Italy a garden of this calibre and beauty.

The plain on which Ninfa lies was until the 1920s part of the Pontine Marshes, which stretched from the mountains to the sea – a distance of some 15 miles. It was largely owing to Prince Gelasio Caetani, who was a brilliant engineer, that this tremendous feat of drainage was accomplished. His plans were used by Mussolini, who took all the credit.

Wintersweet and cypress in the garden.

The lake, which lies just above the gardens and out of which rises the river Nympheus, is fed by many underground springs pouring in from the mountains. The cool, clear river flows at great speed through the garden, over the plain and away to the sea. Many channels have been made, and sometimes they intersect and cross over one another. Where the level permits, the water falls in cascades into pools, or into the river, so that wherever you go there are lovely reflections and sounds.

A bridge of water. An example of the many streams that cross, feed into and finally flow into the Nympheus.

The river is inhabited by a curious species of trout called *Macrostigma*. A legend exists that they are only found here, in Tunis and in the Lebanon. It is thought they may have been brought to Ninfa by Hannibal, who came from Tunis. Alternatively, Queen Dido may have stopped here on her way from the Lebanon to Carthage when she visited Aeneas two thousand years earlier. The trout seem to be endowed with chameleonic powers, for they change colour according to their background. Wisps of emerald green weed wave incessantly in the clear, hurrying river.

Ninfa has been fortunate in having three generations of knowledgeable gardeners to own and care for it. All have planted with infinite

The fast flowing Nympheus inhabited by trout.

fore-thought and good taste. Nothing jars. In fact, it is so perfect both to eyes and senses that one could happily remain there for ever. The late owner, Donna Lelia Caetani, who was herself an artist, inherited the good taste of her American mother, also a knowledgeable gardener. Together with her husband, Hubert Howard (a brother of Lord Howard of Penrith) she worked incessantly in the garden, constantly adding to the already formidable list of trees and shrubs. Several peasants tend the garden, but none are trained gardeners.

Many magnolias, which include *M. sprengeri* var. *diva*, are now tall trees and thrive splendidly. There are twenty or more varieties of prunus flowering from February till April, at which time the scent of huge bushes of viburnums loaded with blooms is intoxicating. There are also a large number of interesting roses, mostly species ones growing with voluptuous abandon. Clematis smother anything they can cling to, *C. florida* var. *bicolor*, 'Sieboldii', *texensis* and *balearica* to name but a few. Ceanothus grow to immense heights, and with wisterias, bignonias and jessamines, array themselves gracefully and prolifically among the ruins of houses and churches. You can see an impressive number of malus and acers. One is frequently coming across unusual plants tucked away under a gothic arch or nestling beside a little bridge.

In an enclosed part of the garden, under the shadow of the apricot-coloured tower, are some ancient fish ponds crossed by stone bridges. Here is a plantation of gigantic and immensely tall bamboos. These handsome and interesting plants were brought there in the nineteen twenties. A few years ago one lot died, and it is thought they must have flowered, this being the way with bamboos, though no one apparently observed the phenomenon. In one part of the garden there is a bank of pinks of every known variety, interspersed with large flat stones to walk about on. In another area are drifts of lavender, and the grass is carpeted with bulbs of every description. Orange, lemon and grapefruit trees abound, and the fruit is stored on shelves of bamboo in the cool undercroft of the house. A particularly lovely sight is the banks of a little stream thickly carpeted with arum lilies.

Above the sound of water, of which one is constantly aware, the strangely tropical song of Cetti's warbler adds an exotic flavour to this extraordinary place. Nightingales abound in the summer months, but the winters, though short, are too cold for them. There is a curious affinity between Ninfa and Sissinghurst Castle in Kent. The setting of Ninfa is, of course, entirely different, yet the way in which plants are encouraged to grow naturally and to scramble up and over trees and walls is very much the same. Sissinghurst was also created among ruins, and both places have an indescribable magic about them.

Ninfa did not escape the ravages of the last war. It was commandeered by the Germans and used as a munitions dump during the many months when the Allies fought for the beaches. Anzio, where the great battle raged, was only 15 miles away. During this time the family, headed by Donna Lelia's father Prince Rofredo Caetani, and followed by a great number of people from the neighbouring farms, took refuge in the wonderfully preserved medieval castle of Sermoneta, some ten miles away in the mountains. Food, however, was scarce. From time to time the peasants would descend to collect what provisions they could. It was mid-winter, and there was no light, or heat. Yet here they camped for several months, watched and waited. When the Battle of Anzio was over and the Germans were gone, leaving a trail of devastation behind, the family returned to Ninfa to restore order and recreate the temporarily shattered atmosphere of serenity.

Donna Lelia died some years ago and her husband Hubert Howard died in 1986. The fate of Ninfa is again threatened by plans for developing and industrialising the plains around it. There are also ominous threats to draw off the water. This would mean death once more, but not this time 'death garlanded with flowers.' There is no doubt that Ninfa is unique, and one can only hope that this extraordinary creation will long continue to prosper and receive protection and help from the authorities. It is unthinkable that something so perfect could disappear.

Photographs by Tim Rees

A Tradition in Clay

JOHN NEGUS

Browse around Harris Farnham Potteries, an enchanting cluster of oak-beamed buildings overlooking the Wey Valley in the Surrey village of Wrecclesham, and you're quickly seduced by a splendid array of superbly crafted terracotta.

Classic Marbella, ivy leaf and Tudor rose vases jostle with ornate patio bowls. Wall pots, pedestal vases, strawberry pots, long Toms, chimney pots, bird baths and finials beckon you to examine them closely and, in your mind's eye, find room for them in your own garden. Admire a handsome arch with a glazed owl keystone. Wonder at the 'slave' wheel, no longer used, and unchanged since the 14th century. Fondle an oak beam worn mirror smooth by potters waiting, patiently, to fire the old bottle kilns.

A family business in the best tradition, with 115 years of expertise to draw upon, fifth generation brothers Philip and David Harris aim to increase their range and satisfy new demands.

But let's start at the beginning, with Absalom Harris, founding father and master potter. On Christmas Eve in 1831, in the Hampshire village of Droxford, Absalom married Martha Cobbett, a niece of politician William Cobbett and author of *The English Gardener* (1829) and the classic *Rural Rides*.

Six years later, when William IV died, Victoria became monarch and Morse Code was invented, Absalom the younger, and the famous, was born. Tragically, typhoid struck and his parents died. Happily, Absalom was adopted by his uncle, George Cobbett, and apprenticed to him at Shorley, Beauworth. Under George's tuition, Absalom's fingers developed great dexterity. His plant pots, seakale and rhubarb forcing pots, ridge, roof and drain tiles and chimney pots were sensitively drawn from the gault clay and admired by many.

He gained experience – working for other potters in the family, such as James Cobbett at Hill Pound, Droxford and David Harris at Fareham Pottery, and his reputation grew. Large milk pans, coloured with white clay on the inside, were a speciality, but the nearest supply was 30 miles away at Claypits Wood, Old Park, Farnham, on the Surrey/Hampshire border. It fell to Absalom to collect this

ABSALOM HARRIS

precious commodity with a waggon and horses.

But visits to Farnham held more for this young, handsome potter than digging for clay. The attraction was Elizabeth, daughter of Mr G. Freemantle, tenant of Old Park, who became his sweetheart. After an endearing courtship they were married in 1858. Absalom was twenty-one.

Two years later, and ever keen to produce the finest pottery, he moved to Elstead, near Farnham, to become tenant of the almost derelict Charles Hill, Elstead pottery. This was a long, single-storey building with a house at one end and workshops and kiln at the other. Absalom was no sluggard. He thrived on the satisfaction gained from working long, hard and creatively . . . and prospered. His kiln, which meant so much to him, was 8ft in diameter. Pots for firing were packed in through a side door and bundles (bavins) of birch and other fine twigs were lit in a fireplace. Flames passed through arches under the floor and up through vents around the edge to fire pots at a temperature of 1,000°C. The stoke hole was closed with bricks and the kiln allowed to cool. The whole process took about six days.

Though a committed potter, he was also a farmer, and life was good . . . for a while. But Absalom's success was observed by his wily, avaricious landlord who so steeply increased his rent that, in 1866, he was forced to find fresh premises.

Determined as ever, he sought a plot of stiff gault clay in Alice Holt Forest, some two miles to the west of Farnham. There he built Holt Pottery and a house – Glenbervie – for his increasing family. Many were the hours spent fashioning his beloved paint pots, stands, feeders, pork pans and lard pots, together with chimney pots and six types of 'fancy-ware' vases. The red firing clay he used, often glazed with lead oxide and sand, gave a pleasing nut-brown finish to his wares.

He also continued farming – crops grew apace on the heavy clay. He sold potatoes, barley and straw to the locals. His horse meant a great deal to him: for journeying around the villages on rutted roads often thick with mire, for pulling his cart and delivering orders, or for working the pug-mill in which the clay was prepared for throwing. But again, he encountered problems. The local clay contained too much lime and the fired pots developed unsightly blisters. A perfectionist, Absalom searched for a better pocket of clay and, close by, found what he needed at Wrecclesham. There, in 1873, he built the present pottery at Clay Hill. Gardening pots and coarse domestic ware were his stock in trade. He also enjoyed fashioning yellow and brown-glazed 'fancy ware'.

With his family growing up and his fame spreading, it was fortuitous that, seven years later, in 1880, the famous water colour painter and illustrator, Birket Foster, then at Witley – some ten miles distant – visited the pottery. His mission was special. He brought with him a badly worn French green-glazed garden vase and wished to have it copied. Absalom, delighted with the challenge, spent months developing this special glaze. It wasn't easy. Many 'hybrids' were fired before he achieved the correct result. And, to Absalom's delight and surprise, these 'oddities' proved popular and sold well.

This novel departure of duplicating customers' faded pieces grew and, in the mid 1880s the Harris Pottery was commissioned to copy a collection of 16th century green-glazed vessels unearthed in London. Incredibly, they were made from white Farnham Park clay. The pits there were far from spent, so Absalom had the clay and the glaze he needed. The superb ewers he produced sold for the handsome sum of 8 shillings each. This was equivalent to the price of 288 2½in. plant pots. They were also much less effort to make.

This Farnham Green-ware, as it was called, was not without its admirers. One W. H. Allen, who, in 1889, became Art Master at the Farnham School of Art, was greatly taken with it. With Harris' co-operation – which stands to this day with the College – Allen inspired his students to create designs to be worked by the potters. Many were copied from pots in the Victoria and Albert Museum which, Allen was convinced, were made in Farnham in the 1500s.

In 1890, this new Green-ware was displayed to the public at the Farnham School of Art. Absalom was amazed at the response it received. Many orders resulted and Heals, Liberty's of London and the Rural Industries Society had Absalom and his team working round the clock.

This heralded a period of expansion. Soon Harris' Pottery was two kilns and twenty workmen strong. Extra workshops, a small kiln for glaze production and a showroom were added. There was also a change in direction, with an emphasis on 'fancy ware', domestic and horticultural pots.

You could buy Green-ware rustic fern pots, green plates and urns, baskets, rustic epergnes (ornamental stands for large dishes), green flower stands, wine casks, fruit dishes and fancy pots. There were owl pitchers, amphora and bouquet holders. By now, Absalom's children were involved with running the pottery. William Freemantle, the eldest, was a skilful potter, Ernest kept an eagle eye on accounts, and Gertrude and Nellie had a flair for fashioning ornamental and architectural pieces.

Things went smoothly. The business continued to expand. Young Ernest travelled to America and learnt about 'push'. But advertising promotions weren't really necessary as the pottery, because of its quality, tended to sell itself. An even greater variety of glazed and unglazed ware, including glazed mantlepieces and hearth tiles, table and toilet ware, and fetchingly designed 'art pottery', was produced and caught the public's imagination. In 1914, a third kiln was built.

Then came the First World War and a reduction in manpower. Production slumped. But not for long. When the war ended, William Freemantle Harris' two sons, Arthur Leslie and Reginald Freemantle, were at the helm. Again production soared. But The Depression was near. In the 1930s, the very close Harris Family tightened their belts. Most of their staff was laid off. Within a few years the Second World War made it impossible for many potteries to survive. But not the indefatigable Harrises. Though there was less demand for the almost iridescent Farnham Green-wares, there was a big jump in the sales of flower pots and other horticultural items.

After the War, Farnham Pottery was ready, and eager, to return to its former strength. And most certainly it would have if more young men and women had realised what a creative profession it is. But few came forward and an otherwise thriving industry, hard put to meet demand and lacking trainee potters, had quietly to realise that it might be some while before another peak arrived.

But arrive it did, a few years ago. It coincided with renewed interest in terracotta. Today, Farnham Pottery, managed by Eileen Harris and her sons Philip and David are working harder than ever. And the earlier bottle kilns, designed by Absalom with loading chambers of around 1,000 cu. ft. and fired by coal and wood, have been replaced by a smaller but more efficient kiln. This was originally fuelled by oil, but this developed an 'aggressive' heat in the early stages of firing and occasionally froze in winter, so has now been converted to gas. The burners produce 1,000,000 Btu per hour and pots can now be fired in under 30 hours.

The Harris brothers tell me they have a burning desire to step-up production. David, for many years a printer, relinquished his profession to help expand the business and widen the range. Philip, an Air Traffic Control Assistant, is an active participant in pioneering new production methods. Together, with a staff of eight, they plan to eclipse their pre-war output. Knowing them, as I do, I have no hesitation in saying – they will.

THE POTTER'S ART

Preparing clay for throwing, drying the finished pottery, glazing it, firing it – takes years of experience to perfect. For centuries, many aspects of pot production have remained unchanged. The clay is mixed with sand, the proportions of which change according to the nature of the clay, to produce a 'body' which shrinks by approximately one eighth during drying and firing. The mix is then soaked and squeezed through a pug-mill – a bit like a mincing machine – which extrudes the clay in a perfectly malleable state for throwing.

Years ago, before there were pug-mills, preparing the clay was a decidedly chilly affair. Layers of clay were put in a pit sandwiched with sand, watered, and left for a day. Rolls of the mix were then taken out and spread on the floor. Barefoot men 'trod it into little ruts'. They picked out any stones their feet found.

Throwing – when a lump of prepared clay, in some instances 'as much as a man could lift', is hurled on to the centre of the potter's wheel – requires a good eye. There are several different wheels at Farnham Pottery.

Plant pots are made on a 'kick' wheel, worked by a treadle and crank, which the potter powers with his left foot. An electric power wheel is also used for general work and its speed is controlled by a foot lever.

Years ago, the very largest pots and other heavy work were produced on a very simple 'slave' wheel – now a museum piece – based on a 14th century design. Here a stick on the crank of the wheel shaft is pushed and pulled by an apprentice, to turn the wheel at the slowest speeds.

To make a 3½in. plant pot, a potter moulds a ball of prepared clay and throws it with some vigour on to a fast-rotating wheel. Quickly wetting his hands, he cups the clay and centres it on the wheel head. In an instant, he hollows and lifts the walls to a height indicated by a gauge above the wheel. When the pot is shaped and perfected, it is cheese-wired from the wheel. The process is a rapid one, taking no more than 20 seconds from start to finish.

Large terrace vases and other bulky items are thrown on a 'bat' – a wooden disc set on the wheel, which is lifted off complete with pot, to avoid risk of distorting the pot when cutting it away with wire.

Drying is the next phase. Before the Pottery enjoyed full 'central heating', winter work was limited to milder days when there was no fear of Jack Frost's icy fingers probing moist, drying pots and crumbling weeks of work. Freshly-made pots are carefully and slowly dried on boards positioned on racks formed by inserting pegs into holes in floor-to-ceiling beams.

If glazing is necessary, it's done before the pots have dried out. With demand growing for terracotta, there is less call for glazed items. But years ago there was a big demand for the special glazes developed at the Pottery. The original glossy nut-brown glaze imparted to red clay, and the pale yellow on white clay, was made from lead oxide and sand.

In the 1880s, Absalom added copper to this mixture to stain it green. By 1905, other glazes – blue, pale yellow, orange, chocolate and brown – were also in everyday use, but it was the 'Farnham Green-ware' that the public was greatly taken by and made the Pottery a mecca for the multitude. The glaze was made by heating scrap lead in a furnace and stirring it to change it into lithage (lead oxide). To get pale yellow, it was mixed with fine sand and a little

The late Reg Harris setting up pots on a platform of pottery supports in the old bottle kiln. *Photograph*: *Farnham Museum*

water. The famous green glaze was achieved by heating scrap copper until it changed into copper oxide, allowing it to cool and grinding it finely in a mortar with a pestle and mixing it with lithage and sand. These glazes required just one firing, but later, when white lead was used, each piece had to be fired twice – to mature the pottery and again to mature the glaze. Modern Health and Safety regulations preclude the methods of glazing described here. Nowadays, a 'safe' leadless glaze must be used. Firing, at around 1,000°C, follows.

The Pottery is living history. Visit Wrecclesham and immerse yourself in a world of wondrous terracotta. You won't regret it.

Gardens in Fiction

Through Elizabeth Bowen's Gardens

JOHN FRANCIS

There are certain authors with whom you are never finished. There is something about a particular author's point of view which is so sympathetic that, once embarked upon, the author turns into a ship which you find so to your taste you decide to stay and cruise with endlessly.

Such an author does not have to be, necessarily, one of the great literary flagships. Some mighty vessels (in my case it is the good ship Hardy) just do not float. One salutes them with the most profound respect. Such workmanship, such capacious holds – why can one never quite bring oneself to buy the ticket? It is because other craft, Jane Austen for example or that superb gilded barge The Ronald Firbank, so seaworthy if inclined to wallow among the billows, are setting out for preferred destinations. For years now I've been promising myself a really long sumptuous cruise on the S.S. Marcel Proust. That great bulk is there with steam up, and many a short trip I've taken; such cuisine, such detail, such luxury; but when the next night I've settled down, I always at the last moment jump ship and embark with happy confidence on Elizabeth Bowen once again.

I like her class of passenger. The edgy, neurotic if not neurasthenic women, well turned out and with cultivated tastes, such as Anna Quayne, seem to have something very particular to say to our edgy, neurotic, civilisation. If Regent's Park is a garden it is, in *The Death of the Heart*, almost a character as well, met on the first page in iron winter. Anna and her friend are standing on a bridge talking and looking down on the miniature ice floes through which a swan moves 'in slow indignation.' Why are they 'making this long summerlike pause'? What keeps Anna from her fireside and the prospect of tea and buttery tea-cakes is the presence of Portia. It is Portia's heart that is doomed to die, you may remember. Often, Bowen characters are possessed of an icy composure and limitless stores of delicate feeling. What has frozen Anna is an adulterous solecism committed by her dead father-in-law, the fruit of which is poor Portia. St Quentin, by now off the frozen bridge, is hungrily eating the tea-cakes, thwarting the rivulets of melted butter with his handkerchief, beady eyed, drinking in every naunce. He is a writer, and old scandals are valued by him.

In another garden, a garden in the country, we are shown a glimpse of Anna's father-in-law as he was, damming streams, a boy at heart, watched with mortifying indulgence by his alarmingly fair-minded wife. It is good to record that, in her turn, the boy-at-heart's wife is subject to the lynx gaze of Matchett the servant, who in most cases prefers furniture to people. When the wronged wife hears about the birth of Portia she picks herself some snowdrops and goes in for a stormy bout of piano playing.

Claustrophobia is the word that comes to mind. Everyone preternaturally aware of everyone else. Vintage Bowen country. When the tension is screwed too tight release is found in tinkling a lustre. A vase of roses will suddenly shed, for no obvious reason, a shower of petals. Anna's mother-in-law, she of the probing, searchlight-like understanding that scythes through everyone's cloud cover leaving everyone feeling as naked as Adam and Eve in the garden of Eden, she with her piano playing and snowdrops, steals a part of Portia's birth. She is like the Eye of God but without the mercy.

Uncle Bill does a little desultory gardening in *The House in Paris*, another novel with its full quota of powerful women. His gardening, rooting out daisies with a spud, is undertaken less for the sake of the lawn than as a way of not thinking about his doomed wife. *The House in Paris* contains a more significant scene in a garden. It is a garden in Twickenham. Someone has died, another aunt, and her house must be cleared. Naomi and Max are engaged. They have tea in the garden with Naomi's great friend Karen. This is a scene which even more than most must be read by the reader with, so to speak, all his antennae fully extended and in tip-top working order. Naomi, proud of her Max, is most anxious that he and Karen hit it off. This they do all too well, outwardly seeming to just not quarrel; as they are seated in sunshine on unmown grass one of those tiresome magnetic attractions stirs and starts to prowl. Artful Bowen handles this scene magnificently. It is rather as if, appalled by what is happening, she feels compelled to point out aspects of the garden to distract us and her. The reader is shown the garden with a sort of alarmed clarity. 'Besides the pink cherry tree, there was not much in the garden: a stretch of lawn, now unmown, between the tree and the window two lolling bloomy borders of lupins not yet in bud. The aunt must have lived indoors. But every blade of grass, pricking up, shone; the wind puffing the poplars in other gardens shook white light from the April sappy leaves.'

Naomi has set something going which, like a runaway train, will end with a smash, but she knows nothing of this. ' "What old friends we are," said Naomi, "telling each other truths." She refilled the teapot happily.' The gardens of *The House in Paris* seem to be full of tolling bells. We have seen how the off-stage aunt, she of the lolling lupins and unmown Twickenham lawn, had died. Nice reposeful Aunt Violet in her Irish garden has not long to go. Absently noting the pile of uprooted daisies, she remarks ' "Poor little things, it seems such a waste." ' Uncle Bill has blurted to Karen that Violet has to have an operation. To the reader it is obvious that this will not be successful. Violet plays Schubert, trails about, expresses faint regret about the daisies, in fact is in the process of becoming a ghost in her own life time.

By contrast the mood of *To The North*, both in and out of the gardens, seems lighter, happier. This is misleading. When you finish *To The North* you realise for all the comedy on the way the plot has been arrow-straight to tragedy. But there is so much laughter: ghastly Gerda Bligh with her pert, pretty ways and her dirndl skirt. Above all there is Lady Waters, a richly comic character who has a skilled nose for scenting misfortunes, an ominous, stately creature with a telephone 'that trilled from the heart, whose dinner gong boomed a warning.' Lady Waters ransacks her young friends' hearts for confidences but sometimes even the young in love find that things are going well, their emotional cellars empty. This does not do for Lady Waters, tirelessly alert for signs of trouble, and people are reduced to inventing quandaries for her to pick over. But in the end this lugubrious sybil is justified; she becomes, as Elizabeth Bowen puts it, 'sheer aunt.' We all know how right aunts invariably are.

Lady Waters has a country house called Farradays where there is a small white dog which, belonging to nobody in particular, belongs to the house and lacks confidence because it is always being left behind. Lady Waters has a Daimler, and a chauffeur who is sent to collect Pauline, an orphan, and a turbot from the station. The chauffeur asks Pauline how she is 'but looks with far greater solicitude at the turbot.' Later that weekend the orphan is commanded to take her uncle to see the view. Because of the rainclouds Pauline cannot find the view. There is a mournful procession around the garden, including the luckless dog, in search of the view; there is a heart-to-heart in an arbour but, owing to the dampness perhaps, the hearts are not properly aligned; as they all retire it is realised that if only there were no clouds there would be a very fine moon.

Another weekend is more fortunate. In part this is due to the fact that Lady Waters takes the more unhappy of her guests to view a ruined Roman Villa, ignoring justified warnings that it will be closed. This leaves the vicar free to take tea under the lime with others who make no bones about their contentment.

Also in *To the North* is a wonderful and appreciative account of gardens in London's St John's Wood, '. . . that airy uphill neighbourhood where the white and buff coloured houses, pilastered or gothic, seem to have been built in a grove. A fragrant, faint impropriety, orris-dust of a century, still hangs over part of this neighbourhood; glass passages lead in from high, green gates, garden walls are mysterious, laburnums falling between the windows and walls have their own secrets. Acacias whisper at nights round airy, ornate little houses in which pretty women lived singly but not always alone. In the unreal late moonlight you might hear a ghostly hansom click up the empty road, or see on a pale wall the shadow of an opera cloak . . .'. What strikes me about this beautifully written passage, beauty apart, is the possibility that, when writing about St John's Wood, Elizabeth Bowen remembered that it was to that neighbourhood, for sinsister reasons of his own, Count Fosco came to further his dangerous plans.

In total contrast there is the glorious account of the garden of the Russian villa in *The Hotel*, her first novel. *The Hotel* is set in Italy and the villa is called Russian because here, before the fall of the Tsar, lived some Russian nobles. The guests of the hotel go to explore the grounds; it is an outing, socially a notch up from a trip around the bay. But it serves much the same function: filling in time before luncheon.

The departed Russians may have gone but their presence, a very Bowen touch, is pervasive. The party, although they come from the same class, have as the common factor merely that they are staying

at the same place. At best they are polite enough to veil their in-
difference from each other. 'A number of disappearing pathways
darted off from the avenue; Corinthian pillars suggested themselves
through a net of undergrowth, and the arch of a stone bridge let one
suppose water. The party hung fire, embarrassed by this choice of
attractions, then continued to move slowly up the avenue in a close
formation.' 'She made for the bridge, appearing, so abrupt was the
turn of the path, to have plunged waist-deep into the dark shiny
leaves that flopped back, heavy as fish, from the sweep of her
skirts.' The phrase 'heavy as fish' is so unexpected a description of
leaves that I really do think I should repeat it. 'Heavy as fish.' It is
an insight that a lesser writer would have not dared employ. She is
also excellent at noting those charming little deceits which a cunning
landscape gardener deploys. 'The path by going up steeply for
short distances and only gradually coming down again, presented a
clever effect of being Alpine: one felt one must have climbed to a
great height.'

There is a luscious description of a tank bordered with yellow
marble full of opaque green water. 'The water looked solid; if a
body disappeared through the surface it might leave a dint, perhaps
a gash, which might slowly heal, but never a ripple.' It is plain that
a clergyman on holiday is just as prone to indulge in morbid fancies
as the rest of us. Holidays, particularly perhaps holidays in Italy
and a time spent in such a lush setting as the garden of the Russian
villa, make people unlike themselves.

Unlike themselves, in her very funny and perceptive essay, 'The
Mulberry Tree', about her old school, Down House, Elizabeth
Bowen notes the power to transform certain gardens wield. 'On
Saturday nights, in modified evening dress, quite a certain amount
of glamour set in. In the week curvilinear good looks were naturally
at a discount and a swaggering, nonchalant air cut the most ice. If
you were not good at games the best way of creating an atmosphere
was to be good at acting. We acted a good deal. On Saturday afternoons, one or two people who could play the piano emotionally had
seances in the music rooms. All this was the best we could put up
in the way of romance. All the same one or two people contrived to
keep diaries, moon round the garden alone and be quite unhappy.'
Then later: 'The other great social occasion was Saturday evening
(as I have said). We danced (we thought) rather glamorously in the

gymnasium to a piano, and dances were often booked up for days ahead. On summer Saturday evenings we walked round the garden between dances, feeling unlike ourselves. The garden was long, with lime trees and apple trees and long grass with cuckoo flowers in it: looked very beautiful in the late evening light, with the sound of the piano coming out through the gymnasium door. On winter Saturday evenings we danced more heartily, in order to keep warm. The staff filed in in evening dresses and sat on a platform, watching the dancing, and occasionally being asked to dance, with expressions of animation which, now I look back, command my respect.'

A tiny point I can't resist making: when Cecilia and Julian have occasion to visit a school in *To The North*, 'it looked pleasant enough, with limes drooping over the wall . . .'. One has only to recall Leopold and Henrietta in *The House in Paris* to see how good Elizabeth Bowen was at understanding children. The look back at Down House is affectionate. Too many literary accounts of school days are dismal welters in self-pity and advertise the author's famous sensibility. Not the Bowen way. Her sympathy with the state, you might almost say the plight, of childhood is light, ironic and without self-pity or self-advertising. Here is a description of the pupils' own gardens in *To The North*, and I suspect that they are an account of similar plots at Down House. 'The gardens were planted like rows of neat little graves, someone had a cement rabbit, someone had built a seat. Pauline looked drearily at some sprouting annuals, said that Dorothea and she had a garden but never won the prize. They turned in by a side door to the gymnasium where Dorothea, with a flash of blue knickers, turned a dignified but *dégagé* somersault on the bar, let down and swung the ropes, displayed a vaulting horse, and said they must see the studio.' The full flavour of a school visit is caught, a blend of strain, fatigue and aching boredom. Note that Elizabeth Bowen does not grind on about games. In 'The Mulberry Tree' she merely observes, 'I never thought worse of anyone for being good at games so long as she was not unattractive in other ways.'

It seems to me that gardens are everywhere in Elizabeth Bowen's novels. There are many Roman gardens in her wonderfully evocative *A Time in Rome*; Regent's Park provides the opening not only for

The Death of the Heart but also for *The Heat of the Day*. In the latter, summer is just tilting towards autumn. There are roses and an open air concert and the mood is tense. This is wartime. Bees are no doubt busy but their soothing buzzing may be replaced by far from soothing sounds when the night shift, the sinisterly droning Luftwaffe, come on station. Two of her most famous short stories, 'Look at all Those Roses' and 'Ivy Gripped the Steps', are redolent of gardens.

There is just not enough space to mention all the gardens which occur in Elizabeth Bowen's work. *The Little Girls* has several, as does *Eva Trout*, so if you want more Bowen gardens I must respectfully urge you to go dig for yourself. What I hope to have done is to point out that, in addition to all her virtues as a writer and despite her refusal to wear glasses, when it came to gardens, as with people, she had no need of an optician's skills. She missed nothing. Looking at tulips in bud she noticed the way the streaks of colour showed when they were still tightly buttoned, and she gets the colour of tulip buds precisely. 'Here stood the tulips just ready to flower: still grey and pointed, but brilliantly veined with the crimsons, mauves, yellows they were to be.' Grey. Not so many people would have seen that.

The Medieval Gardens at Fontevraud Abbey

GILLIAN MAWREY

Many English visitors to the famous châteaux of the Loire Valley in France find that one of the most interesting places is not a château at all, but an abbey. A little off the main tourist route, between Chinon, with its ruined castle and stories of Joan of Arc, and Saumur, where the château still dominates the river as it did in the *Très Riches Heures du Duc de Berry*, they find the Abbey of Fontevraud, and the tombs of four of England's kings and queens.

Henry II, founder of the Plantagenet dynasty, was buried here in 1189, followed later by his son Richard I 'the Lionheart', his widow Eleanor of Aquitaine and his daughter-in-law, Isabelle of Angoulême, King John's second wife.

The abbey had been founded in 1099 and was from the beginning an enormous enterprise – in fact five foundations in one. On a huge site it contained a monastery for Benedictine monks, a convent for nuns, a general hospital, a leper hospital and a house for ladies who wished (or were forced) to retire from the world and where gently-bred girls could be educated. Unusual in always having a woman rather than a man at its head, Fontevraud maintained its royal connections up to the Revolution, when it was dissolved and much damaged.

Napoleon turned the vast buildings into a prison, and when I first visited the abbey in the early 1960s chain gangs of prisoners could still be seen trudging off to work in the grounds. In those days tourists were shown little except the church, the four royal effigies, and the Romanesque circular kitchen with its twenty chimneys, designed to draw well whichever way the wind blew. But since then, successive French governments have subsidised a great deal of restoration and, together with the regional authorities, have established there the *Centre Culturel de l'Ouest*, which organises exhibitions, seminars and concerts in the wonderful stone buildings.

Now that much of the fabric has been restored, the directors of the centre have turned their attention to the gardens, and this year a recreation of a medieval garden was opened to the public. In fact, as Fontevraud goes in for multiples, there are four separate medieval gardens in different areas of the grounds.

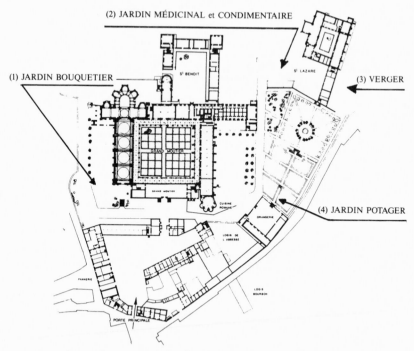

(2) JARDIN MÉDICINAL et CONDIMENTAIRE

(1) JARDIN BOUQUETIER

S' BENOIT

S' LAZARE

(3) VERGER

GRAND MOUTIER

GRAND MOUTIER

CUISINE ROMANE

(4) JARDIN POTAGER

ORANGERIE

LOGIS DE L'ABBESSE

FANNERIE

LOGIS BOURBON

PORTE PRINCIPALE

Near the main entrance to the church is the Jardin Bouquetier (1) or flower garden, to provide flowers for the altar. By the leper hospital, on what is believed to be the original site of the medieval herb garden, is the Jardin Médicinal et Condimentaire (2) – the medicinal garden, which also contains herbs for flavouring. The largest garden is the Potager (4) or vegetable garden, and there is also an orchard or Verger (3) with nut and fruit trees.

The original impetus to recreate a medieval garden on this medieval site came from the French cosmetic firm of Yves Rocher, pioneers of cosmetics based on natural sources. They have large experimental nurseries in Brittany where they breed plants and investigate their potential uses, and before approaching the Cultural Centre at Fontevraud they had already recreated old gardens in Spain and Ireland and were working on another in Belgium. When Monsieur Baugé, the then Director of the Cultural Centre, showed an interest in the idea, they persuaded Professor Claude-Charles Mathon, an ethno-biologist who works at the Universities of Paris and Poitiers, to become involved. He in turn enlisted the help of

Flower garden outside church

Flower garden showing 'fleur de lys'

Dr John Harvey, who has researched early gardens for over twenty years and whose book *Medieval Gardens* (Batsford 1981) was the chief published source of information in the planning of the garden.

At Fontevraud it was decided to make the garden representative of what might have been seen there at the height of the Plantagenets' power. A cut-off date of 1200 was chosen, but such an early date meant much rigorous research to establish the exact plants which would have been grown then and to find the nearest available equivalent. Professor Mathon, with the help of John Harvey, made a list of the plants and trees he thought ought to be in the garden and gave advice on where they might be found, and Monsieur Michel Cambornac of the Yves Rocher laboratories then endeavoured to provide them.

He found particular problems when choosing the flowers for the Jardin Bouquetier, as plants in the early Middle Ages were more often grown for practical than ornamental purposes (even the favourite and highly symbolic roses and lilies were also used medicinally) and those that have survived have been much changed both by chance and by deliberate breeding. Even with what seem obvious survivals care has to be taken. For instance the national flower of the French, the *fleur de lys*, is not a lily in the modern sense, but the Florentine iris. It was adopted as a symbol for his banners by Clovis in the fifth century because he found it growing on the site of one of his battles. When Louis VII decided to make it the symbol of France it became known as the *fleur de Louis*, a name which evolved into *fleur de lys*.

The flower garden is itself divided into two parts. One has the flowers in large beds, while the other has the individual plants set in small beds separated by terracotta tiles. Monsieur Jean Poulain, the deputy director of the Cultural Centre who has done most of the coordinating of the garden, admitted that the tiles were one of the few anachronisms. Plants *were* grown in separate beds in this way in the twelfth century, but the tiles used to separate the flowers here are sixteenth century, older ones being rare and too good to risk outdoors. (Indeed even those used are showing the effects of frost.)

Flowers grown in the Jardin Bouquetier include both lilies and irises, broom (*Planta genista*, the flower of the Plantagenets), bellis daisy, marigold, peony, periwinkle, poppy, and violet.

Gardener working in tiled part of flower garden

The herb garden was the easiest to recreate as the varieties have changed little over the centuries, in part because of the declining reliance on herbal medicine. The use of herbs in cooking has seen a great revival in recent years and there are signs that this is being followed by a renewed interest in their medicinal use. Certainly there is evidence at Fontevraud that medieval medicine and medieval cookery were both more sophisticated than many people believe.

For flavouring there were different sorts of mint, sage, fennel (nearer to our wild fennel than to today's cultivated or Florentine fennel), cumin, rosemary, caraway, aniseed, chives, chervil, coriander, savory, dill, mustard and parsley, as well as now rarer herbs such as gith (*Nigella sativa*). Most of these herbs had medicinal uses as well, while others, such as pennyroyal, rue, agrimony, wormwood, fever-few, betony and squill were grown mainly for their healing powers.

Many French people today drink herbal teas or *tisanes* to cure mild complaints or as a quick pick-me-up where we would prefer a cup of tea. In the Middle Ages they were equally keen. They used tansy and costmary (also known in England as alecost from its use in flavouring ale) and many other plants, but the great favourite, with the nuns at least, seems to have been madder. Better known now as a dye, madder had many uses in the Middle Ages, and so much

Herb garden with old lime trees

madder tea was drunk by the nuns of Fontevraud that when their bones were dug up later, their skeletons were found to be bright orange from the effect of the drink.

The herb garden lies beneath an avenue of old lime trees, pollarded many times in the French fashion. Each plant is clearly labelled with its botanical and common names and the date of its probable arrival in Europe. The early writings which mention it are cited and some possible uses suggested, and there is a small but detailed drawing of the plant in flower to aid identification during non-flowering seasons.

The Potager is the largest of the four gardens and as well as vegetables contains practical plants like flax for linen, hemp for ropes and canvas, soapwort for soap, teasels for carding wool, and woad and madder for dyeing it. Hops and a vine have also been planted in this section. Most kitchens, monastic or lay, brewed beer or made wine as the freshness of the drinking water could not always be relied on.

Fresh meat was something else that was not always available in the Middle Ages, and Benedictines were in any case vegetarian; so vegetables formed an important part of the abbey diet as well as often being used as specifics against disease. The range of fresh vegetables was impressive – cabbage, carrot, beet (of which they ate the tops but not the root), parsnip, celery, lettuce, chicory, landcress (but no watercress until the nineteenth century), kohlrabi, chard, cardoons (the heads were cooked and eaten like those of artichokes or else dried and used instead of rennet in cheese-making, while the inner stems and hearts were eaten like celery), mallow, kale, leeks, chives, onion and garlic (and probably shallots too), horseradish, burdock (cooked like salsify) and cucumber. They also had melons, but of course no tomatoes or potatoes.

Pulses which could be dried and eaten in the winter were particularly important as they provided protein when other sources had run out. In this part of the garden grow peas, chick-peas, lentils and different sorts of beans; it also contains the cereals, although they, like many of the other major sources of food, would obviously have been grown on a much larger scale to support all the inhabitants of the abbey.

Finding the correct medieval variety of all these vegetables and grains again proved a problem for, like flowers, they too have changed greatly over the centuries. Those who try to grow the plants as well as to recreate the layout of old gardens have two ways of obtaining their plants. The first is to search for chance survivals still growing in out-of-the-way places. The ruins of castles and monasteries are good places to look, and Professor Mathon found an old form of beet growing on the slopes of the ruined castle of Moncontour only thirty miles away. But this form of research can prove very frustrating. For instance, although Professor Mathon found early forms of cabbage in Brittany and Cornwall and knew that there were two or three places in the world where even earlier varieties were still cultivated, he has so far been unable to obtain any seed.

The other method of obtaining medieval plants is by breeding back to them. Monsieur Cambornac is unlike most modern plant breeders, who try to create *new* varieties by crossing existing ones. He works backwards to try to get as near as possible to *old* ones; but with such an early cut-off date at Fontevraud he has been unable in a few cases, such as carrots, to get as close as he would have liked to the really early varieties and has had to compromise on later forms. (Of course, most of these old varieties would not taste as good as modern ones. Many would be very tough, the cabbage would be pretty pungent, and the carrots quite pale and spindly, more like the wild carrot found in hedgerows today.)

Trying to find genuinely old forms of fruit trees posed some of the same problems, particularly as grafting is such a slow method of creating new (or in this case old) stock. Although the Verger was begun before the rest of the garden, it is the one area that is still unfinished. Trees will be planted for some time to come, until there is as complete a selection as possible of the many fruits that were available in the twelfth century. Several varieties of apple and pear were grown then, as well as cherry, mulberry, fig, peach, plum, quince, and service (a variety of *sorbus* producing a fruit which is edible only when over-ripe). Nut trees were particularly important as not only was their oil used in both cooking and medicine, but the nuts themselves were a valuable source of protein. The abbey would have had almond, sweet or Spanish chestnut, walnut and hazelnut, but of course the olive would not thrive so far north. Bay trees flourish in the area, often damaged by severe winters but usually shooting again in the spring; lime trees would give leaves for *tisanes* as well as a particularly pleasant shade (unlike the walnut, whose shade is reckoned to be unhealthy); buckthorn was grown for the value of its bark in medicine and for its berries which gave green ink, and elder for its flowers and berries. (A French friend told me that some nuns of his acquaintance make particularly good elderberry wine, which they are quite convinced is non-alcoholic!)

The layout of these four gardens pays equal attention to historical accuracy, although again a few anachronisms have been allowed. The beds in the Potager have been outlined either with low box hedges or with small fences of interwoven reeds. It looks charming, but neither method is strictly in period. Box was not used in this way until the Renaissance, and although we know that fences of reeds (a bit like wickerwork) *were* used, they would have been for keeping animals in or out, and so would have been three or four feet high rather than a few inches.

A by now obvious question is how those involved in recreating this garden could be so sure of what it ought to look like. In fact, until quite recently little research had been done into medieval horticulture. The eccentric Sir Frank Crisp did some work on the subject before making his garden at Friar's Park, near Henley, and

Herb garden, lime trees, box hedges

'Potager' with gardener and wicker fence

published the results in 1914 as a guide to the garden; and there have been chapters in various histories of gardening: but the subject was strangely neglected until 1981 when John Harvey published his *Medieval Gardens* and Teresa McLean her *Medieval English Gardens*. Both books were consulted by those working at Fontevraud, as I gather that there is no book on the subject in French.

There are of course primary sources as well – for those with enough Latin to read them. One of the most important was found in the monastery of St Gall in Switzerland and is known as the St Gall plan, although in fact it is probably an idealised version of the layout of the monastery of Christ Church, Canterbury. Made in the early ninth century, it shows not only the monastic buildings but the gardens as well. Even more helpfully, each flower-bed and tree is labelled, so that we get a list of forty-eight plants. Strangely enough, this period is more fruitful than later ones for plant historians; the Emperor Charlemagne ordered a list of plants to be compiled as a schedule to one of his laws, and a few years later a monk called Walafrid Strabo mentions twenty-three plants in his poem *Hortulus*.

There are other manuscript sources, some utilitarian – legal documents, inventories, recipes and so on – and others poetic. The former are the more reliable, for poets were inclined to write about idealised gardens filled with flowers they may have heard of but not seen. The beautiful miniature illustrations in some manuscripts must also be treated with caution. They can give valuable information about garden design and content, but the artists were naturally inclined to emphasise what was unusual and leave out the commonplace. Aesthetics were considered when gardens were laid out, and the value of shade and water was appreciated even before the Moorish influence of the thirteenth century; but the more exotic gardens in early pictures were at best depictions of an individual patron's taste.

The fascinating gardens at Fontevraud have been largely created in only two years. Admittedly some areas are still a little sparse and need a few more years' growth before they look at their best (I spotted a few modern roses in the Potager, filling in while older plants grew) but it is an impressive achievement in such a short time.

The financial side is interesting, as the costs are remarkably small. The Cultural Centre paid for the planting, funded by central

government and various regional authorities, and the firm of Yves
Rocher provided the plants and trees out of their normal budget.
No great structural work was necessary as the gardens were defined
by the existing layout of the monastic buildings. Where the soil
needed enriching this was done with spent mushroom compost
from nearby growers costing nothing except for sterilisation and
transport. The Cultural Centre pays for the upkeep of the garden,
but this comes to less than £2000 a year as they have only one
gardener for one day a week. One expense is for water, which is
metered in France and nearly always needed in the summer.

Monsieur Poulain is now turning his attention to another garden
project within the grounds of the abbey. This is the creation of a
Parc Bourbon, a formal seventeenth-century garden and park to
tie in with Fontevraud's other great period of prosperity when
Louis XV sent his four daughters to be educated there. This will be
a much bigger and more expensive undertaking than the Jardin
Médiéval as it will cover four hectares and will mostly be laid out
from new. Some potentially splendid avenues of trees have already
been planted, and it is hoped that the garden will be opened to the
public within five years.

Photographs by the author

Graham Stuart Thomas in his garden near Woking, Surrey.
Photograph by Nigel Colborn

For the Love of Beauty

A Conversation with GRAHAM STUART THOMAS

NIGEL COLBORN

Present a small boy with a fuchsia plant and who knows what will happen next? Six-year-old fingers are invariably sticky but seldom green. Even if he was keen on plants, your average little mite would have pulled the plant up a couple of times a day just to see how the roots were growing. But for Graham Stuart Thomas this present, given by a fond godfather, was a lodestar. It helped him to set his course towards a life in horticulture. There was to be no looking back, no compromise, and no consideration of anything else. Several years later, the fuchsia was still thriving – protected under a pile of ashes each winter – and the little boy already becoming something of an expert.

What made him know with such certainty, so early in his life, that gardens and gardening would be his vocation? His answer was succinct: 'A love of beauty.' Sipping coffee in his sitting room, I had no need to ask him to expand his reply. Evidence of a life devoted to aestheticism was plain to see: two pianos side by side with music scores ready for use, attractive furniture, a wall vase containing branches with harmonious leaf textures highlighted with forsythia blossom, and the walls hung with superb copies of sixteenth century drawings. Elsewhere in the house, small vases with late winter flowers were dotted about. 'I'm sorry there's a mess in here,' he told me as I followed him into the kitchen, 'my home help isn't coming today.' The 'mess' looked immaculate and well ordered to me. So did the garden. Glancing through the windows I could see patches of winter heather and above them, bright red stems of *Cornus alba* 'Sibirica' showed well against a backdrop of *Elaeagnus* × *ebbingei* 'Gilt Edge'. It was difficult to tear my eyes away, knowing that the author of such books as *Perennial Garden Plants* and *Colour in the Winter Garden* would be sure to have a feast of treasures to gloat over on this bright March morning. A garden tour was promised for later, so meanwhile we got down to the business of delving into his past. First, I asked him what makes a gardener. Without hesitation he replied:

'Close contact with the soil. A knowledge of plants and how to use them.' He went on, 'teaching the *art* of gardening is much neglected today. Horticulture leans very much in the direction of technology. In all these colleges, the scientific and craft side takes precedence over the art side.'

Graham Thomas was born in Cambridge in 1909. Both his parents were talented artists – the Holbein copies in the sitting room turned out to be by Mr Thomas senior – and were capable gardeners. At first, the little boy was allowed to cultivate a small piece of ground between a laurel hedge and the rubbish area. As he grew older, alpines became his main interest and his father allowed him to plant elsewhere in the Thomas family garden. At school his best subjects were what teachers today call 'humanities' but science seems to have left him cold. He even disliked botany and claims to have been bad at drawing, though it seems likely that the teachers lacked talent rather than the pupil. Childhood illnesses plagued him in those days: 'I wasn't at all a strong and healthy chap,' he said,

Daphne laureola

'eventually I gave up school and had private tuition.' His schoolboy contemporaries must have thought him rather odd – flowers and gardens hardly go with a roustabout image – and his parents were not at all keen on his choosing a career that offered prospects of hard work with but little financial reward.

Between the world wars, the Cambridge Botanic Garden was run on a shoestring. One way of overcoming the problem of under-funding was to take on students who, in return for their work, would receive training. They also had permission to attend botany lectures at the university free of charge. When Graham Thomas was sixteen, he told his father that he wanted to work in the Botanic Garden. It was not a popular decision with the family but they permitted him to live at home for two and a half years while he served what amounted to much more than a mere apprenticeship. During his spell at Cambridge he attended lectures in the company of such gifted undergraduates as John Gilmour who became director

Crocus fleischeri and *Crocus sieberi*

of The Royal Horticultural Society's garden at Wisley, and Tutin and Warburg who subsequently produced the *Flora of the British Isles* – the standard work on our flora for this century, superseding Bentham and Hooker. The garden's Director in 1926 was H. Gilbert-Carter, a keen linguist who invited students to attend reading sessions in Latin and German. As well as puzzling over abstruse German botanical works, Thomas was introduced to the delights of Virgil's *Georgics* with its accounts of Roman agriculture.

I asked him what the Botanic Garden was like in the twenties? 'Penniless,' he said, 'but still much as it had been when designed a century before. Compact. It has been enlarged and, to my mind, spoilt in many places. They spoilt it by putting that gigantic rock garden there and doing away with a lot of the original design. There used to be blocks of evergreen on every corner – box or yew or phillyrea – but that's all gone by the board.' Work at Cambridge, without pay, could have gone on for ever but as Thomas writes in *Three Gardens*: '. . . it was conveyed to me by my father that I had better start earning my living.'

The next move was to Clarence Elliot's famous Six Hills Nursery. A short career here, as it happened, because after nine months an attack of scarlet fever landed him in hospital. In those days of the slump, employees had little legislation to protect them and, after a few weeks away sick, he was sacked. Nevertheless, he had had time

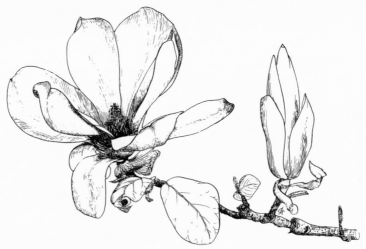

Magnolia × soulangiana

Fuchsia 'Eva Boerg'

to sample life in a busy commercial nursery and to buckle down to the laborious routine. His pay was paltry, even for the early thirties: fourteen shillings (70 pence) per week – about half his real cost of living, so his father was still having to subsidise him. His accounts of dispatches from Clarence Elliot, plant hunting in the Alps, make interesting reading. Boxes containing masses of *Primula allionii*, ramondas or gentians would arrive from abroad to be resuscitated and potted up. Clearly, the concept of conserving these species in the wild by limiting collecting to seed had not yet occurred to commercial nurserymen.

After Six Hills, he managed to land himself a job with T. Hilling and Co. at Chobham, Surrey. Although the area abounded with famous nurseries and Wisley was just round the corner, Hilling was a relatively new wholesale outlet. When he joined them, their production was limited to trees and shrubs. As Alpine and Herbaceous Foreman, his task was to develop a stock of non-woody plants. Working hours were demanding: 7.30 to 5.30 Monday to Friday, 7.30 to 12.30 on Saturdays and one whole week's holiday every year!

With Graham Thomas, Hilling had struck gold. By now in his early twenties, he had not only amassed a sound knowledge of plants, but had also a useful collection of his own from which to propagate. Finding a wide range of stock plants was less difficult in those days because there were so many nurseries with large collections. Although his responsibility was for herbaceous and alpine plants, he also worked in the other divisions of the nursery and eventually became Manager. By that time the business had expanded from fairly humble beginnings to 330 acres. In those blissful days, before garden centres and plastic Georgian urns had come upon the earth, Hilling customers consisted of other nurseries or public corporations. Plants were distributed all over the United Kingdom and overseas. The Royal Parks were among their more prestigious institutional clients.

Successful though his career with Hilling was, the wholesale nature of their business tended to bore him. As an artist he must have found it irksome to spend his days propagating rather than gardening. He had longed to exhibit at Chelsea ever since his first visit there in 1929. He also felt a need to communicate more directly with people who were in the forefront of gardening and garden

Arbutus unedo

design. A perfect opportunity for this presented itself in 1955. He applied for, and landed, the post of Gardens Adviser to the National Trust. This was a part-time appointment, since the Trust held no more than a handful of gardens in those days, and he was quite able to hold down both jobs.

A further opportunity to escape from the wholesale business presented itself when Graham Thomas's good friend James Russell asked for help with his Sunningdale Nurseries. Russell was a distant relative of the proprietor (not the original) and wanted to set the business back on its feet after some years of decline. He was not a trained horticulturist but was an excellent plantsman, who having started with rhododendrons went on to build a unique collection of roses. Although the nursery was badly run down, Graham Thomas recognised its great potential. Much of the soil was good natured, being easy to work, even after rain, and the premises were ideally

placed for London and the Home Counties. He was also mindful of
its famous history. The original founders, Noble and Standish, had
started propagating there in 1847 when the emphasis was on
rhododendrons, especially new species coming in from the Himalaya
and from China. He joined forces with Russell and was to manage
the nursery for fifteen years. Different soil types on the site, from
heavy clay to thin sand and even some black fen, enabled them to
raise a miscellany of plants requiring all kinds of different conditions.

Under their management, artistry emerged in the nursery. There
were display beds, rhododendron woods and many specimen trees
and shrubs. Sunningdale became known as 'The most beautiful
nursery in the country.' In the late sixties, towards the end of
Graham Thomas's spell as manager there, they were taken over by
Waterer Sons and Crisp Ltd. The rationale was that Sunningdale
plantsmanship would be allied to Waterers' business acumen to
make the new, enlarged nursery a great commercial success. What
actually happened was rather different. Over the next few years,
the range of plants grown at Sunningdale was reduced and eventually
Waterers was absorbed into Notcutts, losing its identity as an
individual firm. But both Thomas and Russell had departed some
time before this chain of events took place. Jim Russell moved to
Castle Howard and by now work at the National Trust was making
a much heavier demand on Graham Thomas's time.

The important rôle played by the National Trust in preserving
some of our best gardens cannot be overestimated. Before the war,
the Trust owned several great houses which were set in historic
landscapes. Many of those gardens suffered badly in the war years
but worse, several private owners of less important houses but with
good gardens were confronted with the impossible task of carrying
out expensive repairs during the miserable period of post-war
austerity. The remedy, if these gardens were to be rescued, was to
raise enough money for restoration and maintenance, even though
their houses were not of sufficient stature in their own right for the
National Trust to accept. To this end, a joint Gardens Committee
was set up with members from both the Royal Horticultural Society
and the Trust. It was to this committee that Graham Thomas first
reported in 1955. As the years went by, the number of gardens under
his wing increased. Eventually funds grew larger, but in the fifties
money was short and the heritage 'industry' had hardly started. 'It

was a pinchpenny affair,' he said, 'everything was done on a very tight string. You were lucky if what you decided to plant got planted that year.'

One of the first acquisitions after the war was Hidcote Manor in the Cotswolds. It had suffered badly and took several years to restore. Other examples of early gardens on which Graham Thomas advised were Blickling in Norfolk, Polesden Lacey in Surrey and Trelissick, a Cornish garden that needed a great deal of work. Some gardens, like Sheffield Park and Killerton, were in a sorry state, needing emergency restoration. Elsewhere, the brief was to extend seasons of colour and interest. 'At Trelissick, for instance,' he said, 'the garden consisted of little bits of shrubs in island beds all over the place. As with so many other Cornish gardens, there was nothing to see after June. That caused thought. I built up an *aide-mémoire* of things which flower each fortnight during the year.' Eventually, these notes were developed until they emerged in book form as *The Art of Planting*. Useful information indeed, enabling the garden planner to select plants within various colour ranges to provide a succession of displays right through the growing season and beyond into winter.

I asked whether it was possible to restore gardens a century or more old to their truly original state. 'Up to a point,' he said. 'It depends how involved the design is. There was a certain amount of simplification to be done in some gardens because we were not allowed to take on extra labour.' Looking back, some gardens give him an especial feeling of pride. Hidcote has become world famous and Wallington, in Northumberland, was something of a triumph too: 'It came to us in a most woebegone state. Full of weeds.' Another major achievement was Mount Stewart in Northern Ireland: 'I feel tremendous pride in restoration there because I regard it now as one of the six best gardens in the British Isles. It is so varied in its attractions: formality as well as natural planting, a great lake, good house and a fine collection of rare plants. Its original designer, Lady Londonderry, was not only interested in rare things but in colour and beauty.' Another great transformation was in the 18th century design at Claremont, Surrey which had become totally overgrown.

The influence exerted on National Trust gardens by Graham Thomas can be seen across the country. Although he has always been careful to match planting styles to the idiom of each particular place, his own ideas of colour combinations and plant associations have usually been apparent. In his younger days he met Gertrude Jekyll and walked her garden at Munstead Wood. 'She was a very old lady then,' he said. 'She was just sitting in her chair, hair parted in the middle and smarmed down. She was very quietly spoken. A cultured voice. It was a lovely house, Munstead, not old but with all the old ways about it.' Gertrude Jekyll told him to walk round the garden and bring back a sprig of anything he wanted to discuss with her. 'I'd heard about her borders and read her books, of course, but her garden was absolutely incredible. You see, she'd been working on those borders for forty years. Nobody can get a border right first go and she'd gone on and on, polishing. She knew just how to mix her colours and so on. She was a clever old stick – down to earth as well as an artist.'

Besides his work with the National Trust and his career as a

Rosa damascena var. *semperflorens*

Rosa stellata var. *mirifica*

nursery manager, Graham Stuart Thomas is a name linked with roses – particularly shrub roses. He has written three comprehensive books about them – *The Old Shrub Roses*, *Shrub Roses of Today* and *Climbing Roses Old and New*. His knowledge of them is profound and his love for them manifest in his book illustrations. His original in-

Rosa wichuraiana

terest in them came about like this: At the Cambridge Botanic
Garden he had worked with the nephew of G. N. Smith who owned
Daisy Hill Nurseries in Northern Ireland. Just before the war, they
went bankrupt and, in lieu of payment, Hilling took their collection of
rare roses. Nurseries went dormant during the war but were allowed
to keep stocks ready for multiplication when peace returned, so the

roses sat in a field, keeping the weeds company. Later Beckwiths of Hoddesdon, and Bunyard in Kent gave up, both nurseries having interesting collections of old roses. From that nucleus he went out actively looking for more. There were many at Nymans, in Sussex, and others at The Hon. Robert (Bobbie) James's garden in York-shire. The main influx from abroad came from the Roseraie de l'Haÿ and from Sangerhausen (the German National Rose Garden). There were also imports from America and Holland.

'By and large,' he said, 'the nomenclature was incredibly un-reliable. What I've got are pretty accurate now but there are still two that I want to find with their legitimate names – "Fantin Latour" and "Empress Josephine." There is no mention of either in any of the old books but those names have stuck and I've no doubt they will stay.' I asked him about the Sissinghurst rose and whether it was 'Rose des Maures'. 'I wish they wouldn't keep raking up that *stupid* name!' he retorted. 'There isn't any such thing as "Rose des Maures" in any old book whatever, so it should be called "Sissinghurst". It may have originated there. A friend did find the self same thing in Devon but that may have come from Sissinghurst.' Vita Sackville-West and Hilda Murrell both collected old roses but all from the same sources as Graham Thomas. He is convinced they are here to stay and will not go out of fashion again. 'They are grown so widely now,' he declared, 'their safety is assured by such organisations as the NCCPG with the National Collection housed by the National Trust at Mottisfont.'

Graham Thomas has several qualities in common with Jekyll, including talents for drawing, painting and writing. His illustrations are informative and supremely beautiful. They appear in most of his books – would that there were more! – and several are reproduced in large format in his *Gardens of the National Trust* and at last, the whole collection has been published recently in a single volume – *The Complete Paintings and Drawings of Graham Stuart Thomas* (London, Thames & Hudson, 1987; New York, Sagapress.) Part of their appeal lies in the arrangement of subject matter on the page. In *Colour in the Winter Garden*, for example, a cluster of winter twigs is shown with shades ranging from the silver of *Perovskia atriplicifolia*, through pale and deep greens (*Cornus stolonifera* and *Leycesteria formosa*) to deep red *Cornus alba*. Turn then to the frontispiece of the same book and there is an array of leaf colour: *Arum italicum* 'Pictum',

Bergenia purpurascens and *Elaeagnus pungens* 'Dicksonii'. How simple it would be, after studying the plates, to transpose these ideas to a winter border! He claims to be entirely self taught but open *The Complete Paintings* and you will see a wild rose in the inside cover painted by his father and over the page a peacock butterfly by his mother. Clearly, even if not inherited, something has rubbed off.

Later, we turned to his books. I asked what made him write so well. As before, his reply was: 'Love of beauty.' Beauty in the English language is as dear to him as beauty in a well designed garden. 'You only have to read English poetry to discover that kind of beauty.' As with his painting, he had no special training. 'My parents spoke good English,' he said. 'I realise that more than ever today, when I hear so much sloppy English being written and spoken. I also had to write catalogues. That makes you economical with words.' The books themselves are still widely used and some are in the process of being revised for reissue. The three on roses have become standard works, as has *Perennial Garden Plants*. The value of all his books, both specific plant directories and the instructional works like *Plants for Ground Cover*, is in their artistic advice. Colours and textures and how to juxtapose these for optimum effect are covered so clearly that one longs to put down the book and rush out to rescue one's own planting attempts.

When we turned to his personal life, I sensed that I was trespassing. In answer to the inevitable questions about marriage he said, 'I was wedded to horticulture.' Very much the confirmed bachelor, he is an avid reader and a keen amateur musician. Had he considered a career in music? 'Heavens no! That really would have been hazardous.' But he founded a madrigal group forty years ago, enjoys singing and was an accomplished pianist. His tastes in poetry and literature are akin to his musical predilections – anything up to but not after Vaughan Williams. He enjoys Bach and Brahms but not Britten; Trollope and Galsworthy but not Anthony Burgess or Graham Greene.

Graham Thomas has had a brilliant career. His contribution to horticulture has been recognised and appreciated by his peers. In 1968 the Royal Horticultural Society awarded him the Victoria Medal of Honour – their highest award – and he received an O.B.E. in 1975. He has enjoyed other honours such as the Dean Hole Medal in 1976 from the Royal National Rose Society, and is active in numerous societies. He is vice president of the Garden History Society and of the British Hosta and Hemerocallis Society. He has written numerous articles and thirteen books, most of which are still in print. He is not a large man, by any manner of means, and not in the least aggressive or brusque. However, despite his perfect manners and graceful courtesy, he has strong opinions and an unwillingness to allow any of his endeavours to fall very far short of perfection. This dedication is evident in all his art, writing, gardening – even in his spoken English. His work will be appreciated for many years to come. Much of his literary output deserves its place among earlier classics by such writers as Bowles, Farrer and Jekyll. On my own shelf, his books have the scruffiest spines because they are the most used.

Clematis cirrhosa var. *balearica*

The illustrations for this article are reproduced from The Complete Flower Paintings and Drawings of Graham Stuart Thomas, (*London, Thames and Hudson, 1987*).

Angraecum sesquipedale

Dreaming of Orchids

HEDVIKA FRASER

Close to the modern Mustek metro station in Prague is a small
florist's shop. Years ago, it held me spellbound for days. An enormous
frilled blossom of soft lilac with a deep purple velvety lip appeared
somewhat incongruously in the middle of a few cyclamen plants,
potted ferns, and some vases of cut carnations. The exotic flower
fascinated me: I made a detour every day just to see it. A cattleya.
I was in my early teens, and during the fifties Czechoslovakia was in
a period of austerity. Rather wistfully I determined one day to grow
plants bearing these extraordinary flowers.

A decade later I came across a travel book about Madagascar. Its
Polish author had spent some time in a little Malagasy village, and
the slim book was full of photographs – all black and white – of
charming ring-tail lemurs, weird chameleons and strange plants.
Among them was an orchid. Only this time it was not a cattleya of
course, but a 'Comet Orchid' with a strange name of *Angraecum
sesquipedale*. Large, stiff, presumably white as far as I could see from
the photograph, the star-shaped flower with a very long spur looked
quite different from anything I had ever seen before. To visit
Madagascar and see these plants and animals for myself was another
secret ambition to store for the future. At that time a journey to
Poland or Bulgaria was perhaps possible for an ordinary citizen,
but Madagascar certainly did not exist on the Czech tourist maps
in the early sixties.

All things in good time. Two decades later I was settled in Britain,
a proud owner of a few dozen orchids, cattleyas among them. And
then I saw an advertisement for a three weeks botanical holiday in
Madagascar.

We landed in Antananarivo, the capital, in mid-August. It was not
at all what I expected. Being high up on a mountain plateau in the
centre of this vast island, the temperature was not much higher
than our indifferent British summer. Not until we reached Tulear
in the south-west corner of the island did we feel we were truly in
the tropics. The west coast was impressive, miles and miles of spiny
forest creeping right down to the long deserted sparkling white
sandy beaches. But fascinating as all the Didierea, Euphorbia, and

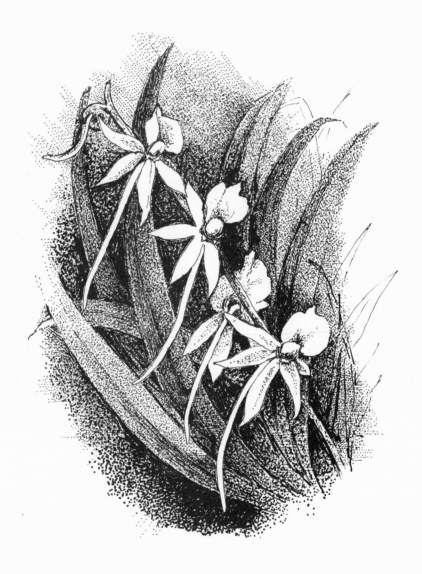

Angraecum eburneum

other genera with their threatening spines, barbs, hooks and nasty sap were, I could not wait to have my first taste of the tropical rain forest of my imagination: hot, steamy, luscious, impenetrable vegetation of Tarzan and Jane type. Even the happy few days of close encounters with the inquisitive, amusing, boisterous ring-tails and their shy, gentle sifaka cousins in the south-east corner of Madagascar were only a wonderful interlude. I longed to see the juicy jungle of my dreams, every tree dripping with water and orchids.

At last we went there, to Perinet and Moramanga, two small towns half way down the eastern strip of Madagascar's tropical rain forest. And rain it did, although not all the time. There was just enough to make the paths slippery with mud and wriggling with leeches, but, oh, the magic surrounding us! Every tree struggling to be taller than its neighbours, every branch weighed down with epiphytes and lianas, every square inch covered by moss, by ferns, by peperomias, by orchids. Scores of them! angraecum, jumellea, aerangis, aeranthes, down to the humble bulbophyllum, all jumbled together in a wonderful mixture. Miniscule plants and huge clumps, all fighting for light and space, all intent on survival, all sparkling with raindrops in the sunshine. And then, above the quiet of the forest, the haunting, wailing, eery calls of a troupe of indri, Madagascar's largest lemur. Unforgettable magic.

Ile Sainte Marie, reached a few days later by Twin Otter, remains in my memory a tiny pocket of paradise left on Earth. Surrounded by a band of coral reef, this lovely little island, once the haunt of pirates, is rich in clove trees, coconut palms, erythronias, Baringtonias, and orchids. Chasing after fireflies and glow-worms on star-lit evenings, we found the air heavy with the scent of dozens of angraecums: *A. sesquipedale* and *A. eburneum* festoon every tree trunk along the beach, their waxy flowers glistening in the dark. A long squelchy march through paddy fields under the blistering sun on the neighbouring tiny Ile aux Nattes brought us another reward: beautiful and rare *Eulophiella roempleriana*. A robust plant nestling in the crowns of pandanus, it has gracefully arching spikes of about a dozen flowers each. The blooms are gorgeous, about 3 inches across, deep pink with a cream lip, and are very sweetly scented. The sight of a pandanus grove richly adorned with these magnificent flowers was worth every step of our long plod in the hot sun.

The attitude of the local villagers to this beauty was rare, too.

Eulophillea roempleriana

Napoleon, the village chief, sent his own grandson to show us the orchids. He warned us: 'Do not pick the orchids. They are beautiful and we are proud to have them growing on our island.' What a difference from the rest of Madagascar! Orchids and pachypodium, another Malagasy speciality, are often offered to tourists, indeed there are open tables full of desiccated plants for sale at roadsides. Good old Napoleon. Perhaps his grandson and the young generation of Malagasy inherit his pride in the beauty of plants surrounding them. So far there is little evidence of it. Like in so many other poor countries, forests fall for firewood, and orchids disappear with trees.

Surprisingly our modern techniques of micropropagation seem not to have touched Malagasy orchids: the famous *Angraecum sesquipedale* is offered occasionally by British nurserymen, sometimes *A. eburneum* also, and some aerangis species, but the others remain undiscovered by our orchid enthusiasts. Yet they are every bit as beautiful as any other genera, and given warmth and humidity, no more difficult to grow and flower than my first favourites, the cattleyas. Indeed in my own orchid house, the two genera thrive side by side: angraecoids to remind me of a wonderful holiday and a dream come true, cattleyas to tempt me to visit more far away countries. Because regardless how well we grow and flower orchids in the controlled conditions of our greenhouses, how tidily we tie their pseudobulbs and prop up their flower spikes, a huge shaggy clump of orchid growing wild on a tree, battling for supremacy with ferns and mosses and victoriously spilling a shower of blossom is a breathtaking, wonderful sight, a sight far removed from that one frilled purple cattleya blossom that set me dreaming by a florist's window almost thirty years ago.

Drawings by Mary Heneghan

John Rose's Pineapple*

HERMIA OLIVER

The celebrated painting showing 'Mr Rose, the royal Gardener presenting to King Charles 2nd the first pineapple raised in England', as Horace Walpole first described it in a label on the back, was exhibited at the 'Glory of the Garden' exhibition at Sotheby's in 1987. It has raised more problems and arguments than, surely, any other painting. What mansion is shown in the background? Where did Rose raise this pineapple? Who painted the picture? Above all, did Rose in fact raise *any* pineapple in Restoration England?

At least three copies of the painting exist, and two engravings. John Rose and the king are on a terrace beside a baroque fountain,

* When I wrote 'Jane Austen's Gardens' (*Hortus 5*, Spring 1988) I followed Horace Walpole's description of Rose presenting the pineapple at Dawney Court near Windsor, but the doubts it raised in my mind resulted in the research on which this article is based.

separated from a garden by a low balustraded wall with two classical statues at its entrance. Rose, then Keeper and Gardener of St James's Park garden, is on one knee, holding up a pineapple by the stalk. The king, standing under a conifer growing in a large pot on a pedestal, is extending his hand towards the pineapple. The *parterre* of the garden is unattractively divided by horizontal lines of low hedging, except for a circle of orange trees in pots around a second fountain at the back. The imposing seventeenth-century three-storied brick house with stone facings in the background has a roundheaded gable on the wing nearest the spectator and has no dormer windows.

The picture was given to Walpole by the Revd William Pennicott, rector of Long Ditton (not far from Strawberry Hill) from 1758 till 1811, who was grandson of the famous nurseryman and garden designer George London (d. 1714). In March 1780 Walpole told his friend the antiquary John Cole that Mr Pennicott had shown him 'a most curious and delightful picture' in which Rose and the king were 'in a garden with a view of a grand private house such as there are several at Sunbury and about London.' It was not until he published his *Description of Strawberry Hill* in 1798 that he said 'the house seems to be Dawny Court [i.e. Dorney Court] near Windsor, the villa of the Duchess of Cleveland. The whole picture is well painted, probably by Danckers.' By 'Danckers' (Pepys called him 'Dancre') he meant Hendrik Danckerts (1630–1678), a Dutch landscape painter who was invited to England by Charles II and commissioned to paint views of the royal palaces and seaports of England and Wales. Pepys had panels in his dining-room painted by him in 1668.

Dorney Court, Buckinghamshire, built *c.* 1510 and partly rebuilt in the eighteenth century, was from 1624 the seat of the Palmer family. Sir James Palmer, who died in 1657, was a royalist and Chancellor of the Order of the Garter. He inherited Dorney Court through his first wife. By his second wife he had a son, Roger, whom he did his best, though without success, to dissuade from marrying Barbara Villiers – hence, it seems, Walpole's belief that Dorney Court belonged to the Duchess of Cleveland, which in fact it never did. The notorious Barbara Villiers, as Lady Castlemaine by her husband's elevation to the Irish peerage (to compensate Barbara for the king's marriage), was installed by the king in Whitehall, and her husband separated from her. Dorney Court was inherited by the son of Sir James's first wife and has remained the property of the Palmer family. But although there is no resemblance whatsoever between this Tudor timber-framed building and the house in the painting, the long-held belief that Rose had raised a pineapple there caused its owners to install a large carved pineapple on the table in its Great Hall, and the village inn is called The Pineapple. Not until 20 February 1948 was it reported in *Country Life* by Wyndham R. Dunstan that the late Colonel Henry Palmer had recognised that the mansion in the painting was not Dorney Court.

The lines had already been crossed by the existence of Dorney House, near Weybridge. A copy of the painting at Ham House was made in 1787 by Thomas Hewart, aged 20, and given by Walpole to his niece Charlotte, who had married the fifth earl of Dysart; this copy appeared in the 1959 guide – and no doubt earlier – with the title 'Rose, the royal gardener presenting Charles II with the first pineapple grown in England at Dorney House near Weybridge, Surrey.' And some writers added to the confusion by writing 'Dawney Court, Surrey', while Ralph Dutton in *The English Garden* (1937) and Mollie Sands in *The Gardens of Hampton Court* (1950) wrote also of pine-pits existing until recently at, according to Sands, 'Dawney Park, Surrey'. It looks as if Dutton had read Dunstan's letter in *Country Life* in which he said that he, Colonel Henry Palmer, and Sir Lionel Cust agreed that the house in the painting could be identified with Oatlands or The Manor House in the same neighbourhood, where Major Benton Fletcher (in *Royal Houses Near London*, 1930) had thought he detected pine-pits among the ruins of old gardens. As if Rose would have had time to ride out to Weybridge (or Windsor) to tend pineapples!

The house in the painting does not resemble any known house in England. Sir Lionel Cust, former Keeper of the King's Pictures, believed that it was an imaginary one (*Apollo*, February 1926) and Sotheby's 'Glory of the Garden' catalogue regards it as 'uncertain'. And while the portraits of Rose and the king are, to quote Cust again, 'worthy of a practised portraitist', Danckerts painted views and not portraits. It was Walpole who made the attribution to Danckerts stick for so long, but in the far more expert opinion of Sotheby's, the painting is of the English School of the 1670s, thus independently confirming Cust's suggestion that possibly John Michael Wright, a personal friend of Evelyn, was the artist. Another portrait of Charles II from his studio with the King's head in exactly the same position is in the National Portrait Gallery in London. These findings, and the fact of the contemporary Dutch wars, dismiss the unlikely suggestion that the picture may have been painted in Holland, made in Philip Miller's *Gardeners Dictionary* (first published in 1724) and followed without acknowledgement by David Stuart in *The Kitchen Garden* (1984).

Rose, 'esteemed to be the best of his Profession in those days' in the words of Stephen Switzer's *Iconographia Rustica* (1718), was born at Amesbury, Wiltshire, in 1619 and went on to become head gardener to William Seymour (1558–1660), marquis of Hertford, at Amesbury House. Seymour, an active royalist, was restored as duke of Somerset in 1660, the year he died. As Rose was later described as 'the ingenious keeper of the garden at Essex House [in London]' in John Rea's *Flora seu de Florum cultura* (1665), since at least the 1896 edition of Lady Amherst's *History of Gardening in England*, all horticultural authorities have believed that Rose was the gardener of Arthur Capel (1631–83), created earl of Essex in 1661 – after Seymour's death. The truth was that Seymour married the eldest daughter of Robert Devereux, the second earl of Essex, who was co-heir of Essex House. She was certainly living there in 1648 and 1652 and probably permanently after her brother's death in 1646 (see *Archaeologia*, vol. 23) while her husband was at Oxford and, after its surrender, attending Charles I during his imprisonment. Hence, Rose was in London a good deal earlier than has been believed, and had established his own nursery before 1655 when the seventeenth-century horticulturalist Sir Thomas Hanmer, then in Wales, noted in his pocket-book that he sent 'a very great mother root' of the Agate Hanmer tulip to Lord Lambert 'by Rose'. This nursery, where Rose grew the vines which he sold 'at very reasonable rates', must have been in the parish of St Martin in the Fields, where a monument was put up to him. George London, starting as Rose's apprentice, was a fellow parishioner, for John Harvey has shown that his nursery was 'near Spring Garden' (*Early Nurserymen*, 1974). Rose was Keeper and Gardener of the St James's Park garden from November 1660 (*Calendar of State Papers 1660–1* Dom. Ser.), not from October 1661, the date usually given, so that he was royal gardener when a pineapple was presented to Charles II in August 1661.

If Rose did raise pineapples in England, where did they come from and what equipment did he have? The first pineapple seen in England was 'the famous Queen Pine brought from Barbados' which is mentioned in Evelyn's diary on 9 August 1661, though Evelyn was wrong in saying then that the first pineapples seen in England were those sent to Cromwell 'four years since'. It is clear from his entry under 19 August 1668 referring to 'Capt Liggon's history' that he had either misremembered or read too hastily Richard Ligon's *A True and Exact History of the Island of Barbados* published in 1657 – the 'four years since'. For Ligon, who described the Pine as 'all that is excellent and superlative degree, for beauty and taste', said it was impossible to bring it from Barbados 'by reason of the severall Climates between. We brought in the ship seventeen of severall growths, but all rotten before we were halfe the way.' Since in 1661 and as late as 1667 the return voyage from Barbados took 7–10 weeks (*Calendar of State Papers 1661-8*, Col. Ser., *America and the West Indies*), it is hard to believe that the Queen Pine of 1661, or for that matter the King Pine from Barbados Evelyn recorded on 19 August 1668, which the king cut up at a banquet for Louis XIV's ambassador Colbert, can have been fruits brought from Barbados and not fruits from plants brought in to the country. And what did Evelyn mean by 'famous'? Ligon said 'the Queen is far more delicate', but it just might have been 'famous' because it was being grown in London. This pine was 'presented to his Majesty' and it has been believed that the painting represents this event. An engraving of it made in 1823 describes Rose presenting it at 'Dawney Court'. W. Roberts in the *Gardeners' Chronicle* (70, 3rd ser.), believed that Rose 'was chosen to present the pineapple from Barbados' to the king, but he had evidently not read Ligon. Why in any case should the gardener be chosen to present a fruit he had not grown? Others believed that Rose raised a pineapple from a slip of this 1661 pine. Miller (and again Stuart) believed that the fruit shown in the painting 'might come from Holland', for there are authentic records to show that Pieter de la Cour of Leyden raised pineapples about the middle of the seventeenth century, after repeated trials. It is generally believed that these were the first raised in Europe. However, none of these authorities so much as ask, let alone attempt to answer, the question why young pineapple plants are included among those shown in the painting; why, if it was decided to present the king with a fruit of the utmost rarity, the gardener should present it; perhaps above all, why any royal gardener should have agreed to being shown presenting a fruit grown by someone else, or why the painting should have been cheished by George London. Moreover, the Dutch scarcely wished to confer choice gifts on a king cultivating relations with Louis XIV.

Where did the pineapple plants, as opposed to fruits, come from? What seems likely is that some time after 1657 Ligon, who had described how the fruits could be grown fron 'a Slip' or from the Crown, discovered that crowns and suckers could be brought from Barbados. Mr F. A. Roach, whose *Cultivated Fruits of Britain* does not deal with crops under glass, has been so kind as to send me some notes on the pineapple, including a quotation from J. W. Purseglove's *Tropical Crops – Monocotyledons*: 'The plant, suckers, slips and crowns withstand considerable desiccation and resume growth when planted.' Hence, Mr Roach himself adds, they 'would have been much easier to transport to new countries than many other plants which had to be planted in soil.' The extensive relations between Barbados and England occupy ten columns of the index of the relevant volume of the *Calendar of State Papers 1661–8*. Ligon could also have given practical advice on succession plants, watering and withholding water, and other details described in his book and, as Cust asked, 'To whom would Capt Ligon have entrusted so precious a plant but to John Rose?' However, it is impossible to be certain. The plants might have come from Holland, since as Mr Roach points out, the great many trials made by de la Cour show that pineapple plants must have been available in Europe some years previously. But there is no record of Dutch pineapple plants being brought into Restoration England, and in fact the authentic record is that the first Dutch plants did not arrive in England until 1690 – after the accession of William III – imported by William Bentinck, earl of Portland. Professor Richard Bradley, in his *General Treatise of Husbandry and Gardening* (1726), said he saw about forty plants at the Richmond Green garden of the wealthy Dutch merchant in London Sir Matthew Decker (1679–1749), whose gardener Henry Telende produced edible fruit in 1715. He used a hot-bed of tanner's bark, regulating the temperature by a mercurial thermometer – then very

new in England. Decker had this recorded in a painting by Netscher
and a memorial tablet in the Fitzwilliam Museum, Cambridge.
Hearing of this claim through Gough's *British Topography* (1780), in
a letter of 11 November that year Walpole said he could authentic-
ally contradict the assertion that Sir Matthew Decker had first
introduced 'ananas'. 'My very curious picture . . . proves the culture
earlier by several years.' But all the authorities have credited
Decker's claim and denied the possibility that Rose raised a
pineapple.

Walpole of course knew nothing about pineapple culture but
believed, as have others, that the painting was a record of a real
event. On this it is important that Sotheby's team of experts independently concluded 'it is clear that an event, in which a pineapple
plays a significant part, is here being recorded.' The painting is in
no sense the equivalent of a media photograph of our own day. It
is a true seventeenth-century portrait, in which, besides the likeness
of the person, his chief interests and achievements were portrayed;
as for instance in the well-known Van Dyck portrait of the 14th earl
of Arundel and his wife, in which the earl is surrounded by objects
denoting his interest in art, history and exploration. Looked at
closely, it will be seen that the garden in the portrait of Rose was
got up, like a stage set, to show off his most renowned skills. One
of the pots contains a dwarf fruit tree. In their translation of a French
work, *The Retir'd Gard'ner* (1706), London and his partner Henry
Wise recommended planting dwarf pears and apples on the borders
of a fruit and herb garden and said 'Whoever will satisfy their
Curiosity may further inform themselves by viewing those in the
Royal garden at St James's Park, which were planted in the Reign
of King Charles the Second and are now in the greatest Perfection
of any Plantation of Dwarfs here in England.' Other pots contain the
'choice greens' Rea recorded Rose growing, including orange trees,
then very much in vogue. The Treasury money warrant of 14
October 1661 to John Rose, 'Keeper and Gardener of the garden
plotted and laid out and to be formed and made in St James's Park',
specifically mentioned 'all orange trees and other trees and greens
therein to be planted.' And it is notable that at least two pots in the
painting contain young pineapple plants. While no attempt has
been made to include a *parterre de broderie* like that shown in the
garden of Essex House in Hollar's map of west-central London, the

painting was evidently devised to portray Rose's skills, culminating in raising the pineapple presented to the king. The finding by Sotheby's experts, that the king's costume of 'rarely seen simple day dress' dates the painting shortly before Rose's death in 1677, strikingly confirms this. The artist's portrait of the king would of course have been made from sketches. As for the pineapple, it might represent one Rose at last succeeded in fruiting *c.* 1677, or an earlier one. At least it does not seem credible that London would have treasured a painting that was mainly fanciful, or that he would have passed it to his eldest son George, whom he recommended in his will to 'stick to his trade'.

London had every reason to be grateful to Rose. Switzer said that after he had been Rose's apprentice for four or five years, Rose 'sent him (if I am rightly inform'd) into France, the greatest school of Learning at that time in the World.' Although this can be no more than speculation, London may well have wanted his large family to remember Rose who – as his memorial tablet showed – had no surviving wife or children when he died. It thus seems not unlikely that it was London who commissioned the painting.

Has not the time come to reconsider the question whether or not Rose could have grown pineapples? Since this seems eminently a question for experts who grow bromeliads in the English climate, I referred it to Mr J. B. E. Simmons and Mr Brian Halliwell, Curator and Assistant Curator of the Royal Botanic Gardens, Kew, who have both been so kind as to make valuable contributions to my findings on the equipment available to Rose. The indispensable item was a hot-bed. According to the *OED*, in England hot-beds date back at least to Bacon's *Sylva sylvarum* of 1626, but possibly earlier because melons were raised at Hampton Court for Henry VIII. John Rea described making a hot-bed by casting horse-dung and wet litter on a heap, then putting it with more litter between stakes, treading it down, putting on sufficient good sifted earth and covering with mats, hair-cloth or canvas. Fermentation would then heat it up in four to five days when it was given air and the process was repeated. The hot-bed was covered with bell jars or frames to retain heat. This is how melons were raised. They need a temperature of 64°F to germinate and Mr Brian Halliwell does not expect that much higher temperatures would be required to produce pineapples. It would be possible in his view to maintain a temperature of *c*.74°F by making up a series of beds at regular intervals and, as the temperature fell below the critical, pot-grown plants could be transferred to new beds. Contemporary conservatories were not suitable because, as he points out, heat in them was provided by an open charcoal brazier 'which resulted in low fluctuating temperatures and a rather noxious atmosphere.' Evelyn described a subterranean stove, but although this would produce a sweeter atmosphere, 'heat would be too low in winter for the successful cultivation of pineapples.' Mr Simmons points out that pineapples do not need tropical conditions. They are grown most extensively in Queensland and Hawaii and plants at Kew 'have to tolerate a winter minimum of about 60°F.' In his monograph *The Pineapple* (1960), J. L. Collins said that in some regions temperatures may drop to or near freezing point for short periods without permanent damage to pineapples. Mr Simmons concludes: 'On technical grounds it would seem possible for Rose to have cultivated pineapples'. Surely Rose should now be accorded the honour of producing the first pineapple in England, which has been denied him in all works of reference, including the *Dictionary of National Biography*?

Acknowledgements

I should like to thank Mr J. B. E. Simmons and Mr Brian Halliwell, Curator and Assistant Curator of the Royal Botanic Gardens, Kew; Mr F. A. Roach, OBE; Dr Brent Elliott of the Royal Horticultural Society's Lindley Library; and Katharine Duff.

Illustration

John Rose, the royal gardener, presenting to King Charles II the first pineapple raised in England. English School, formerly attributed to Hendrik Danckerts.

Day-lilies

Hemerocallis in the wild and in gardens

STEPHEN G. HAW

The common orange day-lily is a familiar old garden plant, which has been cultivated in Britain since the sixteenth century. Its flowers are of a distinctive shade of brownish-orange rarely seen in any other group of plants. It is something of an oddity even in its own genus, the other species all having flowers of various shades of yellow.

The orange day-lily *Hemerocallis fulva* is one of just over a dozen species in this rather small genus. All the day-lilies occur in Asia, mostly in China, Japan and Korea, with some extending into the Soviet Far East and Siberia. Two can be found wild in parts of Europe, *H. fulva* and *H. lilioasphodelus* (*H. flava*). Whether they are genuinely native, however, is open to doubt. It is almost certain that *H. fulva* was brought from China across Central Asia at an early date, and became naturalised in Europe as an escape from cultivation. *H. lilioasphodelus* is unquestionably native to parts of Siberia, and might perhaps extend naturally as far as eastern Europe. But it too has been extensively cultivated throughout Europe since before 1650, and most wild populations are certainly the result of naturalisation.

The taxonomy of day-lilies is difficult and confused, as several of the species are variable and distinctions between some of them are small. Thus, some species now considered distinct were in the past treated as varieties of other species, while a number of forms once accorded specific rank have been reduced to varietal status or synonymy. Many problems of classification still remain to be resolved, but there seems to be a reasonable consensus about currently-used nomenclature. This recognises about fourteen species. These are quite evenly distributed across the Far East, with some three species endemic to south-west China, two species widely distributed through southern China, a couple of Japanese endemics and most of the remainder widespread in parts of Japan, Korea, northern China and neighbouring areas of the Soviet Union. China boasts a total of no less than eleven species, with doubtful records of a couple more.

Day-lilies have a long history in China. They are first mentioned in a text dating from several centuries BC, though it is not clear from the context whether they were already cultivated at that date. After about AD 200 they were certainly widely grown, for they are mentioned in many texts, including poetry, and seem to have been greatly admired. *Hemerocallis fulva* was the species usually cultivated at this early period. It was not planted solely as an ornamental, for it also had other uses. The flowers, worn in the belt of a pregnant woman, were supposed to favour the birth of a male child. It was also said that the day-lily could make people forget their worries. This was brought about, according to one account, by eating the young shoots of the plant, which induced a state of intoxication. There were also more serious medicinal uses, mainly of the dried roots. They are still utilised in Chinese medicine today. Virtually all parts of the day-lily are in fact edible. A Chinese famine herbal of the fifteenth century recommended eating the shoots in times of scarcity, and the flower-buds of some of the yellow-flowered species, especially *H. citrina*, have been eaten as a delicacy for several centuries at least. They are picked and dried before being cooked, for it is said that eating too many fresh flowers causes indigestion.

Hemerocallis fulva was undoubtedly commonly planted in gardens in the capital city of the Tang dynasty (AD 618–907), and may well have been carried westwards along the trade routes across Central Asia at about this time. Its fleshy roots, which will shoot again after some time out of the ground, would have facilitated its spread even in those days of travel at the pace of the Bactrian camel. It would first have reached the Middle East, and from there have been carried across the Mediterranean into Europe.

A Chinese gardening manual called *The Mirror of Flowers* of 1688 describes not only the ordinary form of *Hemerocallis fulva*, but also its double variety and a fragrant yellow day-lily which may have been *H. minor*. Evidently there were several day-lily cultivars already being grown at that time, for there is mention of one with a particularly late period of flower.

In the wild in China *Hemerocallis fulva* is very widespread in the region south of the Qinling Mountains, about 34° N. Its exact natural area of distribution is uncertain, however, because it has been cultivated for so long and is likely to have become naturalised in many places. I have personally seen it growing wild in the Lu Shan range on the south bank of the Yangtze River in Jiangxi province, where it was common in open areas, especially where the soil was moist. In late July its brightly-coloured flowers attracted notice even from a considerable distance.

The common yellow day-lily of southern China is *Hemerocallis citrina*. This species is the main source of dried flower-buds for eating, and is widely cultivated for that reason. Many different cultivars are recognised, including one with white flowers. The period of flowering varies between cultivars, the earliest beginning to bloom in May and the latest still being in flower in September.

In northern China the common species are *Hemerocallis lilioasphodelus* and *H. minor*. These are very similar, being distinguished basically by the number of flowers and the extent of branching of the inflorescence, together with the form of the roots. There seems to be some doubt as to whether these are sufficient differences to merit recognising two species, and it may be that *H. minor* should be accorded no more than varietal rank. The two species have similar areas of distribution, extending from Manchuria across north China as far west as Gansu province. I have seen both growing in mountainous areas of Shandong province, usually in damp ground near streams. They have most attractive flowers of a clear pale yellow, which are also fragrant. They are somewhat less easy to cultivate than the two preceding species.

The other Chinese day-lilies of most interest are those from the south-west. These have flowers which are darker yellow, sometimes more or less orange. They are rather small species, *Hemerocallis forrestii* and the very similar *H. plicata* reaching to one to two feet in height and *H. nana* rarely attaining as much as a foot. They are all quite distinct from the other species of the genus, and are very pretty plants.

Both *Hemerocallis fulva* and *H. lilioasphodelus* have been long cultivated in Europe, as has been noted. Other species arrived later, mostly in the nineteenth century from Chinese and Japanese gardens. *H. forrestii* was not introduced until the first decade of this century, by the great collector after whom it was named. It is not very often seen in gardens today, but.is a very desirable plant. Like most of the day-lily species, it has been eclipsed by the numerous hybrids which began to be produced as early as the 1890s. Hybridisation was much

Hemerocallis lilioasphodelus (H. *flava*) from Curtis's Botanical Magazine,
Vol I, 1793, Plate 19.

taken up in America. Day-lily cultivars have now come to be numbered in thousands, with flowers of various shades of red, pink, orange and yellow. It must be said that many of the reds have brownish or purplish tinges, and that a good clear pink is rare. My own personal preference is still for the plain bright yellows of some of the species, particularly when their purity of colour is combined with fragrance.

Day-lilies are generally very easy to grow, adapting readily to a variety of soils and positions. But as with all plants, they will only look their best if conditions really suit them. A little attention to their preferences will ensure the most rewarding results. Although individual day-lily flowers last for no more than a couple of days (often for a day or less, as the name suggests) a well-established plant should produce a profusion of bloom over a period of several weeks in summer. Day-lilies are long-lived, and if planted with reasonable care in a suitable site should need no more than a minimum of attention for many years.

The main requirement of day-lilies is for a reasonable amount of moisture. There is no great difficulty in growing them in dry soils, but they will never do as well as in a good moist loam. They will flourish even in marshy conditions, and look good planted beside water, where they will associate well with other moisture-loving plants, including ferns. *Hemerocallis fulva* and its many forms and hybrids can, because of the strong and very individual colour of the flowers, be difficult to associate well with other flowering plants, but the pale green, arching leaves can make a very pleasing contrast with the fronds of larger ferns. They will also mix well with many of the cultivars of their close relatives, the hostas. It is always well to plant day-lilies generously, a small isolated clump having little impact, while a large colony can be very impressive. Hemerocallis appreciate sunlight, though partial shade is quite acceptable. In heavy shade flowering is reduced.

The planting site should be well prepared by digging and incorporating large amounts of well-rotted manure or compost. If this is done thoroughly, day-lilies should need no attention after planting for at least ten years, except for an occasional mulch with more compost or manure. Occasionally the clumps may become congested, especially in poor soils, with a reduction in flowering. Such clumps should be lifted in autumn or early spring, divided and replanted.

Most of the day-lilies available from the nursery trade today are hybrid cultivars, and it will be very much a matter of personal taste which are selected. My own choice would fall on those which are not too strident in flower colour. The influence of *Hemerocallis fulva* on its progeny has often been rather unfortunate, bequeathing them a brownish-purple tinge which can be quite unpleasant. Some of the newer American hybrids are great improvements in this respect. The best of the day-lilies are those with unmarked flowers of pure coloration, which is most common among the yellow shades. It is still hard to better the original *H. lilioasphodelus*, with its strongly scented, pale gold blooms, which may last for almost three days and are worth cutting for indoor decoration. This has now become one of those old garden plants which an effort must be made to conserve. There is no good reason for such neglect, as it is so adaptable a plant and an asset to any garden. *H. forrestii* should also be tried, if it can be obtained. It is distinct from the larger day-lilies, but just as attractive and most useful where a smaller plant is required. It has also begun to be used in hybridisation, and some of its offspring are now becoming commercially available. Little *H. nana*, from high altitudes in the mountains of south-west China, is the only day-lily with a good claim to a position in the alpine garden. It would be an attractive rarity to grow, though it may no longer be in cultivation. It is certainly worth trying to seek out some of the hemerocallis species, as well as being selective when choosing hybrids. There must be a place in any garden for at least one or two clumps of these lovely plants.

Painswick Rococo Garden

PAUL MILES

One of the arts of which we can be particularly proud in this country is the maintenance of fine gardens.

In the twentieth century gardens are being made more frequently and on a smaller scale than in preceeding centuries, and along with this increasing interest has come a finer appreciation of earlier schemes and a developing skill – that of restoring old gardens of which we have more than any other country.

The Painswick Rococo Garden, near Stroud in Gloucestershire, is a rare survivor of a dizzy and exuberant style which is found in architectural decoration and has all but vanished out of doors. Even at Wurtzburg in Germany, where Rococo reached a peak in the eighteenth century, the garden is well mannered and formal with no reflection of the richness of the decoration in the palace itself.

At Painswick House we find the bones of a scheme illustrated in a painting of 1748 by Thomas Robins (1716–1770), The Limner of Bath, which captures the spirit of an Arcadian landscape, and which is gradually being brought back to life by Lord Dickinson with the help and advice of the landscape architect Paul Edwards.

The painting (reproduced above) shows a garden behind the house and stable block (from which it is now reached) running down the valley and with views to architectural incidents in the surrounding landscape.

If we enter on the east side from the garden of the old stables we can see across the valley to a sheltered seat with what was the flower and vegetable garden (now down to grass prior to restoration) in-between.

But let us take an anticlockwise tour of the garden, which is a unique survivor of a style of gardening developed between the formal gardens of the Renaissance and the flowing English landscape movement of the eighteenth century.

Paul Edwards has written that 'the garden at Painswick can be fairly accurately dated as being laid out between 1738 and 1748 by Benjamin Hyett (1708–1762)'. He inherited the property – a fine stone mansion built in Palladian style in 1738 – from his father, Charles Hyett (1686–1738) and who had purchased a house called 'The Herrings' from the Adey family and then built the present house.

The layout of the garden is clearly shown in the painting by Thomas Robins. Roger White and Tim Mowl in their article for *The Journal of Garden History* hint at the possibility of Robins being the designer and having produced his picture as a statement of intent rather than one of an existing scene.

Our path runs up the side of the valley referred to by Bishop Pococke who visited the property, then known as Buenos Aires, in May 1757:

'We came to Painswick, a market town prettily situated on the side of the hill, and esteem'd an exceeding good air; just above it Mr. Hyett built an house of hewn stone, in a fine situation, and made a very pretty Garden; before it is a court with statues and sphynxes, and beyond that a lawn for the grand entrance; the Garden is on an hanging ground from the house in the vale, and on a rising ground on the other side and at the end; all are cut into walks through wood and adnorn'd with water and buildings, and in one part is the kitchen garden.'

We come first of all to a Gothic summer-house known as The Red House, which is at the head of the valley and approached by serpentine paths although there is a straight central walk from it down through the newly replanted shrubbery and orchard.

The shrubbery has been kept to bold groupings of species known to have been in cultivation in this country in the eighteenth century,

and includes bold plantings of our native guelder rose (*Viburnum opulus*) and the Stag's-horn sumach (*Rhus typhina*) which was introduced from the east coast of North America in about 1629. There are also several bushes of *Philadelphus coronarius*, a long cultivated mock orange which is well suited to dry soils, and surprisingly hard to obtain from nurseries, with a single specimen of *Calycanthus floridus*, the Carolina allspice, which was introduced in 1726 and has reddish-brown flowers during the summer and autumn.

Nearby clumps of the sea buckthorn (*Hippophae rhamnoides*) contribute narrow grey leaves which fall to reveal persistent amber berries on the female plants in the autumn and into the winter.

Between the shrubbery and one surviving and recently excavated fishpond lies the orchard containing a collection of apple and pear trees with one or two plums, some morello cherries, medlars, mul-

berries and Portugal quince.

A charming feature of the garden in February is the abundance of snowdrops, which were established in large quantities especially in The Grove. There are old photographs which show villagers visiting the garden on Snowdrop Sunday, when they were allowed to pick a bunch of twelve flowers each. This may have some connection with James Atkins (1804–1884), who was a noted grower of snowdrops and who came to live at Rose Cottage, Painswick. His name lives on in *Galanthus nivalis* 'Atkinsii' which is a tall and graceful member of the genus.

Following the perimeter path past the sheltered seat we can look down onto the bathing pool, which has been cleared and survives together with the wellheads and, ram. It is in the area of this pool that Thomas Robins shows a figure of Pan set in a rustic arbour. This figure is now located at the front of The Stables.

Five buildings in all have survived the years of neglect and are gradually being restored as funds become available and with grants from English Heritage and donations from the Georgian Group and other well wishers.

It is remarkable that so much of the garden, the national importance of which was not realised until 1983, and which was buried in forestry planting after the second World War has been recovered.

The path leads down into the valley and then up to another seat in an alcove from which a straight path runs uphill towards the house and thence via the pond to The Eagle House, the ground floor of which is intact but which has lost its timber framed superstructure.

Also lost is The Gothic Exedra shown in the painting, but that could be reconstructed.

It is a garden of considerable interest to garden historian and designer alike and it is very much to be hoped that sufficient funds will become available for the completion of the scheme. The garden is open to the public from May to September and also at snowdrop time.

REFERENCES

Gardens of Delight – The Rococo English Landscape of Thomas Robins the Elder, by John Harris, Basilisk Press, 1978.

'Thomas Robins at Painswick' by Roger White and Tim Mowl, *Journal of Garden History,* vol. 4, No. 2, p. 163–178.

'The Strange Lost World of Pan's Lodge', *Gloucestershire and Avon Life,* November 1982.

The Travels Through England of Dr. Richard Pococke, ed. J. J. Cartwright, Camden Society, 2 vols. 1888–89.

Painswick House Garden and its Restoration, by Paul Edwards 1986.

Acknowledgement
The author is grateful to Lord Dickinson for assistance in the preparation of this article.

Photographs of the garden by the author

Gardens in Fiction

Jane Austen's Gardens

HERMIA OLIVER

One attraction of a novelist's gardens is that, unlike those described in garden histories, they are lived in by people of the kind we either know in person or at least by repute. If, in our own day, the self-satisfaction of a garden owner comes from his collection of rare plants or his design and not from his greenhouses, we all know someone like General Tilney who said 'He is a very happy man' on learning that Mr Allen had only one small hothouse, 'with a look of very happy contempt.' Jane Austen (1775–1817) portrayed 'with a brush so fine' on what she called 'her little bits of ivory' a series of gardens dating from the 17th to the late 18th centuries and also superbly encapsulated Humphry Repton's revolutionary 'improvements'.

She herself lived in three gardens, and her family connections and friends made her familiar with many more, including those of Manydown Park, near Basingstoke, Hampshire, Goodnestone Park and Godmersham Park, Kent, Stoneleigh Abbey, Warwickshire, Chawton Manor near Alton, Hampshire and Adelstrop in Gloucestershire. She spent the first twenty-five years of her life at Steventon Rectory, Hampshire, where her father was rector. Its garden had a turf terrace which in *Northanger Abbey* must have inspired Catherine Morland's delight in 'rolling down the green slope at the back of the house.' And the possibilities for a story-teller of one of Steventon's hedgerows clearly impressed her deeply. These were not thin lines but irregular borders of copse-wood and timber, often wide enough to enclose a winding footpath. Jane wanted to include such a hedgerow in a scene in *Mansfield Park*, set in Northampton which she never visited. In January 1813 she asked her sister Cassandra, then staying at the Bigg-Withers' Manydown House, 'If you could discover whether Northampton is a county of hedgerows I should be glad again.' But Cassandra may have found out from 'those enormous great stupid quarto volumes which one always sees in the breakfast parlour there' that there were no hedgerows of this kind in that county. So the hedgerow comes in the later *Persuasion*, set in

Somerset, where on a walk to Winthrop Captain Wentworth and Louisa Musgrove were gathering nuts when Anne Elliot, sitting under the hedgerow, heard them 'as if making their way back along the rough, wild sort of channel down the centre.' This was how she overheard them saying that it was Lady Russell who had persuaded Anne to refuse Charles Musgrove.

The next garden Jane lived in was in Castle Square, Southampton, from 1807–09, after her father's retirement to Bath in 1800 and his death in 1805. In a letter of February 1807 she said this garden was being put in order. The gardener said that the shrubs bordering the gravel walk were only sweetbriars and 'an indifferent sort' of roses. Jane asked him to procure some syringas (philadelphus) and spoke also of laburnum (both introduced in the late 16th century). She 'could not do without syringa' because her favourite poet William Cowper (1731–1800) in *The Task* wrote of

> Laburnam, rich
> In streaming gold; syringa, ivory pure.

Another border was being cleared for currants and gooseberry bushes and a spot was being found for raspberries.

The third of Jane's home gardens was that of the cottage at Chawton, which her brother Edward offered to his mother in October 1808. In this garden Mrs Austen, by then aged 70, worked vigorously, dressed in a green round smock. As early as 1798 Jane had reported that her mother 'sometimes complains of an asthma, a dropsy, water on her chest, and a liver disorder,' but she lived until 1827 – a splendid advertisement of the therapeutic effects of gardening. In May 1811 one of Jane's letters tells us that some of the flower seeds were coming up well, and that 'our young piony [*sic*] at the foot of the fir-tree has just blown and looks very handsome'; the whole of the shrubbery border would soon be 'very gay with pinks and sweet-williams, in addition to the columbines already blooming.' The 'piony' also featured in *The Task*. In a seond letter written that May Jane said 'You cannot imagine what a nice walk we had round the orchard. The row of beech looks very well indeed, and so does the young quickset hedge. ... I hear today that an apricot has been detected on one of the trees.' It is to be hoped that it tasted better than Mrs Norris's in *Mansfield Park*, which had no more flavour than potatoes. On 6 June the Austens had begun 'pease' and on the day before 'had the agreeable surprise of several scarlet strawberries quite ripe.' Did they suggest Donwell's strawberries in *Emma*? At any rate, this was a true cottage garden, with vegetables, flowers and fruit. The main gardens in the novels however were gentry, not cottage, gardens which in the 17th and 18th centuries were either flowerless or grew flowers in separate enclaves, like the 'flower' gardens in Mansfield Park, at Kellynch Hall in *Persuasion*, and that planned at Norland in *Sense and Sensibility*. Except for the roses picked by Fanny Price in *Mansfield Park*, no flower is named in any garden in Jane's published fiction.

The earliest gardens must be those of the two abbeys, which would have had monastic foundations. *Northanger Abbey* (written 1798–9, published 1818) is set in Gloucestershire, and the abbey is owned by General Tilney, 'tall and handsome' but who always seemed 'a check upon his children's spirit'. Catherine Morland, one of ten children of a clergyman, was invited to stay by Eleanor Tilney, with whom she had become friends in Bath when she was the guest of the well-off Mr Allen and his wife. The general, who 'loved a garden', was only too pleased to show her his great walled kitchen-garden. Its size was more than double the whole of Mr Allen's garden as well as her father's, including the churchyard. 'The walls seemed countless in number, endless in length; a village of hot-houses seemed to arise among them and a whole parish to be at work within the enclosure.' The general was so odious that he forced her to tell him in words 'that she had never seen any gardens at all equal to them before; and he then modestly owned that . . . he did believe them to be unrivalled in the kingdom.' He loved good fruit, but 'the utmost care would not always secure the most valuable fruits.' The pinery had only yielded one hundred the last year. (Pineapples, *Ananas comosus*, were first introduced in the mid-17th century and immortalized in a well-known painting atributed to Hendrik Danckerts. It shows Rose, the king's gardener, presenting to Charles II at Dorney Court, Bucks, near Windsor, the first pineapple grown successfully in England.) General Tilney's 'look of very happy contempt' on learning that Mr Allen had only one hot-house turned into 'a triumphant smile of self-satisfaction' when he heard that Mr Allen did not care about his garden or go into it. The general's garden had nothing else of note except 'a thick grove of Scotch firs' but when Catherine went down to breakfast the first morning there were hyacinths on the breakfast table. (It was March.)

Donwell Abbey in *Emma* (1815), a mile from Highbury where Emma lived at Hartfield with her father Mr Woodhouse, was 'low and sheltered', nearly at the foot of 'a considerable slope', so that it 'had scarcely a sight' of its ample gardens which 'stretched down to meadows washed by a stream', but Emma thought its situation was 'suitable, becoming, characteristic.' It had abundant timber 'in rows and avenues, which neither fashion nor extravagance had rooted up,' an allusion to the 'clumping' of avenues by Bridgeman, Kent, and Lancelot Brown. The house was rambling and irregular, with many comfortable and one or two handsome rooms. It belonged to Mr Knightley, 'a sensible man of about seven or eight-and-thirty' (whereas Emma was not yet 21). He issued an invitation to a large Highbury party in the middle of June, when the gushing, vulgar Mrs Elton – who never allowed the world to forget that her elder sister had married Mr Suckling, of Maple Grove, Bristol – had been disappointed because a lame carriage horse prevented a visit to Box Hill. The party included Emma and Mr Woodhouse, Jane Fairfax, Mr and Mrs Weston, Harriet Smith, Frank Churchill (who arrived very hot and late) and Mrs Elton.

Donwell was famous for its strawberry beds, and Mrs Elton was

> very ready to lead the way – gathering, accepting, or talking. Strawberries, and only strawberries could now be thought or spoken of. 'The best fruit in England – everybody's favourite – always wholesome ... hautboys infinitely superior – no comparison – the others hardly eatable – hautboys very scarce – Chili preferred – white wood finest flavour of all.'

The strawberry beds must have been brought up to date quite recently because 'Chili', *Fragraria chiloensis*, was the first large fruited strawberry introduced into England, a seedling being raised by Keens in 1806. (Jane was working on *Emma* in 1813–15.) Hautboys were *Fragraria elatior* and white wood the wild strawberry.

After the strawberry picking the party – with the exception of Mr Woodhouse and Mrs Weston – walked all over the gardens, following one another 'to the delicious shade of a broad short avenue of limes, which stretched beyond the garden', a reminder of John Evelyn's 'perfection of the lime' and 'its unparalleled beauty for walks.' The Donwell avenue led to 'nothing but a view at the end over a low stone wall with a high pillar which seemed intended ...

to give the appearance of an approach to the house which had never been there,' but the view was 'exceedingly pretty.' At the bottom of a bank about half a mile distant rose the Abbey-Mill Farm, with meadows in front and 'the river making a close and handsome curve around it.' In describing the farm Jane made a mistake. Too late her brother Edward annoyingly pointed out, when he next saw her, that she wrote of its 'orchard in blossom' – in June. (He reportedly said 'in July'.)

Sotherton Court, Northampton, in *Mansfield Park* (1814), had an interesting early 17th-century garden. The house, built in the reign of Queen Elizabeth I, must have replaced a previous manor house, because it was the 'ancient manorial residence' of the Rushworth family, 'with all its rights of Court Leet and Court Baron.' Its owner, Mr Rushworth, was 'a heavy young man, with not more than common sense' (then meaning the minimum), who had recently succeeded to 'one of the largest estates and first places in the country.' His widowed mother was a 'well-meaning, civil, prosing, pompous woman,' who thought of nothing 'but as it related to her own or her son's concerns.' The situation of the house was 'dreadful' because it stood on one of the lowest spots in the park: 'We go down hill to it for half a mile.' From the west front an oak avenue led to the top of a hill, with beyond it tall iron palisades and gates. In front a flight of steps led immediately to turf and shrubs. Mr Rushworth explained that the greatest number of their plants were there – unfortunately none are named – as well as 'the curious pheasants.' If these were Amherst pheasants, they were of course a later addition. The lawn, bounded on each side by a high wall, contained a bowling-green and beyond that a long terrace walk, backed by more iron palisades. The bowling-green must have been made in accordance with the Act of 1541 laying down that those who owned land worth £100 or more could obtain licences to play bowls on their own private greens. From the terrace could be seen the tops of the trees of the 'wilderness', a planted wood of about two acres, chiefly of larch, laurel and pollarded beech ('beech cut down'), laid out 'with too much regularity' but providing darkness and shade and 'natural beauty compared with the bowling-green and terrace.' The very long lawn and terrace walk ended with a ha-ha into the park – another later addition.

Mr and Mrs Rushworth had invited a party from Mansfield to

visit Sotherton. Those who came were the two daughters of Sir Thomas Bertram and his younger son Edmund, Fanny Price (an adopted niece), Mrs Norris (Lady Bertram's sister), Henry Crawford (brother-in-law of the Mansfield parson) and his 'remarkably pretty' sister Mary. After seeing the house and its James II chapel, the young people walked in groups to the ha-ha, where Fanny Price sat on a bench for what seemed an age while Edmund and Mary Crawford set off 'to try to find the dimensions of the wood by walking a little more about it.' Fanny was not found until Maria Bertram, Rushworth and Henry Crawford came to the ha-ha. In the meanwhile the detestable Mrs Norris met the gardener, 'who had shown her all his choicest nursery plants' (alas unnamed), and had presented her with 'a curious specimen of heather.'

But for garden buffs Sotherton's chief claim to fame lies in the improvement Mr Rushworth was determined to carry out. Just before his first visit to Mansfield since the arrival of the Crawfords, he had been to see a friend, Smith, 'in a neighbouring county' whose place, Compton, had been laid out by an improver. 'The approach *now* is one of the finest things in the county. You see the house in the most surprising manner.' Later he says that the place 'was a mere nothing before Repton took it in hand.' He hoped to have some good friend who would help him with Sotherton.

> 'Your best friend upon such an occasion,' said Miss Bertram calmly, 'would be Mr Repton, I imagine.'
> 'That is what I am thinking of. As he has done so well by Smith, I think I would like to have him at once. His terms are five guineas a day.'

At Compton two or three fine old trees that grew too near the house were cut down, 'which makes me think that Repton, or anybody of that sort, would certainly have the avenue at Sotherton down.' Only Fanny, thinking of Cowper's 'Ye fallen avenues, once more I mourn your fate unmerited,' said 'What a pity!'

It is believed (see Dorothy Stroud's *Humphry Repton*, 1962) that Jane's model for Compton was Harlestone House, Northampton. Repton described his improvements there in his *Fragments on the Theory and Practice of Landscape Gardening* (1876). The centre of the south front had been taken down and a bow added, with pilasters. The entrance was changed from the south to the north side and some new rooms added to the west. Jane, who cannot have seen this house, may well have seen the Northampton volume of John Britton's *Beauties of England and Wales* (1810), in which it appeared. Yet she herself did not situate 'Smith's' house in that county, nor would the improvements to Harlestone House have done anything for the 'dreadful' situation of Sotherton. However, a house that Jane must have seen often on her frequent journeys to Rowling, Goodnestone and Godmersham Park in Kent (the successive homes of her brother Edward) was Sundridge Park, whose 'Red Book' Repton supplied before 1795. There was a site difficulty caused by a sharp rise in the ground from a valley which ran through the park. This was solved when Repton cut a shelf into the hillside to a depth of about thirty feet, thus forming a plateau for the new Nash house, which must indeed have meant that 'you see the house in the most surprising manner.' As for Repton's charge of five guineas a day, Jane would undoubtedly have known this because Repton worked at Adelstrop for her cousin J. H. Leigh, who eventually succeeded to Stoneleigh Abbey.

There is a glimpse of another, though small, 17th-century garden in *Sense and Sensibility* (begun 1797, published 1811). This is Colonel Brandon's Delaford. He was a friend of Mrs Dashwood's relation Sir John Middleton, who offered a cottage in Devon when she and her three girls were turned out of Norland Park by her daughter-in-law. The colonel was 'silent and grave', though his appearance was not 'unpleasing', in spite of his being, in the eyes of the girls, 'an absolute old bachelor', for 'he was on the wrong side of five-and-thirty.' He was a shade younger than Mr Knightley in fact. Lady Middleton's mother described Delaford as

> What I call a nice old-fashioned place . . . quite shut in with great garden walls that are covered with the best fruit-trees in the country; and such a mulberry tree in one corner! . . . Then, there is a dovecote, some delightful stewponds, and a very pretty canal.

Thus this garden seems about the same date as those described by Evelyn which had stewponds, and in September 1667 he himself designed 'the plot of his canal and garden' for Mr Howard's villa at Albury. Delaford was only a quarter of a mile from the turnpike road; it was never dull because it had 'an old yew arbour behind the house.' If you sat in it, you could see 'all the carriages that pass along.' Though this arbour is not a *mise en scène* of the kind featured by Nancy-Mary Goodall in *Hortus 3* (Autumn 1987), it was evidently put into Jane's head by the sitting-room window at Chawton which looked on to the Winchester road. (The novel was completed while she was there.)

A second garden in *Sense and Sensibility* is the only one in the novels which, like Godmersham Park, has a mound with a 'Grecian temple', so reflecting the influence of Kent and Vanburgh. Cleveland belonged to Mr and Mrs Palmer. Charlotte Palmer did not so much ignore as seem totally unaware of her husband's studied rudeness. It was he who, when first invited to Mrs Dashwood's cottage, 'did not raise his eyes from the newspaper.' Asked if there was any news, ' "No, none at all" he replied, and read on.' The grounds of Cleveland were older than the house, described as 'modern built'. As the novel was begun in 1796, this must have meant later 18th century, a date strikingly confirmed by one species of tree which was interspersed with others to form a 'thick screen' near the house shutting out 'the offices', the Lombardy poplar (*Populus italicus*), not introduced in England until 1858. The other trees in it were 'the fir, the mountain ash and the acacia' (*Robinia pseudoacacia*).

Cleveland was thirty miles from Combe Magna, the home of John Willoughby with whom Marianne ('Sensibility') Dashwood had fallen desperately in love, only for him to marry a rich heiress instead. Her emotion at being so near Combe Magna made her walk through the shrubbery to the top of the mound with the classical temple. From it she gazed at the furthest ridge of hills on the horizon, fancying that Combe Magna might be seen from their summits. As a result of two later twilight walks there, she caught so violent a cold that she was laid low for several days. Thus the temple is an important device for moving the story along.

In *Persuasion* (written 1815–16, published 1818) there is only a brief glimpse of Sir Walter Elliot's Kellynch Hall, Somerset. As might be expected from one who 'never took up any book but the Baronetage', where 'his faculties were roused into admiration and respect by contemplating the limited remnant of the earliest patents,' Sir Walter hoped when he let the Hall to deny his tenant access to the garden: 'The park will be open to him of course ... but what restrictions I might impose on the use of the pleasure-grounds is another thing. I am not fond of my shrubberies being always approachable; and I should recommend Miss Elliot to be on her guard in respect of the flower garden.' Evidently his eldest daughter, 'very like himself', endorsed his recommendation because we learn later that his younger daughter Anne had been several times in the garden 'with Mackenzie, trying to understand and make him understand which of Elizabeth's plants are for Lady Russell.' (Then, as now, the gardener was a Scot.) There are even briefer glimpses of the walled garden of the mansion at Upper Cross, with its great gates and old trees, and of the compact parsonage, 'enclosed in its own neat garden, with a vine and pear-tree trained round its casements.'

Garden details are also absent in *Pride and Prejudice* (written 1796–7, published 1813). The arrogant and conceited Lady Catherine de Bourgh, when she called at Longbourn to try to prevent Elizabeth Bennet from marrying her nephew Mr Darcy, spoke of a 'prettyish kind of little wilderness on one side of the house' where she could speak – with the utmost severity – to her, but the text goes on to mention 'the copse' they entered, so that there does not seem to have been a Sotherton-type of 'wilderness'. Mr Collins's Hunsford rectory had a 'large and well-laid-out' garden, but we know only how thankful Charlotte Collins was that her pompous husband spent a good deal of time in cultivating it. Like nearly all Jane's gardens, Longbourn had a shrubbery. The most celebrated of them was at Mr Woodhouse's Hartfield, where Mr Knightley proposed to Emma, and this is the only one where any indication is given of the shrubs in it. Mrs Elton announced that 'the laurels at Maple Grove' were 'in the same profusion' as at Hartfield and stood 'very much in the same way – just across the lawn.' The Longbourn and Mansfield parsonage shrubberies were ideal for the exchange of confidences between Elizabeth and Jane Bennet and Mary Crawford and Fanny Price, while that in Mansfield Park was a dry place for walking.

Jane of course was far more interested in people than in gardens, but part of her genius lay in devising precisely the right setting for each of her characters. Where else but in the shadow of Lady Catherine de Bourgh's Rosings Park could there be a more perfect exercise ground for Mr Collins's mixture of servility and self-importance? Supposing that Delaford were situated only a mile from Highbury, how impossible to imagine Mr Knightley cooped up in it. Is it not also a splendid index of his character that Mr

Rushworth, who had only just inherited it, should apparently be longing to have his Elizabethan house and its avenue pulled down? And Jane's series of well-observed gardens and her lively sketch of a typical Humphry Repton 'improvement' make a not unimportant contribution to English garden history.

Partal: *Roses and Box*, charcoal, 28″ × 22″. 1987

On drawing at the Alhambra
JOHN HUBBARD

John Hubbard is an artist whose garden in Dorset was included in Penelope Hob-
houses's Private Gardens of England *(London, Weidenfeld & Nicolson, 1986).*
He has recently completed a series of drawings of the gardens of the Partal and the
Generalife in Granada. Five of the drawings are reproduced here together with the
artist's own description of working in the gardens and tips for other visitors who may
wish to work there.

Raleigh Trevelyan has added a short history of the gardens and further information
may be found in a new English translation of Spanish Gardens *by Marquesa de*
Casa Valdes (Woodbridge, Suffolk, Antique Collectors' Club, 1987, first published
in Spain, 1973) and in John Brookes's Gardens of Paradise *(Weidenfeld &*
Nicolson, 1987).

I have visited the Alhambra three times, in 1958, 1983 and, in early
May 1987, I spent a week living there, drawing in the gardens every
day. It is, without question, an earthly paradise, even on those
days when there are visitors in such numbers as to make Sissinghurst
seem like a secret garden. If you take your time and plan wisely,
none of that really matters, particularly outside the courtyards.

What impressed me the most forcefully in 1983 was colour: the
roses and the underplanting, in a riotous profusion which escaped
vulgarity only because of the ambient light and the discipline of the
evergreen hedges. I returned determined to concentrate on that, to
search for a way of dealing with it pictorially but in the event, I
found the key to the gardens to be *form*. I was – quite literally –
pushed in that direction by the hordes of tourists in the rose gardens
of the Generalife but in fact the three principal gardens are all
marvels of formal structure with flower beds scattered about like
jewelled carpets. Arches, paths, steps, cascades, channels, jets,
reflecting rectangles of water, walls, topiary, hedges of every shape
and variety, the whole illuminated by the most seductive light,
particularly in early morning and late afternoon.

The drawings I made there are not meant to be descriptive and
are most certainly not botanical or topographic. They are intended
to be explorations of the essence of the place, its volumes, mysteries,
excitements, and the inter-action of foliage and light with the

geometry of the hedges. Out of them have come a small number of oils on paper and, I hope, the beginnings of something more substantial.

For anyone interested in drawing at the Alhambra, here are some practical tips: no stools, folding chairs or anything larger than a small sketchbook are allowed within the palaces or courtyards, for practical reasons. For rather more obscure reasons, no oil or watercolour is permitted anywhere. It would be prudent to obtain a permit to draw within the garden complex by applying at the Director's office in the palace of Carlos V. There, you will be told that a permit isn't necessary; but it is. It is because any group of guards contains a small proportion of bully-boys who make their life more interesting by persecuting visitors and, if the number of regulations disappoints them, they invent their own. (The permit is free.) The Partal is particularly well suited to artists because it attracts fewer visitors who linger and it contains a large number of nooks and crannies where one can lurk undisturbed. There are hazards: small boys, always, and amateur artists who insist on prying. It is worthwhile gabbling incomprehensibly at these so that they think you are either Finnish or mad. (The latter is better, as a lot of Finns seem to visit Granada, for some reason.) One of my favourite corners turned out to be just below a refreshment kiosk, so that I suffered a rain of breadcrusts and orange skins, but fortunately no bottles. As expected, the best time (and best light) is during the first hour after opening and the last two hours. There is nowhere quite like it.

An introduction to the Partal and Generalife gardens
RALEIGH TREVELYAN

Domes of heaven, water, gardens: these are the three main themes of the inscriptions that decorate the Alhambra. The Arabian association of a garden with paradise has its origins in dreams of an oasis, with its fresh springs and lush foliage under a timeless, infinite sky. The European travellers of the Romantic period fell under the spell of this meeting between East and West in Spain, but for them part

Partal: *Mock Orange and Box No. 1*, charcoal, 27½″ × 22″. 1987

Generalife: *Rose Trellis*, charcoal, 28½″ × 22″. 1987

Generalife: *Fountain and Water Jets No. 3*, charcoal, 29″ × 22″. 1987

Partal: *Twisting Trees*, charcoal, 28½″ × 22″. 1987

of the enchantment of the Alhambra also lay in the dilapidation of those once royal buildings. 'Here we are,' Richard Ford wrote in 1831, 'with the most delicious breezes from the snowy mountains above, perfumed by a thousand groves and gardens of vine, orange and pomegranate, carolled by nightingales.' Later he was lucky to live in the crumbling Casa Sánchez, with its superb view across the River Darro to the Albaicín and the Sacromonte: once part of the Partal palace. That building, restored now, is known as the Tower of Las Damas, and he would be amazed by the transformation.

In reality the Alhambra was a series of palaces, erected by successive sultans. The Partal was built by Mohammed III, early in the 14th century. The present gardens also cover the site of the palace of Yusef III, dating from a hundred years later and taken over by the Marquis of Mondéjar after the Conquest. In 1923 excavations began there under the architects Cendoya and Torres Balbás, and it was the idea of the latter that the ancient patios, pools and canals should be preserved in the form of a series of gardens, designed in the tradition of the sultans. The great pool that today so beautifully reflects the arches of the Tower was empty in Ford's day, since the water supply of the Alhambra had been blown up by Napoleonic troops. At the far end, sit two strange chimaera-like beasts, removed from the old Marestán hospital in the town. The Mondéjar garden on the terrace above has a geometrically shaped pool full of lilies and surrounded by pots of flowers and a decorative pebble pavement, somewhat reminiscent of Pompeian frescoes.

For the Arabs their gardens were a place for contemplation and retreat, usually on a small scale. They tended to be closed, like patios, but generally with vistas and views opening out from them. The plants would be scented or aromatic, such as jasmine, honeysuckle, roses, orange blossom, myrtles and rosemary. Above all, the gardens had to be cool, with shade from vegetation or pergolas and, of course, from pools and fountains. Leopoldo Torres Balbás followed these precepts. The views, especially from the Partal mirador, are marvellous – towards the Generalife, the Sierra Nevada, the red fields and olive groves of the plain of the Vega, with hazy blue mountains beyond. A number of other sites of ancient buildings were discovered, and each of these form quite distinct gardens, some sparkling with fountains, some modest, some shadowed by cypresses. Plants tend to be placed asymetrically, in order to 'heighten the individuality'. In the Albaicín and outside Granada there are many private gardens of Arab origin, their preservation owing much to the inspired example of Torres Balbás at the Partal; they are known as *carmenes*.

The traveller today, wearied perhaps by crowds and sightseeing, enters the Patio of the Fountains in the Generalife and is immediately revived by the amazingly vivacious gushes of water. The Generalife dates from before 1319; strategically placed, it was also designed as a summer retreat. As with the Alhambra buildings, its pavilions were altered in Christian times, and recent architects have tried to eliminate inconsistencies and clumsy restorations. A fire in 1958 gave an opportunity for new excavations, and the Patio at last approximates to its original plan, with smaller shrubs than hitherto, and with paths and a central fountain. Fragments of newly discovered poems and inscriptions have provided further clues about the original plan. As in the Partal, the Generalife consists of a series of contrasting terraces and garden patios, the most famous being the garden of the sultana, where the lovely wife of Boabdil was said to have been discovered with her Abencerrage lover. Beneath the mirador is a simple water staircase, probably just as it was seven hundred years ago, with two rushing streams twisting along the balustrades, intended to cool the royal wrists on the long climb to the oratory.

The Generalife gardens were extended in the 1930s and again after the inauguration of the Festival of Music and Dance in 1952, to connect with the open air theatre designed by Francisco Prieto-Moreno. In a certain degree these gardens follow the plan of the Patio of the Fountains, but are surrounded by cypress hedges. The Alhambra was floodlit for the Festival, and for the first time. But now, on many other summer nights, you can wander through the illuminated courtyards and the Partal gardens: an unique, magical experience.

Tulips in the Orchard Grass

MIRABEL OSLER

Rose-madder streaked with viridian, cadmium flecked with sulphur; mulberry, coral and ochre, or opalescence stippled with jet. Deep crimson ruffles with tracings of silver, smudged amethyst leaking into gold. Only blue is missing. But who's checking? Once you have laid your hands on these emperors amongst bulbs, infinite possibilities open up and no season is long enough to contain all your ambition.

Tulips have been around for centuries. From somewhere in the high Pamirs, in the mountains of Sinkiang or from the far pastures of Persia, they have been collected, coveted and sold for outrageous prices. Tulips have been hybridised and auctioned, they have been etched, embroidered or wrought in iron, immortalised on tiles and engraved on glass. And amongst the Dutch painters only Rembrandt seems to have ignored them.

Out of our eight years of gardening, half have already been frittered away without taking these plants into account. How could we? How could we have looked the other way instead of almost making our garden around them? From the beginning we did plan for bulbs, but they were the other ones. The snowdrops and crocuses, the aconites and narcissus. All that lot have been accounted for from the start and every year they perform the way they should with immense spirit and a loveliness of behaviour. But tulips? Why were we unreceptive to their enchantment for so long? After all, they detonate across page after page in bulb catalogues. But somehow I had a blocked mind. Association with childhood walks through St James's Park made a lasting imprint. Tulips went with discipline. With patterns and conformity, with blocks of colour under bare branches and turbid skies. Nothing rousing came through those pages so I searched for pools of blue amongst the anemone blandas.

It was coming across a mention of species tulips in a wholesaler's catalogue that started us off. The word 'species' has immense power. It sounds good, whatever it is; at least, among plants it does. Our first autumn planting was of several hundred of these feral tulips, in the rough grass between shaggy bushes of filbert hazels. Names and

descriptions were all we had to go on. We'd never seen them growing anywhere but they sounded right and we totally ignored the
catalogue advice that they were suitable for rockeries.

   Tarda, turkestanica, clusiana and *praestans* 'Fusilier'. They came up
that first spring and dumbfounded us. Could they really be what
we had ordered? Members of the tulip family? Relations of those
sane, stiff-stemmed flowers so subjugated and prim? These of ours
were tentative, with nodding heads of gentle yellows and milky
light. Star-shaped and almost greenish, all creamy centred and rosy
petalled they appeared unobtrusively among the grass. The only
species tulips to produce a passing reminder of London parks were
the *praestans* 'Fusilier'. Stupidly that first year I'd planted them too
closely. They formed scarlet carnage, dense and unrelieved. Their
dominance was intensified by lack of colour elswhere, by the leafless
trees and chalky skies. Later we moved them to an informal orchard
where we planted them well apart so that now in spring they
sprinkle the land with intriguing brilliance.

   That was our initiation into tulips. Since then we have been
devoted. Their versatility, their beauty, their astonishing habit of
flowering so protractedly, has made the annual ordering an agony
of indecision. What choices, what names and what previously un-
imagined effects can be achieved if only we get it right. We next
ordered hundreds of Lily-flowering tulips and we chose at random
by descriptions. How lucky we were. 'Ballade', 'Captain Fryatt'
and 'China Pink' appeared the following spring, with ravishing
perfection. Mauves, soft purples and fragile pinks with their chalice-
shaped buds came up in such profusion we could hardly take our
eyes off them. Their reflexed petals opened into curling delicacy,
light-weight and buoyant. Slowly over the weeks the grasses grew
up to them, blurring and fuzzing their colours. Even in a small
unkempt patch these bulbs would give this effect when the sun is low,
of an almost floating translucence. And like so much in gardening,
quite by chance not only had we chosen the right colours but,
fortuitously, our five wild cherries bloomed above them at the
same time.

   Alas, our second year's planting of Lily-flowering tulips was not a
knock-out. This time we thought another few hundred of other,
though similar, tones would embellish the first plantings. 'Jacqueline',
'Lilac Time' and 'Mariette', again chosen from their descriptions,

were really nasty. The pink was too magenta, the deep rose too crass and the purples too livid. They curdled hopelessly and that diaphanous look was lost. It is true that as the weeks went on their colours bleached a little and even, towards the end, we thought them passable. But I had wanted perfection for every day of those six weeks. For surely, after all that labour of planting, the aching back and flagging commitment could only be worth it if each flower was superb, blending one with the other to create iridescent radiance?

Moving into the world of tulips requires space, for once you have succumbed to their charm your longing becomes almost insatiable. Because we have no formal garden, no flower beds, but only shrubs planted into the meadowy grass and underplanted with certain flowers that don't mind such treatment, we decided last year to lop off a piece of our six-acre field and bring it into the garden. This land tilts towards us so that on icy days in April we can be indoors but clearly see the robust thrusting of our next choice of bulbs – the Double Early tulips.

These are twelve-inch-high 'Peach Blossom', 'Garanza' and 'Schoonoord', with a quite different manner to the fine elegance of the swaying twenty-two-inch lily tulips. There is none of that noble precision from these sturdy tulips with densely ruffled petals, and sensual colours that shine across the still wintery waste with compelling dominance. Carmine, flush and creamy whites which like the others last for weeks. Before ordering I was apprehensive about white. But white 'Schoonoord' (described forlornly as an ideal 'bedder and forcer'), being diffused by grass, added a luminous contrast which was not too emphatic.

There is no going back on tulips now. Somehow their versatility and range raises our planting schemes to reach for further possibilities. Already for next year I am overwhelmed with recklessness. We can no longer ignore the existence of the hybrids, Fosteriana or 'waterlily' Kaufmannianas. A place must be found for Viridifloras with their green dappling, for the frilled Parrots. What too of Cottage and Peacock? Paeony, Fringed or Triumph with their white hems, and all those streaky Rembrandts? Who goes through a spring without a scoop of Greigi with mottled leaves or without a handful of black tulips murky as sloes?

One aspect of tulips which should not be overlooked is the sheer unmitigated hell of planting. It is far worse than putting in roses. For where we have chosen is in rough, tufted turf made up of sorrel, cocksfoot, buttercups and clover. Generations of unploughed herbage have grown into impenetrable density. Bulb planters, the short- or the long-handled kinds, trowels, crowbars and pickaxes are all equally inefficient. With bad temper and irritation, with an increasing weariness and muscle fatigue, I have finally decided that the only way is with a spade. First I lift a great scud of turf, in itself an excruciating chore, and then dig out the earth, under which I bury six inches deep three to five bulbs according to the area. And now, maddeningly, I've just read that we should plant our bulbs *twelve* inches deep. This will give them a chance to withstand the rapacious appetites of the mice and moles which surround us; and the deeper they are, the less the small bulbs form to exhaust the parent plant. Twelve inches! One foot down – the prospect is unthinkable. (And imagine the boost needed for those colours to reach the air.) It is only the vision as we are planting, of what these amber and golden stones will turn into, that keeps up our resolve. I do know there will come a day in spring when we will be confounded and we will stand amazed at our achievement.

There is a kind of sorcery to tulips. The process works in well-defined phases and it is the sequence of these phases that ensnares you. First, as in all plant ordering, there is the heady pleasure of choosing, filling in forms and spending more than you intended. It becomes a late summer self-indulgence. Months after, when we've long since forgotten them, the bulbs arrive. Vigour and resolve are short-lived when faced with the packets of hundreds to be planted. This second phase can't be dodged: the bulbs menace us, lying in their bags with all that potential. But then comes the third phase – the reward. Long after the blissful months of winter, when gardens are only in the mind, comes that triumphant recompense bursting through the grass. The subtlety and motley tones, the lustre and abundance far surpass our most outlandish plans. Memories of planting are easily forgotten as April, May and June reveal what we laid under the ground so long ago.

There is only one sneaking flaw, which at present is no more than a tiny seed of doubt as we haven't been tulip growing for more than three seasons. When we first started I thought tulips would flourish like daffodils, appearing reliably spring after spring. But have we been receptive enough to what they need or have we overlooked, in our enthusiasm to create splendour among the long grass, one crucial point? That is, their origins in the arid steppes of Asia. Tulips may not be resigned, nor may they approve of our wet Shropshire hills. Will next year's folly prove to us that we really have to treat our tulips as annuals?

Lily-flowered tulips in unmown orchard grass in Mirabel and Michael Osler's Shropshire garden, first week of May, 1988. *Photograph by David Wheeler*

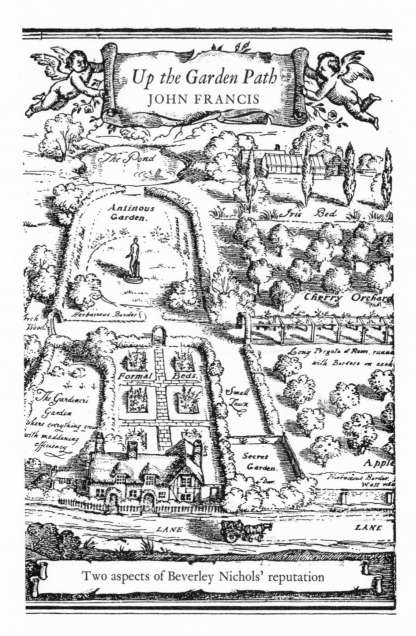

Up the Garden Path

JOHN FRANCIS

The Pond

Antinous
Garden.

Iris Bed

Heather Bed

Herbaceous Border

Cherry Orchard

Inch
Wood

Herbaceous Border

Long Pergola of Roses, running
with Borders on each

Formal Beds.

Small
Lawn

The Gardener's
Garden
where everything grows
with maddening
efficiency

Secret
Garden.

Door

Apple

Herbaceous Border.
Wall whe

LANE

LANE

Two aspects of Beverley Nichols' reputation

I was afraid of Mr Nangle and Mr Nangle despised me. He taught arithmetic at school, my worst subject, by terror, stealth and wintry smiles. The stealth part came from his habit of prowling behind the desks. Accoutred like a crow in black academic draperies, made of a special rustle-free material, he would crash down the knob of his silver propelling pencil on your head while you were actually making a mistake in your exercise book. On one occasion at least he swerved away from his subject and asked the class, one by one, to name their favourite author. He came to me after a long litany of names, Conan Doyle, Farnol, Sabatini, Wodehouse, Austen, Captain W. E. Johns. With mad candour I told the truth. 'Beverley Nichols, sir.'

There was a stupified silence. The Tram took off his glasses and gave them a polish with a silk paisley handkerchief. (Mr Nangle was known as The Tram because of his amazingly unvarying customs.) 'Whom did you say, Francis?' 'Beverley Nichols, sir.' The more sensually alert in the class sniggered, doubtless hoping that this Beverley Nichols would turn out to have written *Forever Amber* perhaps or *No Orchids For Miss Blandish*.

The Tram shuddered and raked me with a long stare from his bulgy brown eyes. '*I see.*' The awful moment passed in a slow flash of eternity and ever afterwards when we met in the grounds or corridors of the school, despite the grave salutations, I knew that Mr Nangle knew I was a lost soul.

I had lapped up *Down The Garden Path* and *A Thatched Roof*. Here was a writer who wrote rhapsodically about the pleasures of gardening, who conveyed the excitement of bulbs pushing up through the earth. I loved and laughed at the neighbours, Mrs M. and Undine Wilkins, who lived just down the lane from B.N. in Allways. Nor did I wince or even notice the purple patches in the Nichols prose. I gloried in the purple and asked for more. Even as a tot I had enjoyed pottering in the garden. When I was down in the dumps with measles my mother, thinking to cheer me, bought in Salisbury market a prize pink geranium and at once I had felt much better. Being young I had a sweet tooth. Shallow called unto shallow. Beverley Nichols's style, breathless, gushing, you could almost say girlish, exactly found the spot. I knew nothing of *Cry Havoc*, his fervent pacifist plea. No doubt Mr Nangle did. I don't know what Mr Nangle did in the war but he would have done it with a grim gusto. Again, B.N. wrote with huge success for the more down market end of Fleet Street about his cats, about what the modern girl was thinking, of flower arranging. None of these abhorred activities would have escaped the steely Nangle eye. You could not, and after all these years cannot, imagine old Nangle letting old Nichols take him by the hand in order to scamper to a special spot in the garden where a madonna lily was doing something rather special. All the fountains of adjectives, all the rhapsodies, would have had Nangle reaching not for his garlic and crucifix but rather for his gun. Murder in the garden? And not a jury in the kingdom would have dared convict.

Murder in the garden. By 1972 B.N. was a fading star. Because his time had gone by and he knew it and no doubt sick at heart but still game and resolved like some star of the opera determined to make one more triumphant come-back, Beverley Nichols published *Father Figure*. It made a stir. Alas for Beverley there was not to be a prolonged outburst of stormy applause. A whistle or two of the 'well I'll go to the foot of our stairs,' variety and, oh dear! not a little jeering laughter. The decision to tell all, to bare your tortured soul, to cry, '*Mea culpa, mea culpa, mea maxima culpa!*' is a healing one and often received in a respectful silence. What you cannot, what you must not do is emotionally and, heedless of buttons, wrench apart your Jermyn Street shirt, get down on one knee, expose your best profile and shrill, '*Mea culpa, mea culpa, mea* slightly *culpa!*' And that is what B.N. did.

Now, in *Down The Garden Path* we had been introduced to a loveable old party who stumped about the Nichols demesne saying things like 'H'rumph,' and 'Pshaw,' who screwed in his eyeglass and who was a storehouse of pithy and earthy wisdom. Old man Nichols told Beverley – who was only too apt in particularly rhapsodic moments to lose his head – how to whip out a pen-knife and take cuttings. Beverley, you see, had had a sheltered upbringing and had been on the point of buying a whole grizzle of weeping willows from the nursery. With a scornful 'H'rumph,' Nichols senior had advised Beverley to cut a few twigs and to stick 'em in a nice squelchy bit of Huntingdonshire and lo! he could have his grizzle for free. Beverley is struck all of a heap – and, the canny reader will infer, a pretty picturesque heap at that. Incidentlly, B.N. was apt to be dumbstruck by this business of cuttings. I remember an amusing passage where he has a slight accident with a geranium and daringly sticks the severed limb into the earth. This is done fairly tremulously and he hovers crooningly over it – you do wonder sometimes how on earth he ever found the time to accomplish so much in the way of gardening and book writing – until in time the sprig establishes itself and becomes *another* geranium. B.N. points out, quite reasonably really, that if you snapped off the leg of an actress you could not, by popping it into the richest of composts, acquire another actress. No, indeedy.

In *Down The Garden Path* father Nichols sounds the ideal dad for a dreamy but talented lad such as Beverley. The reader of that funny and entertaining book could never have known the fact that B.N. loathed his father and had, already, tried to murder him not once but thrice in, as it happens, the garden. It would have been enough to make the nice gentle lady readership measure their collective lengths on their *Ideal Homes*, circa 1930, crazy paving. Beverley Nichols a would-be, not very successful patricide? You can almost hear the gasps in the Surrey gardens. And father so helpful about cuttings too! In a jarring phrase, for upper middle class B.N. is anxious to know that you know that he has not sprung from the loins of an ordinary farmer but from those (as we learn in *Father Figure* somewhat fat and hairy loins – he goes on rather about dad's Esau-like limbs which is . . . interesting perhaps) of a 'gentleman farmer'.

Always keen on flowers, as a tot, possibly even in his perambulator, he had been taught how to collect and press wild specimens and could distinguish while still in rompers between a primrose and cow parsley. To such an instinctive gardener who knew all about bone meal and the virtues of dried blood, a ghastly drunken father must have seemed the ideal, the ultimate mulch.

In *Father Figure* B.N. sets out to make our flesh creep and, in ways he never dreamed of, succeeds. Life with father must have been sordid and dreadful and socially right off the Richter scale and yet as pitilessly recounted by beady Beverley I find giggles keep breaking in. There is Dad stretched out yet again, foamingly drunk at the foot of a grassy bank on the lawn, the eyeglass glittering in the moon-light. Dangerous moonlight, but it is interesting to note that, though he was far from being a gentleman and equally distant from the honourable calling of farming, he did wear an eyeglass. However, to follow the narrative, there, as I say, is drunk father, dead drunk and unconsciously deadly. The cook has, as cooks will, gone, taking with her the parlour maid: 'Never heard language like it, Ma'r'm!' Young Beverley is in despair. But soft! What's this? A garden roller! Adept at pressing flowers as he is by his own admission from earliest tothood – it is easy to follow his thoughts, might not pressed father, like pressed beef (with added brandy for flavouring) not be the ideal solution? Straining his little muscles Beverley heaves and pulls and puffs and . . . lets go. Down the bank the roller plunges directly towards prone Nichols senior. The peaceful Torquay night is sundered by a cry. (Rather more than an 'Ouch!' presumably.) Beverley peers into the night. Drat! Missed him but got the brute's leg at least. If at first you don't succeed . . .

The fact is, Beverley's style, overwrought perhaps and a wee bit gushy, is fine for describing the epiphany of a snowdrop or the advent of a lupin but quite unsuited for describing attempted murder. Where he should be penny plain he is threepence or even sixpence coloured. His old friend/enemy Somerset Maugham would have handled it much more drily and we would have been quite moist with alarm.

Somewhere in his writings B.N. remarked, 'Good taste is like a thin purple line over which even the nicest of us may sometimes stray'. As he grew older B.N. did not just stray. Stray is not the word. Helpless as a pin in the aura of a powerful magnet, poor Beverley lurched and crashed again and again. As I say, stray is not the word unless you feel that Hitler *strayed* into Poland or the Japanese *strayed* into Pearl Harbour.

His first great success was *Twenty Five* (still, I find, a good read by the way). He got the title from his age at the time of composition and it was his preferred perch for too long. St Paul, that bracing man, had some shrewd words to say to those who linger too long, who inhabit lingeringly, their youth. B.N. must have missed them. *Twenty Five* was a great success, achieved perhaps too effortlessly.

Clever Beverley perhaps found it like falling off a log. His friend, in so far as, by all accounts, she possessed any, Mrs Maggie Greville, that well-heeled harpy of Polesden Lacy always called him her 'dear Twenty Five'. Another title for *Father Figure* could have been *Sobs In The Confessional*. You wonder as you read, is he getting something nasty from off his chest or is he hoping to put something large and useful into his bank account? It is to his credit perhaps that a reader of B.N. will almost certainly feel that a large part of any useful sum would be spent on his garden.

His love of gardening seems to have lasted until the end. Shortly before he died I happened to hear Beverley Nichols talking on the BBC radio to an interviewer. He insisted that his companion come with him to a certain spot in the garden where the sun would be striking the blooms of, I think, an azalea. 'Promise me,' he bleated cajolingly, 'you'll gasp'. As they rounded a corner the sun was seen to be doing what was right by the petals. He got his gasp. This listener found the moment touching and irritating. How, I've since wondered could such an old party be at the same moment sincere *and* affected?

You would not, or at any rate, should not, go to *Down The Garden Path* or *A Thatched Roof* for useful, technical hints about gardening. But a weary or jaded gardener will, I fancy, on coming across these books and flipping through them, become excited. Read him on water divining or how he brought his vine indoors and you seem to experience, so skilful a writer was he, these things for yourself. You seem to have made a friend.

Of course while he was writing the Allways books he was coping with his odious father, and father was, despite Beverley's best efforts, still very much alive. This was a secret part of his life and we now know that over the click of the garden shears, the purring of the mower and the buzzing of bees there was always at Allways another more sinister sound which B.N. heard all the time: the ticking of that disgraceful old time-bomb of a father ever ready to detonate.

But the feeling that through his books you had made a friend was not, alas, a trustworthy impression as, years later, B.N. was to show when he wrote *A Case Of Human Bondage*. Of course like most things he wrote it was fatally readable. His aim in writing the book was to defend Syrie Maugham, he said. The desire to write a sensational best seller was, he implied, not a consideration at all. When Arthur

Marshall reviewed the book he called it 'a sad little pile,' an arresting phrase and a stern judgement all the more striking for having come from such a sunny and charitable source. His old journalistic skills had not deserted him but where was loyalty? Once more Beverley had strayed across that purple line and got himself drummed out of the Brownies. He had betrayed all the friendship and hospitality he had enjoyed at the Maugham villa and, from my point of view, justified Mr Nangle's spite and scorn.

It must have come as a shock to all those he had so beguilingly and charmingly encouraged to go down his garden path or shelter under his thatched roof that it was in the famous garden at Allways that the third and final attempt to murder his father had taken place. The years had gone by and I no longer would have rated B.N. so highly as I had when adolescent. But I had not thrown his books out and I even picked them up from time to time. I read again the account of how he had discovered at the Huntingdonshire cottage a Sheraton alcove which had been concealed and which had been found to contain a Staffordshire lady with a white hat, all white in fact, the only colour being in the green china grass at her feet and the yellow of corn sheaf in her arms. It was a charming idea, this finding of an eighteenth century alcove in what had been a labourer's cottage and Beverley descants prettily upon it. Why was it hidden? Who hid it? But when I re-read it I became somewhat cynical. I wondered if B.N. hadn't invented the alcove and the Staffordshire lady as a device for gingering up *A Thatched Roof*. But in 1972 in *Father Figure* the Staffordshire lady makes a further and final appearance.

B.N. returns to his cottage on the evening of 31 March 1929 having dreamed all the way up the Great North Road of making his garden tour. This tour, something he greatly enjoys, is made by torchlight and is to discover what has happened in the garden while he has been in London. He soon finds out. Once more the servants have deserted. Father has been at it again. 'He was lying in a heap by the empty grate. His fly-buttons were undone; he had been sick on his waistcoat.' All this enrages him as it has done so many times before but this time an extra detail fills him with murderous resolve; in his father's hand is the shattered ornament which he had found walled-up in the alcove. The first thought that strikes B.N. is to leave him in the cold room to die. But in this uncertain world it is best to leave nothing to chance. So Beverley administers a double dose of sleeping tablets and then hauls the unconscious figure of father out into the garden through the french windows. As he is dragging father across the floor to his doom one eye clicks open. A good touch this, bravo Beverley. 'The best place would be just outside the window, among the tangled branches of an old rose-bush. They would lacerate his face, and if there were any odd bloodstains to be accounted for, they would confuse the issue.'

The murderous author then goes and lights a fire in his study and composes a wild torrential *étude* on his piano, an act of breathtaking self-dramatisation. More perhaps to the point, since after all he was such a very keen gardener, would be to dash down on to his jotter a reminder that he really must sort out those tangled branches of his neglected rose and, while he's at it, fork in some really good manure. But this would have to wait for father's body to be removed and for the warmer weather. Anyway, he gets the *étude* down somehow, though in a rushed manner, admitting that he put in quavers where he should have used semi-quavers. The fire dies down too but he is nicely warmed by all these exertions and has a satisfactory sense of having done himself justice. 'It [the *étude*] was rough and amateurish but some of the pain and passion came through.' Thoughtfully he provides a copy of the work at the end of *Father Figure* so the reader can make his own judgement. Just one more thing before going to bed, better see how frosted father is fairing amongst the tangled rose branches before heading up the wooden hill. Evidently the 'tour' was an ingrained habit. But, what's this? 'And then – there was a crash and a splintering of wood, and he [father] fell into the room, covered with snow, with blood streaming down his face.'

I suppose by making fun of what poor B.N. and his family endured I'm being rather tasteless, but remember, 'Even the nicest of us . . .' But there is something absurd about his accounts of his murder attempts. He's like someone in a pub who has been the centre of attraction, who senses that he is losing his hold on the other drinkers' attention. They are beginning to talk amongst themselves, elaborately mime yawns and say with theatrical surprise, 'Goodness! Is that the time?' Instead of accepting, the pub bore raises his voice, 'Have I ever told you about the time . . .?' he asks and he adds lurid little touches like the scarlet petal of a fuchsia that fell into the poisoned cup that he was carrying upstairs to his father while humming something by Brahms. (Cradle Song perhaps?) That was murder attempt number two. He invents for himself the sort of role that Joan Crawford at the height of her career would have relished. All great fun while disbelief is suspended but downright silly when you consider it.

What he needed was a candid friend, 'Oh do shut up, Beverley.' Someone who would have told him when some pruning would have done not just the roses but his prose a great deal of good. But if you have never encountered Undine Wilkins, Mrs M. and Mrs Wrench and all the other characters in the Allways books you will have missed one of the minor delights of gardening literature. If Mr Nangle was partly right, so, I think, was I.

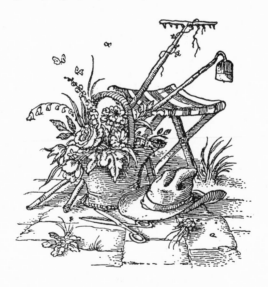

The map and vignettes which decorate this article are by Rex Whistler from
Down the Garden Path, *Jonathan Cape, 1932*

Relighting our Brightest Beacon

STEPHEN LACEY

Wasn't it interesting that of all the gardens designed for Chelsea this year, the Sword of Honour went to an old-fashioned cottage plot complete with straight brick paths and mixed rows of fruit, flowers, herbs and vegetables? Not for the judges the colour co-ordinated banks of shrubs and groundcover, the varied paving materials and subtle level changes, the arty sculpture and *treillage*, and the blueprints for modern outdoor living which littered the rest of the show. Not for me either. And yet, I couldn't help stifling a yawn at the prize-winning Women's Institute/Bridgemere exhibit. Expertly constructed and laid out as it was, it was ultimately only a replica of something we are all familiar with anyway (and it wasn't pretending to be anything more than this). And since I go to Chelsea, even on its 75th anniversary, for new ideas and fresh interpretations,

The 1988 Chelsea Flower Show prize-winning exhibit, 'A Country Woman's Garden' designed by Jacqui Moon and John Ravenscroft for the National Federation of Women's Institutes. *Photograph: David Wheeler*

new plants (new to me, I mean) and new inventions, I rather lost interest in it after a while.

Nevertheless the W.I. garden served a useful purpose. It reminded us at a timely moment and in the clearest possible way of our own special gardening tradition, a tradition of which today's designers seem to have lost sight. The cottage garden is the jewel of our horticultural heritage. It is our main contribution to international garden design and from it has descended, in ever more sophisticated guise, that informal, plant-orientated style of gardening which the world recognises as quintessentially British. It has been developed and perfected by a nation of down-to-earth souls who love the practical challenges of cultivation, the taste of home produce, the scent of roses over the door and the sting of cold fresh air on their ruddy cheeks.

Other nationalities have seen their gardens as places for spiritual contemplation, as theatres of entertainment, as showcases of wealth, and as havens from hostile environments. For the cottage gardener a garden was simply somewhere where you grew plants. There was no carefully conceived ground-plan, no guiding artistic influence; the design sprang from a series of chance occurrences and *ad hoc* decisions. If paths followed straight lines, it was because that was the shortest route from *a* to *b*; if they changed from brick to cinders, it was because the supply of bricks ran out; if there was a clump of delphiniums in a strategic position, it was because Mrs Muffin at the bakery had some spare and that was the only space free.

Of course, British gardening has moved on since the early days. We have become more cosmopolitan and more conscious of design matters. We think about focal points and axes, vistas and 'hard landscaping'. But underlying all our sophistication remains that straightforward attachment to the soil and the things that grow in it. Aren't we still simple plant lovers at heart? And aren't our greatest twentieth-century gardens just highbrow versions of that cottage idyll of happy, colourful, scent-drenched vegetation?

British gardeners are not much interested in cold-blooded design. Since the cottage-garden style took hold two centuries ago, all our famous designers have been plantspeople in disguise. William Robinson, Gertrude Jekyll, Lawrence Johnston and Vita Sackville-West were all, give or take the odd York paving stone and lead urn, concerned principally with the study of plants and the intricacies of planting. And you have only to take a tour of our island to see that the great majority of gardens, whether they be in woodland, suburb or window box, are still little more than homes for plants.

We are told that British garden design is currently in a state of confusion. Anyone who has visited Chelsea Flower Show recently is able to confirm this. I think – and it is only one gardener's humble view – that the reason for the turmoil is that designers have forsaken this rich plant-based cottage-garden heritage. Instead of looking in their own backyard, where they would find some of the most beautiful gardens man has ever made, they have wandered off to China, Japan, the United States and even Scandinavia in search of a new approach to the British garden. And now we must endure pagodas and wooden rafts and gravel twirls, features which had purpose and integrity in their own environments, in the midst of our meadow flowers and lush greenery. The resulting hybrid (I could have used a stronger word) compositions have, not surprisingly, failed to strike a sympathetic chord with ordinary gardeners.

The way forward is surely to adapt our own style of gardening to the needs and circumstances of today and not to abandon it in favour of someone else's style. Since it is plants and the arrangement of plants that is at the core of our gardening, it is this area of design which we should be looking at, allowing the inspiration for modern gardens, small and barbecue-ridden as they are, to come from the flowers, leaves, berries and barks which inspired Gertrude Jekyll and Mrs Muffin before us.

Alas, how we have fallen from those great heights which the cottage garden attained in the hands of our predecessors. The lessons taught by Hestercombe, Hidcote and Sissinghurst are largely ignored and subtlety and sensitivity in the treatment of plants, which are now mere adjuncts to the manmade features, are seldom practised. Since there is no room for a quantity of plants, only the most striking individuals are allowed in – the Chelsea gardens bristle with exotic phormiums, golden robinias, purple-leaved maples, flaming azaleas, gaudy roses and bright blue conifers – and associations are engineered for the maximum contrast in colour and character.

Of course, it isn't easy for today's gardeners, many of whom have plots only 15 feet by 60 feet, to relate to the scale of the planting at gardens like Sissinghurst, to read and interpret the principles behind the compositions and translate them to their own needs. The walls and statues, the great lawns and orchards, the lakes and moats, give such a sense of grandeur that the visitor tends to drift around in silent awe instead of furiously scribbling on a notepad.

But everybody who goes to Sissinghurst (let's settle on this as our example of perfection in mid 20th century cottage gardening) is excited and stimulated. People return again and again. Since it has such an irresistable draw and fascination, oughtn't we to attempt an analysis of its content and construction and try to discover why it has so much appeal? We might then see a way to reproduce some of this enchantment in our own tiny plots.

The first point to acknowledge is that the abiding interest in the place is in its planting. Once you have paid homage to the tower, your eyes are drawn to the ground or just above it and kept there for most of your visit. It is the sheer variety of plants and the ways that they are juxtaposed that wins your heart. Every border is filled to overflowing with shrubs, perennials and bulbs of every conceivable shape and size. This encouragement to wallow in flowers and foliage is bliss for the plant-sensitive gardener, and it seems to me that any blueprint for small garden design that forbids us from surrounding ourselves with a mass of plants is destined to fall on stony ground. In any case, we have a climate which, though not ideal for humans, happens to suit a huge proportion of the world's flora rather well, and it would be a crime to take a vow of abstinence.

All the plant associations at Sissinghurst are sensitively contrived, with attention paid to every individual's personality and impact. There is always some sort of harmony between neighbouring plants so that, even if they have striking contrasting features too, the borders retain their unity and apparent simplicity. In spite of the great diversity of plants present, the eye is never irritated nor the senses made to feel uneasy. Colour is the main unifying device – every border has a strong colour harmony – but the other important factor is natural compatibility. Vita Sackville-West would never have put heathers next to hostas, rhododendrons in gravel, or purple-leaved ligularia behind dwarf conifers – all examples of plant mismanagement on show in the Chelsea gardens this year – because such associations defy every natural and artistic principle. They just look wrong.

The arrangement of plants is casual and informal. Individuals are permitted to seed themselves about, to weave their way through their neighbours and to flop over the paths. There are no artificial blocks, no straight lines and formal tiers. The plants look as if they are enjoying themselves and growing exactly as they might in the wild; the gardener's hand is concealed. It is an idealisation of nature, a benevolent jungle of scented creepers and colourful undergrowth, the stuff of dreams and fairy tales.

This tangled planting creates a series of strong seasonal moods and impressions. With so many flowering plants coming and going, the borders are never the same from one week to the next. There is always variety. The sense of anticipation and adventure that this engenders would be lost were the borders clogged with the permanent cover of evergreens or with modern varieties of plants that bloom on and on. Today's gardeners are inclined to over-use conifers and foliage plants and the resulting planting, though always presentable and labour-free, lacks that element of the unpredictable which counteracts boredom and complacency.

And lastly, the 'bones' of the design, which are for the most part divorced from the planting, never try to compete for attention; the structure comes from the definite geometry of the ground-plan, the symmetry of clipped box and yew, and the furniture and sculpture used as focal points; the border plants could be reshuffled without affecting the composition very much, an important factor in the plantsman's garden, where new plants and schemes are always being tried out and indifferent ones jettisoned. The mellow colours of brick and stone and the sombre tones of yew and box are foils for the brilliant flowers, the straight lines of paths and hedges antidotes to the carefree planting. The structural elements, vital though they are to the overall design, remain – at least during the growing seasons – accompaniments to the planting, not rivals. Today's structural additions – Caribbean blue swimming pools, white planting tubs, yellow patio umbrellas, fancy summerhouses and aluminium greenhouses – do not so easily take a back-seat role, and planting has to be adapted accordingly. This may mean confining yourself to one colour, maybe just green, and seeking variety in shape and texture instead. You will be surprised how much fun you can have operating within a tiny slice of the spectrum.

Reshaping the cottage-garden style for the 1980s is not just a matter of scaling down the Sissinghurst ideal. Today's small 'outdoor room' presents its own special problems and opportunities. The shortage of space, which becomes acute as patios and sand pits elbow their way in, imposes severe limitations on the design and necessitates some hard decisions about what plants to include. But we might use Sissinghurst as a beacon to illuminate our path.

Today's designers might continue to revolve the groundplan of British gardens around a varied collection of plants, informally and sensitively grown. They might consider colour and natural compatibility as the basis for their associations; in the smallest gardens, one strong planting theme (wild flowers, Mediterranean subjects or Myles Challis's tropical exotica, perhaps) will be enough. They might think in terms of a series of seasonal floral incidents instead of an abundance of long-lasting foliar features. And they might seek harmony between man-made features and flora (wherever possible making the man-made features foils for the planting, instead of vice versa) so that, as Gertrude Jekyll advocated, the garden has a simplicity of intention. They might then recapture some of the flavour of our unique gardening style in the modern garden, and so light another beacon for the future.

Gardens in Fiction

Opportunity Lost

NANCY-MARY GOODALL
tours Milton's *Paradise Lost*

There are many ways that a journalist can tackle the vast field of gardening. One tried and tested angle is the conducted tour of a particular garden. The reader is told its history, situation and aspect, is introduced to the owner and often to the gardener, and is taken on a walk round which is as interesting, or as boring, as the writer makes it. Main features are mentioned, trees and plants are described and peppered with a few Latin names. By the end of the piece the reader should feel a sense of having visited a garden without leaving his or her armchair and can turn the page to some other aspect of the second most popular hobby.

Keen gardeners must often wish they could be given similar guided tours of the great gardens of the past. Xenophon left an interesting but short report on the landscape park of Cyrus the Persian and there are fragmentary accounts of some others but these are few and far between. How fortunate we are, then, to have a description of the first and greatest garden of them all, the Garden of Eden. Its exact location is doubtful, the Bible simply tells us that "The Lord God planted a garden eastward in Eden: and there he put the man whom he had formed. And out of the ground made the Lord God to grow every tree that is pleasant to the sight, and good for food; the tree of life also in the garden, and the tree of knowledge of good and evil. And a river went out of Eden to water the garden; and from thence it was parted and became into four heads . . . And the Lord God took the man, and put him into the Garden of Eden to dress it and keep it." God, then, was the owner, and Adam the gardener. So far as I know the garden has never been written up in the form of a gardening article.

For more information we must turn to Milton. Unfortunately he wrote in poetry which is not a very suitable medium for horticultural accuracy and the garden is first seen through the eyes of Satan, hardly the guide we would choose as he has just come from bottomless perdition in a dungeon horrible and has "gestures fierce" and a "mad demeanour". Satan sets out on a reconnaissance, determined on revenge for reasons too complex to go into here. At first, excluded, he sees an "enclosure green . . . a steep wilderness, whose hairy sides with thicket overgrown, grotesque and wild, access denied; and overhead up grew insuperable heights of loftiest shade, cedar and pine and fir, and branching palm". All this is enclosed by a high wall. By "branching palm" is probably meant the doum palm, *Hyphaene thebaica*, much used in Ancient Egyptian gardens.

So Paradise had a very mixed flora, like the volcanic island of Tenerife where palms and oranges flourish at sea level, and where, as you ascend, you pass through deciduous and then coniferous forests until you reach a wide, dry crater, with cacti and other desert plants. In Paradise the higher levels are different. There is a "circling row of goodliest trees loaden with fairest fruit, blossoms and fruits at once, of golden hue . . . with gay enamelled colours mixed." These may be citrus trees which bear fruit and blossom at the same time, or some more tropical species. Gentle gales fan their odoriferous wings and dispense native perfumes and balmy spoils such as may be encountered by ships off the shores of Africa and which, incidentally, enter through the ventilation systems of aircraft approaching Bombay and other odoriferous airports long before one touches down.

Satan ascends "that steep savage hill" apparently on foot, but the undergrowth is "so thick entwined" that rather than search for the only gate he "high overleaped all bound . . . as when a prowling wolf . . . leaps o'er the fence with ease into the fold . . . thence up he flew and on the tree of life", the middle and highest tree, "sat like a cormorant." We can see him perching there, hunched with malevolence, as "Beneath him with new wonder now he views . . . a Heaven on earth." It was evidently a comprehensive arboretum in which grew "all trees of noblest kind" among them "the tree of life, (just mentioned) high, eminent, blooming ambrosial fruit of vegetable gold" with the tree of knowledge growing "fast by". He notices the river mentioned in the Bible: "Southward through Eden went a river large" of which part seems to have been diverted, passed under and "through the shaggy hill" and "rose a fresh fountain, and with many a rill watered the garden." These rills united, "fell down the steep glade, and met the nether flood" where it emerged from a "darksome passage" and then flowed on and divided into the four streams which occur in myth, legend, poetry and art all over Europe and Asia Minor.

The poet continues in lapidary terms: "from that sapphire fount the crisped brooks, rolling on orient pearl and sands of gold . . . ran nectar, visiting each plant, and fed flowers worthy of Paradise, which not nice art in beds and curious knots, but Nature boon poured forth profuse on hill and dale and plain, both where the morning sun most warmly smote the open field, and where the unpierced shade embrowned the noontide bowers: thus was this place a happy rural seat of various view." An informal garden then. This breathless vision has influenced garden designers ever since, showing the importance of irrigation and the contrasting use of different levels, water, light and shade, warmth and coolness. From the horticultural point of view Milton is disappointing; he mentions again "fruit burnished with a golden rind . . . and of delicious taste" but is vague when it comes to flowers. He generalises, mentions "flowers of all hue" but does at least specify "without thorn, the rose" which is sensible in the context of a naked gardener. He tells us that there are "umbrageous grots and caves o'er which the mantling vine lays forth her purple grape and gently creeps luxuriant" and that there are "murmuring waters" and a lake, its "fringed banks with myrtle crowned." A reference to "that sweet grove of Daphne" evidently means the nymph who was turned into a bay tree when pursued by Apollo, not the plant, and one wonders how this pagan lady got inside.

At this point Satan sees Adam and Eve walking hand in hand. "They sat them down and after no more toil of their sweet gardening labour than sufficed to recommend cool zephyr" made a light supper of nectarines before indulging in some "youthful dalliance". Satan feels left out, is tormented by envy – he even says "Oh Hell!" He alights from the tree, assumes the forms of several of the animals sporting in the vicinity, lions, bears, a tiger, an elephant with a "lithe proboscis", a serpent etc., and so disguised listens to the couple's conversation and learns the secret of the tree of knowledge; that God has forbidden Adam and Eve to taste the fruit. He decides to "excite their minds with more desire to know" and then says: "But first with narrow search I must walk round this garden, and no corner leave unspied". So saying he begins "Through wood, through waste, o'er hill, o'er dale his roam."

"Now came still evening on" and all the animals retire to rest. Adam and Eve stay chatting a while, a revealing conversation since Adam, who seems a casual fellow, mentions his work as a gardener, saying: "With first approach of light, we must be risen, and at our pleasant labour to reform yon flowery arbours, yonder alleys green, our walk at noon, with branches overgrown, that mock our scant manuring." A footnote hastily interpolates that manuring is not to be understood in the common sense but as working with the hands, as in the French *manoeuvrer*. ". . . and require more hands than ours" says Adam "to lop their wanton growth: those blossoms also, and those drooping gums, that lie bestrown, unsightly and unsmooth, ask riddance if we mean to tread with ease." Plainly very little gardening has been done which may be partly explained when he says "With thee conversing I forget all time."

They pass on to their "blissful bower" and here we get a better idea of the plants. The roof was "inwoven" of laurel and myrtle. We can assume the laurel was *Laurus nobilis,* the bay, and not *Prunus laurocerasus,* the common laurel, certainly not the speckled aucuba. Anyway, it was "of firm and fragrant leaf: on either side acanthus and each odorous bushy shrub, fenced up the verdant wall" . . . "iris all hues, roses and jessamine, reared high their flourished heads" while underfoot were violet, crocus and hyacinth. There were also some sweet smelling herbs which, with flowers and gar-lands decked the bed – and there we must leave them for the moment, one cannot spy on one's ultimate ancestors.

To a gardener it is a pity that the story distracts the writer so that it obscures the horticultural details, but there is much to be read between the lines. Next morning Adam and Eve get up, say their prayers, then "to their morning's rural work they haste . . . where any row of fruit-trees overwoody reached too far their pampered boughs and needed hands to check fruitless embraces; or they led the vine to wed her elm" a flowery way to describe pruning and tying up. It is surprising to find that Eve also worked in the garden and that fruit trees grew in rows.

God has told Raphael to go and talk to Adam during his lunch break "in what bower or shade thou find'st him from the heat of noon retired to respite his day labour with repast" and while Eve, who has also been working all the morning, "prepared for dinner savoury fruits of taste to please" and "nectarous droughts" Adam, who is something of a chauvinist – "he for God only she for God in him" indeed! – is sitting in the door of his cool bower. He sees Raphael in the distance, flying "into the blissful field, through groves of myrrh and flowering odors, cassia, nard and balm." (By nard the poet probably means *Nardostachys fatamansi* from the root of which spikenard was distilled. Some say the expression to "spike" a drink may come from it.)

Adam calls Eve to look: "What glorious shape comes this way moving?" he cries, as well he may for Raphael, the archangel who travelled with Tobias, has six wings of "downie gold and colours dipped in Heaven" and when he shakes his plumes a "Heavenly fragrance fills the circuit wide." "Perhaps, says Adam" "he will vouchsafe ... to be our guest" and sends Eve out to rustle up a better meal. As records of meals can help historians to work out what crops were grown we should like more detail but Eve does well at short notice "for drink the grape she presses ... fruit of all kinds, in coat rough or smooth rin'd or bearded husk, or shell she gathers, ... and on the board heaps with unsparing hand" while "from many a berry, and from sweet kernels pressed she tempers dulcet creams." So nuts were certainly grown and probably included coconuts.

It is interesting to find that their table was "raised of grassy turf" and had "mossy seats all round" – perhaps the earliest reference to the turf seats so common in medieval gardens – and nice to know that they ate "with keen despatch of real hunger." During the meal Adam and Raphael have a long talk, partly about Creation, which fills 70 pages of small print.

That night Satan returns from his walk, which Milton does not record, and puts on the guise of a serpent, "the subtlest beast of all the field."

After prayers next morning Eve suggests a division of labour: "till more hands aid us ... what we by day lop overgrown, or prune, or prop, or bind, one night or two with wanton growth derides" and suggest that while he is winding woodbine or directing ivy where to climb she could work among the roses and myrtles. Adam does not like this but she persists and the rest we know. The serpent is looking for them when "beyond his hope ... thus early, thus alone" he spies Eve in the rose garden or "flowery plat". He tempts her, she plucks and eats the forbidden fruit and returns to Adam who is rather touchingly weaving a wreath to put in her hair "as reapers oft are wont [to crown] their Harvest Queen". When Eve tells him what she has done poor Adam "Astonied stood and blank, while horror chill ran through his veins . . . the garland . . . down dropped, and all the faded roses shed: speechless he stood and pale." He knows that all is lost. "How can I live without thee?" he asks, even if he could "another rib afford" so he too eats the "fair enticing fruit" and now "enflamed with ardor" leads her – and here we get another little plant list – "to a shady bank, thick overhead with verdant roof embowered . . . flowers were the couch, pansies and violets, and asphodel, and hyacinth." It will be noted that the plants mentioned by Milton seem to owe more to his knowledge of classical literature than from practical experience of gardening. But the visit to the bank is not the same, Adam and Eve now feel guilty. Adam makes a speech in which trees are mentioned: "Might I in solitude live savage in some glade . . . cover me ye pines, ye cedars, with innumerable boughs etc." and both set off "into the thickest wood" to look for a fig tree and find one with leaves as broad as an "Amazonian targe" a variety of *Ficus* which might be identified. The book continues but ends here for the garden enthusiast. We could wish Milton had been a trained botanist and that he had said more about garden equipment.

Adam evidently had a cutting tool for lopping and pruning but a spade may have come later when he was obliged to delve – unless it was he who planted the fruit trees in rows. Many questions must remain unanswered until the site of Paradise is discovered and properly excavated. We do know that there is a plant found in India, *Tabernaemontana dichotoma* the fruit of which is described as 'pendulus, orange-yellow, half round, with a clear cut depression along one side which, supposed to resemble a partly eaten apple, suggested the popular names, Eve's Apple or The Forbidden Fruit'.

To sum up we can be grateful to Milton for his work although *Paradise Lost* may seem an opportunity lost to the garden historian, and one cannot help wondering if Adam might have been allowed to remain in the garden if he had been a better gardener.

Cushion Saxifrages and Cameras

A Portrait of Valerie Finnis

NIGEL COLBORN

Something – who knows what? – separates the high achievers from the rest. It is not necessarily intelligence, money or power, though they often help. Education has little to do with it and talent alone will not suffice. In the case of Valerie Finnis, there were few inherited or acquired advantages – no silver spoons at birth, an interrupted school life and no university. But there was plenty of talent and, by combining that with a lifetime of grinding hard work, she has won the respect and admiration of everyone in the plant world.

Most eminent gardeners have strong memories of incidents, often going back to early childhood, which mark the start of an unswerving route to horticulture. More often than not, it begins with a fascination for plants – the smell of wintersweet on a dank February morning perhaps, or a flash of field poppies moving in the summer breeze amongst ripening barley. For Valerie Finnis, one of the earliest memories was of a garden with drifts of gentians. Though she could only have been about three at the time, she still recalls being fascinated by the intensity of their colour. Later, but still as a little girl, the smell of potting sheds and greenhouses – that unique blend of earthiness and vegetation – was enough to stir up the beginnings of a gardener's enthusiasm in her. Luckily, her mother and grandmother were both keen gardeners and were quick to recognise the spark of interest. Her mother, Constance Finnis, who raised the strain of Iceland poppies bearing her name, allowed her to cultivate a small piece of ground, not tucked away so that the childish attempts might be hidden from visitors, but in a prominent spot where growing conditions were good.

Valerie Finnis was born in Crowborough, Sussex in 1924 but soon afterwards, when her father, Steriker Finnis, retired early from the Navy to spend more time with his wife and two little girls, the family moved to Glastonbury. There was an unfortunate career setback when the owner of the timber company which he had joined died suddenly and the firm closed. Another move, this time to Earlswood, near Reigate in Surrey, enabled him to commute daily to London.

'The Gardner in embreo' Valerie Finnis photographed and captioned by
her mother in 1928

Earlswood was where the five-year-old was allocated her own
garden plot, in the middle of which flourished a large *Daphne
mezereum*. Her grandmother gave her the double daisy 'Rob Roy'
and told her to 'treat these plants reverently – they're people'.
Besides tending her own little garden, she would earn herself a few
pennies laying and weeding crazy paving for neighbours. On
Sundays there were long walks up Reigate Hill or Box Hill or sometimes along the Pilgrim's Way. The flora in that chalky countryside
was rich and varied so picking bunches of wildflowers enabled her
to learn more about plant identification. Her favourites were hare-
bells but she also loved finding heartsease (*Viola tricolor*).

After the false start in Glastonbury, proper school began at the
Kerri School, Reigate. There was a kitchen garden there with
greenhouses and potting shed so that by the time she was ready to
move on to secondary education, she had become caught up with
the excitement of growing things. At thirteen she was sent away to
boarding-school at Hayes Court, Kent. She suffered intense home-

sickness, and for her parents, finding the fees was quite a struggle. However she found solace in the garden and, as some of the girls were given their own plots to cultivate, she was soon able to get her hands into the soil. In former days Hayes Court had had a great garden and in 1938 there was still plenty left to enjoy. One of the first plants she noticed was a yellow Banksian rose which peeped into the dormitory windows and later, to her joy, erythroniums came up in her garden plot.

Academic life did not come naturally to her. 'I was very dim,' she said, 'below average in some subjects.' But she was good at sport, especially tennis and lacrosse, and had a considerable talent for acting. (The drama teacher there was a young actor called Alec Guinness.) But it was at gardening that Valerie Finnis really excelled. Guided by the head gardener – a Mr Jones – she managed to achieve outstanding results. The headmistress at Hayes Court, Katherine Cox, who was herself a great plantswoman, was able to recognise that gardening was as important a school activity as sport or drama and awarded marks accordingly. For her success in that department, the young Valerie was awarded ten out of ten, two stars and an accolade from the whole school. Then disaster struck on several fronts.

At the outbreak of war in September 1939, Hayes Court was deemed to be too near London for safety and had to be closed. Pupils were evacuated to schools in the provinces and Valerie found herself, after missing two terms, at Downe House, near Newbury, Berkshire. 'I was shattered to leave that garden at Hayes Court,' she said, but worse news was to follow. Her father was 'dug out' – recalled to Navy service – to rejoin the Naval Land Base in Newcastle-upon-Tyne. It became necessary for the family to move from Earlswood to Gosforth near Newcastle and there to live in a block of flats.

There was no garden but the apartment looked out onto some rather neglected allotments. Constance Finnis was able to take these over and, with Valerie's assistance during school holidays, created a productive and attractive garden. As well as food, this provided essential therapy to help the family through what must have been a difficult period, not only for personal reasons but also because of air raids and all the other vicissitudes of wartime England.

Meanwhile, school at Downe House continued as before. She took up small-bore rifle shooting and was soon in the first team – evidence

of the steady hand and sure eye that would help her to wield a
camera with such unerring accuracy later on. She also got to know
one of the school employees, Mary Young, who had been trained
at the Waterperry Horticultural School for Women.

There was a link between Downe House and Waterperry. From
1922 to 1927, a certain Miss Beatrix Havergal had worked as
gardener at the school. Among other things, she had laid out a set
of tennis courts which are still known as the Havergal courts. In
1927, Miss Havergal joined forces with the housekeeper at Downe
House, Avice Sanders, and together they founded a horticultural
school for women. The first headquarters were in the gardener's
cottage at Pusey House, near Faringdon, Oxfordshire but by 1932
the school had outgrown its premises and moved to Waterperry,
near Wheatley in Oxfordshire. Mary Young allowed Valerie to help
her with garden maintenance work around the school grounds – 'I
was prepared to do anything to get out of playing cricket' – and
during these chores, told her about life at Waterperry.

When the time came to choose a career, friends at home assumed,
as her father was a naval officer, that she would become a Wren;
people at school encouraged her to consider a career in drama; but
horticulture had the strongest pull. She was accepted at Waterperry, after an interview in which Miss Havergal expressed doubt
that she would be able to face such unpleasant tasks as barrowing
manure, and was reassured by Valerie and both her parents that
she would relish all forms of heavy work.

So began, in 1942, a twenty-eight-year stint at Waterperry, first
as a student, then as a working and teaching member of staff. Since
the school was involved not only with training young women to be
practical gardeners but also with volume food production, it was
allowed to continue throughout the war and contributed handsomely
to the War Effort. The total area ran to about eighty acres (32 ha.)
of which 38 (15 ha.) were devoted to market garden crops and the
remainder to agriculture. There were extensive walled gardens,
glass houses, frames, orchards and seven acres of soft fruit, as well
as a large flower garden and herbaceous nursery. Right up to the
1970s the school had close links with the fruit research stations at
East Malling and Long Ashton and enjoyed a sound reputation for
distributing virus-free stocks, particularly of Royal Sovereign
strawberries.

Soon after joining, Valerie Finnis struck up what was to become a lifelong friendship with a Land Army staff member, Rosemary Dobereiner. In addition to their studies, the two girls were given the job of looking after a twenty-five-acre field. The course-work itself consisted of practical training in all departments by day and lectures in the evenings. Becoming familiar with horticultural theory was only a small part of the education for Miss Havergal was, by all accounts, a perfectionist. Two staff members who had particular influence were Joan Stokes, who became an Associate of Honour with the Royal Horticultural Society and was in charge of the greenhouses, and Jo Cockin who looked after the fruit. The girls had to be neat and tidy in all things. Lining out plants in the fields was done with geometric precision, frames and greenhouses had to be immaculate at all times, and even the girls themselves were expected to look spick and span. There was a uniform of green dungarees and white blouses, with breeches and tweed jackets for winter. On weekday mornings, Miss Havergal took prayers in the little Saxon church.

After completing the course, Valerie stayed on as an employee. Her day began at 7 a.m. – earlier if taking produce to market – and went on until early evening. 'We were supposed to finish at five,' she said, 'but Rosemary and I usually went on until dark.' In winter, their first daily job was to see to the coke boilers for the green-houses. 'We used to faint in the sulphur fumes sometimes, pulling out the clinkers,' she told me. Neither did responsibility end at night: 'If you woke at two in the morning and weren't sure whether you'd put the boiler's damper in, you had to light your hurricane lamp and go down to make sure.'

During the soft-fruit season, she and three other girls left regularly at 4 a.m. to drive a three-ton truck loaded with strawberries or blackcurrants to Covent Garden market in London. It is difficult, for those of us who have not experienced such gruelling hard work, to imagine how much these girls had to do. Even as students, their days were over-full. A sample of a single day from her diary reads as follows:

March 31st 1943
Tomatoes. Planted in border in No 4. Border limed and raked level. Plants in 6in pots, staked with small bamboo plus 1 tie to prevent them

falling over when taken out of pot. Never plant when dry. Put line
across – 2 ft between rows, deep hole dug with trowel – soil covering all
parts of stem – firmed with trowel handle harder than usual to prevent
too much leaf growth. 11 rows on right, 10 on left . . .

Cold Frames. Scratched and loosened to help drainage.

Potatoes. Planted in big field.

Cauliflowers. Planted in South Field. Finished in S(outh) F(ield). 18
'Snowball'.

Rhubarb. Planted under bush apples, S(outh) F(ield). Rather late.

Gooseberries. Pruned.

Spring Cabbage. Planted 10 in apart. First pulled for market.

Because their training was so thorough, Waterperry girls were
always in demand. Too many went on to pursue successful careers
to list them here, but two fine examples are Pamela Schwerdt and
Sibylle Kreutzberger who went to work for Vita Sackville-West at
Sissinghurst and stayed on. Their total dedication to that magnificent garden is self-evident.

After the war, Valerie began to collect and propagate alpines.
Starting with a wooden grocer's box, half-filled with sand and
protected with a sheet of shaded glass, she gradually expanded
production from tiny beginnings to 50,000 plants per year, of which
7000 were cushion saxifrages. In 1947 she began to exhibit her
plants at the Chelsea Flower Show and elsewhere, using one end of
Waterperry's allocated stand space while the famous pot-grown
Royal Sovereign strawberries occupied the other. Her collection
was interesting enough to attract the attention of several eminent
horticulturists and as well as winning orders she was earning
recognition.

From the late nineteen-forties onwards, she was to make a great
many friends, some of whom were of enormous help to her and many
of whom, no doubt, were glad to share some of her own deepening
knowledge. Bill MacKenzie, former Curator of the Chelsea Physic
Garden in London is, she says, to this day her 'guide and mentor.'
When she first exhibited he gave her useful tips, such as dampening
the rocks to freshen things up just before judging. At Waterperry
in 1968 he noticed a self-sown yellow-flowered clematis growing

Working with alpine plants at the Waterperry Horticultural School near Oxford. *Photograph:* Nicholas Meyjes

between mature plants of *C. tangutica* and *C. orientalis*. When he remarked on it she persuaded him to allow her to name it after him. It won an Award of Merit in 1976 and is still one of the finest of the orientalis types in cultivation. MacKenzie provided her with many valuable plants and, though he has a special place in her heart, there were many others. When she runs through the list, it sounds rather like a horticultural *Who's Who*. There were legendary names like

Percy Picton – one of William Robinson's gardeners – and Clarence
Elliott. Cecilia Christie-Miller gave her cuttings of all her saxifrages,
Nancy Lindsay, a friend of Lawrence Johnston at Hidcote, gave her
rare plants; E. B. Anderson left her a *Rhodothamnus chamaecistus* in his
will; Ruth McConnel gave her a collection of rhodohypoxis; David
Shackleton introduced her to the great Irish gardens. There are
scores of others: G. P. Baker, Captain Gerald Mooney, Stuart
Boothman, Ken Aslett, Margery Fish and of course, Sir David
Scott – but more of him later.

By the mid nineteen-fifties, with Waterperry thriving, she had
become a valuable member of staff. She still worked hard, marketing
crops as well as growing them. Her alpine nursery was flourishing,
she was exhibiting at several shows, besides Chelsea, and winning
good awards for her limestone rock garden displays. Photographs of
those fifties exhibits show just how the quality has declined lately.
At one spring show, she made a table rock garden with 180 different
varieties of cushion saxifrages. Though her income was still very
small and the hours far too long for her own good, she was clearly
enjoying the active life she had chosen. Then another major setback
occurred.

When she was 31, a serious illness culminating in a dangerous
operation left her in need of gentle convalescence. At that point,
several friends stepped in to help. One of them, Margaret Ridge,
gave her a camera and sent her with another student, Mary Ebbs,
to the Dolomites for a holiday. Walter Ingwersen gave her a letter
of introduction to Wilhelm Schacht, Curator of the Botanic Garden
at Munich. 'When you get to 63 Menzinger Strasse,' she was told,
'knock on the door of the little lodge.' She received a warm welcome
and stayed for several days. It was Schacht who got her started as a
photographer. 'Not only did he know more about plants than anybody else in the world,' she said, 'he is still the finest photographer.'
Schacht's first advice was to change her camera, and he gave her
one of his Rolleiflexes. Within a short time, armed with the better
camera, she had built up a small but choice collection of transparencies. Without any formal or technical training – 'the less you
know, the better' – she was soon to become a successful professional
photographer. Her knowledge of camera techniques to this day
remains rudimentary. 'I can't do black and white,' she says, 'its too
difficult.'

When, in 1971, she gave a lecture on plant photography to the Royal Horticultural Society, she had a Mr Lassam from Kodak on hand to answer some of the questions. A decade earlier, Lassam had been so impressed with her work that he had allowed her a large display at Kodak's head office in Kingsway, in central London. Thanks to him, she also had an exhibit at London's Royal Festival Hall, and, in 1961, won a Gold Medal for her photographs at an R.H.S. Vincent Square flower show.

She has to thank Dr Warburg, co-author of *Flora of the British Isles,* for her first picture sales. He commissioned her to illustrate an article he was writing for I.C.I. on crocuses. Also with Warburg's help she founded the Oxford Group of the Alpine Garden Society. During those years the health of her father, now living again in Reigate, was failing, and since she was called upon to make frequent visits there, her meagre income from Waterperry fell short of her needs. She sent two rolls of film to Gordon Frazer to see whether any of the pictures might do for greetings cards. They were most impressed and bought the lot. Encouraged by this she approached E.M.I. who promptly bought twelve transparencies to use as record sleeves. J. Walter Thompson was the first advertising agency to buy and use some of her vegetable shots to advertise fertiliser. By the mid sixties, her income from photography quite overshadowed the wage from Waterperry. She still stayed loyal however, working almost full time there although Miss Havergal allowed considerable latitude in her hours. Travelling regularly from Oxfordshire to Reigate enabled her to make frequent stops both at the Savill Garden near Windsor and at the R.H.S.'s Wisley garden in Surrey. By keeping her camera busy at these gardens, and returning each weekend, she began to develop a picture library which now runs to about 50,000 transparencies.

In 1960 her father died and her mother's health continued to decline. Friends were supportive, as ever, and continued to en-courage her and to supply her with various alpine desiderata. John Wall, for example, gave her, among other plants, a cutting of *Daphne cneorum* 'Eximia'. Oliver Wyatt and Elliot Hodgkin were generous with plants as was a great friend, G. W. Robinson, who had been Curator of the Oxford Botanic Garden.

As her reputation grew she became sought-after. She appeared on television, first as guest presenter in Percy Thrower's 'Gardening

Club', a forerunner to 'Gardeners' World', and later at Pebble Mill studios in 'The Garden Game', with Norman Painting. All this meant taking time off from Waterperry. Beatrix Havergal was accommodating in this respect, and also happy to let her take the odd Tuesday for visits to the R.H.S. flower shows – by now she was on the Joint Rock Committee and called upon to judge regularly – and to travel about the country in the evenings, delivering illustrated lectures.

These began modestly, at local village halls and in private houses to raise funds for charity. But she was soon invited further afield, first in Britain and later overseas. In 1961, word came from Sir Mortimer Wheeler that a botanist was needed for the Swan cruises of the Greek Islands. 'I was alarmed,' she said, 'because I didn't know very much about the Greek flora. I owe a lot to the late Patrick Synge and to Chris Brickell, both of whom taught me so much about Mediterranean flowers.' By the end of the sixties her life was full to overflowing. She was still working hard at Waterperry, her pictures were in demand everywhere – not just in advertising and for greetings cards, but in magazines at home and abroad – *The Field*, *Le Figaro* and Japanese garden magazines for example – in books like Anna Griffith's *Guide to Alpines* (Collins) and in calendars and catalogues. She was on several committees and submitting a steady stream of plants to the R.H.S., many of which received Awards of Merit or First Class Certificates.

Then came a change of direction. In a way, Bill MacKenzie was responsible, albeit indirectly. Among many other gifts, he had given her a specimen of the spiraea-like *Gillenia trifoliata* – not a common plant, but gardenworthy nonetheless. One afternoon in 1968 she was working in the potting shed near the alpine nursery at Waterperry when she heard someone say, 'Goodness me! There is Gillenia trifoliata!' This surprised her because until then, no visitor had been able to identify the plant. 'I wouldn't have come out of the shed if I hadn't heard the voice saying it,' she said. The voice belonged to a great gardener and veteran plantsman, Sir David Scott. A firm friendship began and they were married in 1970. 'We didn't really have a proper honeymoon,' she said, 'in fact we went weeding later that evening.' However, she had been invited to lecture in Tokyo that year so the couple prolonged their stay there

With her late husband, Sir David Scott, and Sophie

The garden at The Dower House, Boughton House, Northamptonshire

to two weeks, returning with 300 plants – gifts from Japanese alpine plant enthusiasts.

Her influence on the garden at the Dower House, Boughton House, near Kettering, Northamptonshire is recorded by Sir David himself in *The Englishman's Garden* (Allen Lane, 1982), where he wrote:

> ... with her advent the whole garden was transfigured. The patch by the house was embellished with interesting and beautiful plants ... The vegetable garden, while still, thanks to intensive cultivation, producing enough for the house, spawned 200 yards of raised beds, seventy yards of them made up with imported acid soil, making homes for thousands of small hardy plants ...

In 1975, Valerie Finnis received the Royal Horticultural Society's Victoria Medal of Honour.

With representative plants from all her stocks at Waterperry, plus Sir David's superb collection of shrubs and trees, not to mention the constant stream of new introductions, the garden at the Dower House became an internationally important collection. There is only space here to mention a few of the many garden plants which bear the name 'Boughton' or 'Scott' or 'Finnis'. *Hebe* 'Boughton Dome' was discovered by Sir David, as was *Hepatica transsylvanica* 'Ada Scott', and one of his latest plants to receive an award was *Berberis darwinii* 'Boughton Red'.

The Dower House began opening to the public for the National Gardens Scheme, and by the early eighties had an average attendance of twelve hundred visitors on each of the open days. Sir David propagated plants for the visitors, selling no fewer than 3000 within the first couple of hours of opening. All this enabled them to raise more than £3000 a year for the charity.

In 1980, a further compliment was paid to her when BBC Radio 3 invited her to take part in a twelve-episode programme called 'A Gardeners' Dozen'. The idea was for each gardening personality – Christopher Lloyd and Roy Lancaster were two of the others – to describe their gardens during one month of the year. November would have been considered something of a short straw by many, but Valerie Finnis managed to convey the feel of late autumn to perfection as she described the different-coloured carpets of fallen leaves under the deciduous trees – bright scarlet for maples, dingy white for a sorbus, yellow for *Tilia petiolaris*, and so on.

Sir David died in 1986. 'Since then,' she said, 'things, of course, are not the same. There are plants, bulbs, trees and shrubs here, as before, but now there are memories too.'

A FEW GARDENS

IN CHILDRENS
BOOKS

BY
NANCY-MARY
GOODALL

Gardens in children's books make a fascinating study, perhaps because when writing for children people may drop their guard and express their own memories, dreams and fantasies. We need not look for Freudian explanations such as have been foisted on the Alice books by people who did not know their Oxford; they have been competently dealt with by Mavis Batey in *Alice's Adventures in Oxford*. It may be, however, that making a garden is an unconscious attempt to recreate a golden age, and the same may apply to writing books about gardens, especially when there are children in them.

In *Alice in Wonderland*, published in 1865, there is a glimpse of an unattainable garden which, like Lewis Carroll's photographs of little girls, may express no more than a yearning for the lost paradise of childhood. Alice falls down the rabbit-hole and finds herself in a long, low hall with locked doors all round. Behind a curtain is a little door about 15 in high, while on a glass three-legged table lies the tiny golden key which opens it. Kneeling down, she can see along a passage 'into the loveliest garden you ever saw' and longs to wander in it, but she is too big to get through the door. Then she finds a bottle marked DRINK ME, drinks the contents and at once shrinks to ten inches tall – but the door to the garden is locked again and the key is back on the table. More than half the book that follows is about her adventures as she searches for the garden. At last, after the Mad Hatter's tea party, 'on a table set out under a tree', she finds a door that leads back into the hall and discovers that she can now get through the little door along the dark passage and into the beautiful garden. Even then she is not free to wander among the splendours of Tenniel's illustration, but becomes involved with playing-card gardeners painting white roses red, the ferocious

'O Tiger-lily!' said Alice, addressing herself to one that was waving gracefully
about in the wind, 'I *wish* you could talk!'
'We *can* talk,' said the Tiger-lily, 'when there's anybody worth talking to.'

Queen of Hearts shouting 'Off with their heads', and the famous
game of croquet played with flamingos for mallets and hedgehogs
for balls. It is not until *Through the Looking Glass* (1872) that she
finds herself in a looking-glass garden, where you must walk in the
opposite direction to get anywhere, and has an admirably un-
sentimental conversation with a tiger-lily and other flowers.

Gardens in children's books are often walled, which gives them an
added mystery, particularly if one cannot get inside. A walled
garden forms the background to a children's classic that must have
started many people on the road to gardening. *The Secret Garden* by

Frances Hodgson Burnett was first published in 1911. It is old fashioned, moralising, sentimental and a bit too long – but it has hardly ever been out of print and, once read, is unforgettable.

It starts in winter. Mary, a sickly, ugly little girl, orphaned in India, finds herself in Brontë country, living on the edge of the Yorkshire moors in a vast old house that belongs to her uncle and guardian, a grief-stricken and often absent widower. Waited on by servants but without occupation or friends, she first spends her days wandering in the 'great gardens, with wide lawns and winding walks with clipped borders ... trees and flower beds, and ever-greens clipped into strange shapes, and a large pool with an old grey fountain in its midst.' She hears rumours of a secret garden and the book is the tale of how she finds it and with it companions, beauty, health and happiness.

Many images of mystery and secrecy come into the story, the principal one being a locked garden door, hidden by ivy, and a lost and buried key. As you would expect, she finds the key and enters the secret garden. 'It was the sweetest, most mysterious-looking place anyone could imagine' but, unused to the English winter, she thinks all the roses may be dead. 'There seemed to have been grass paths here and there, and ... there were alcoves of evergreen with stone seats or tall moss-covered flower-urns in them.' She finds 'some sharp little pale green points' ... 'sticking out of the black earth', which she rightly guesses are the bulbs described by the old gardener, and tries to weed around them. A week later she hears crying in the night and, through a door hidden behind a tapestry – we have just seen a door behind a curtain in *Alice* – finds a child ill in bed, overprotected and spoiled; he is her cousin Colin, her guardian's son. Everyone, including himself, thinks that he may die – but Mary will have no such nonsense. Eventually, in the secret garden, the children weed, dig, prune, sow seeds and grow healthy, and in this they are helped by Dickon, a country boy who plays the flute and charms wild animals. We are led through part of the gardening year, starting with a moving account of the miracle of spring and ending with a paean of joy in high summer. When the garden is at its best Colin's father appears, finds him well and strong, and because it had been his wife's garden and it has cured his son, his heartbreak about her death is also cured and all ends well.

The secret garden

But is this enough to account for the great appeal of the story? I wonder if it touches on ideas of which the writer may have been unaware. Dickon seems to be an evocation of Pan – who is never out of place in a garden – and there are many of the ingredients that appear in other stories. At all events *The Secret Garden* can be read as a parable of the beauties and wonders of nature, of death overthrown, sickness cured and the triumph of hope rewarded. Ostensibly a simple tale about children in a garden, it touches us with the force of a revelation.

There are more gardens in the fifteen or so children's books by E. Nesbit, a wonderful, warm, intelligent woman, for whose life see *A Woman of Passion* by Julia Briggs. Born in 1858, nearly ten years after Frances Hodgson Burnett, she died in the same year, 1924. I adored her books as a child and find I still own eleven of them. Dated now, unconsciously snobbish, often wordy but still readable, they paint a convincing picture of late Victorian and Edwardian childhood in a class that is never rich but always well-brought-up and with high ideals of honour. We are soon familiar with their lives, their meals, their clothes, their speech. They say things like 'O Jimminy!' or 'Krikey!' and 'Don't be such a muff'.

One essential for a good story of the genre is that the children should be isolated from normal family life. As in *The Secret Garden*, the mother or both parents have died or are abroad, often in India (an indication of the numbers of people who were sent out to that great sub-continent), so they are boarded out with strangers or relatives. The charm and humour of the stories are often spiced with magic, although not in the celebrated tales of the Bastable family.

The Wouldbegoods starts with a description of the havoc wrought by the Bastables in their uncle's Victorian garden at Blackheath, 'with vineries and pineries ... and shrubberies and stabling.' On the lawn under a cedar they try to recreate *The Jungle Book*, and as this involves a hose, a lot of water and a channel dug across the lawn, getting all the stuffed animals out of their glass cases and the rabbits out of their hutches, and the boys half naked and painted brown – not bad for a book published in 1901 – the children soon find themselves spending the rest of the holidays in disgrace at the Moat House (which is based on the author's much loved home, Well Hall, in Kent).

'How beautifully everything grows here'

The Wonderful Garden (1911) is about three children who go to stay with a scholarly great-uncle in an old house with four-poster beds and a park. They have just been given *The Language of Flowers* and soon they find two old herbals full of magic spells. At first they cannot find the garden. Then they are shown the secret entrance which leads down steep stone steps and through a dark passage ending in an arbour. Before them lies a walled garden: 'The lower half was a vegetable garden arranged in squares with dwarf fruit trees and flower-borders round . . . half-way up the garden came steps, stone balustrades – a terrace, and beyond that a flower garden with smooth green turf paths, box-edged, a sundial and . . . more flowers than I could give names to. . . . "How perfectly perfect!" Charlotte said. . . . "How awfully tidy everything is!" said Charles.' Naturally they get into mischief with their spells and potions and meaningful bouquets. The book ends when the learned great-uncle, delighted with the herbals, gives them all stephanotis flowers signifying 'Will you accompany me to the East?' He will take them out to India to visit their parents, 'bringing to each child its Heart's Desire'.

E. Nesbit lets rip with the garden in *The Enchanted Castle* (1907) which is also entered by way of a stone tunnel from which the children emerge to be faced with a spectacular view: 'everyone's breath was taken away . . . A short avenue of cypresses led . . . to a marble terrace that lay broad and white in the sunlight . . . blinking, [they] leaned their arms on the broad, flat balustrade and gazed . . . a lake – just like a lake in *The Beauties of Italy* . . . with swans and an island and weeping willows . . . amid the trees gleamed the white limbs of statues . . . a round white building with pillars, and to the right of it a waterfall . . . and in the distance enormous shapes of grey stone.' The children find a maze and in it a little girl dressed as a princess, who leads them into the castle and through a door hidden by a tapestry. This time the story revolves round a magic ring and a hoard of jewels; the children become invisible one by one, statues come to life, there is a splendid scene where the children swim in the lake with a marble Phoebus and then enjoy a celestial moonlight feast with the other marble gods. '. . . by day those gardens were like dreams, at night they were like visions.'

In this book the children are spending their holidays at a girls' school because of measles at home, but there is a delightful, romantic French governess whose English is a joy: 'My beautiful flowers – put them to the water, Kathleen. I run to buy the cakes. Wash the hands, all, and be ready when I return.' The wit and invention of

'This is an enchanted garden and that's an enchanted castle'

the writer seem endless, as this tale also involves burglars and a stone
dinosaur that wallows in the lake, as well as the alarming episode
of the Ugly Wuglies, figures with painted paper faces that the
children have made from coats and hats, pillows and bolsters, coat-
hangers, hockey sticks and golf clubs, with gloves stuffed with
handkerchiefs for hands. When through the magic ring these
creatures come to life, it is enough to leave a mild scar on the memory
of any reader. Who can forget the pointed paper face peering out
from a rhododendron bush? Yet, almost to the end, they are harmless
and polite though speaking in a frightening manner because they
have no roofs to their mouths.

Half a century later comes *Tom's Midnight Garden* by Philippa Pearce (1958), a fascinating tale in which the theme is not only a garden but also the nature of time. Tom's brother has measles so he is staying with his uncle and aunt in a big old house that has been engulfed by a housing estate. When the grandfather clock strikes thirteen at midnight he opens a big door at the back of the hall, which by day leads only to the dustbins, and finds an old garden, walled on three sides. He goes back to the garden every night, never knowing what time of day it will be, what season or what year, and there he makes friends with Hattie, a little girl from the Victorian past. Her parents are dead and she has been adopted.

The garden is so lovingly described that you feel the writer is revisiting scenes from her childhood: 'Along the sundial path, heavy red poppies came out and roses: and, in the summer dusk the evening primroses like little moons.' We seem to remember the lawns and flower beds, the summerhouse and the pond, the gravelled paths, clipped box and asparagus beds. Hattie shows Tom all her hiding places, and with them we climb the old yew trees, explore the greenhouse, visit the orchard and the potting shed and see the gardener eating a bacon sandwich, then venture further through the hedge and across the meadow to the river. The story is set in the fens and there is a winter scene when they skate all the way to Ely and climb the cathedral tower. The time theme is brilliantly sustained and the end is entirely satisfactory.

Rumer Godden's *An Episode of Sparrows* (1956) is not strictly a children's book but can be read by any intelligent teenager and is mentioned here because of a haunting little garden and the elements of gardening that it teaches. The scene is London soon after 'Hitler's War'. Lovejoy, a little cockney girl with an absent 'theatrical' mother, is left on the hands of a lovable pair whose unsuccessful but aspiring restaurant is a joy to read about. With agonising difficulty she makes a secret garden in a hidden corner of a bombed and ruined church; she is helped by a boy, Tip Malone, the leader of a juvenile street gang and a very different character from Dickon. Much of the book is about the grown-ups, the high-powered people in the Square and the Dickensian inhabitants of Catford Street, but it centres on the children and it is Lovejoy and Tip that we remember.

Finally, from a long list, the children's books of Lucy M. Boston, which usually have gardens in them. *The Children of Green Knowe* (1954), first of a series, is aimed at younger children. Toseland, aged six or seven (parents in Burma), goes to live with his great-grandmother, and arrives dramatically in a flood, at night, by boat. The weather is often violent: there is also heavy snow and a tremendous thunderstorm in which a malevolent tree is destroyed. The house is ancient, panelled, moated, full of strange things: a mysterious mirror, a locked box, a bird cage, an old rocking horse and a doll's house. Toseland's great-grandmother is not quite a witch, they soon make friends, and she tells him stories and teaches him the flute. Wild birds come into the house, while through a door with a heavy curtain is a very strange garden, with a huge statue of Saint Christopher festooned in old man's beard, many topiary animals and an ancient fish in the moat. There are ghostly children from the Restoration period and, in the stables, a magic invisible horse.

Patterns emerge from all these stories. Are these the things that children like? Or are they things that we all like? – walled gardens, locked doors and locked boxes, lost keys, doors behind curtains or swags of creeper, dark tunnels that end in secret gardens, children alone in strange and challenging places? Are these memories of childhood when all things seemed possible, or the normal trappings of Romance? It certainly suggests that we could all read children's books with more pleasure than we imagine, and that some of us may feel inclined to write one.

The illustration and head and tail pieces from *Alice through the Looking Glass* are by John Tenniel. The illustration on page 87 is from the watercolour by Charles Robinson for the 1911 edition of *The Secret Garden*, whose title page has been adapted for this article. The line drawings by H. R. Millar are from E. Nesbitt's *The Wonderful Garden* and *The Enchanted Castle*.

John Fowler as a Garden Designer

CAVAN O'BRIEN

Although much has been written on the subject of the late John Fowler as an interior designer (he began the celebrated firm of Colefax and Fowler with Sybil Colefax in 1934), little has been written about his interest in gardens and plants. Yet, in the words of the National Trust, it 'was on the basis' of his garden at The Hunting Lodge near Odiham in Hampshire that they accepted the house and grounds before he died in 1976. The house itself was created as a folly for the nearby Dogmersfield Park, when the newly enriched Mildmay family acquired in one fell swoop an heiress, a wife, a hugely enlarged house and according to the existing paintings, a long series of follies in the park.

The Hunting Lodge is the only survivor. There are remains of an Ice House, four lakes, a bit of park as well and the largely rebuilt main house. The reason for the survival of The Hunting Lodge was simple. When the Basingstoke Canal was constructed in 1779 the Park was cut into two; The Hunting Lodge was on the far side from the house, and it became a gamekeeper's cottage. Isolated, with its own small lake and a couple of cottages, it slumbered away until by serendipity it was discovered, or rather re-discovered, by John Fowler in the winter of 1946. He moved into the house in 1947, and very shortly afterwards the actress Rachel Redgrave moved into the cottages.

In the words of the first of what were apparently always called the Garden Boys, and on the evidence of the photographs, there was nothing there except the shell of the house and five old apple trees.

Work went ahead rapidly on what was to become a lifetime's task of forming a new garden as a setting for the folly. The ground was cleared. The clay on which the house and lake are based was dug up into heaps and then burned in a way rather akin to charcoal burning, to render it more friable. In the first year the outlines of the present garden were mapped out. Ditches, followed by hedges, were created. The old apple trees became the supports for a collection of climbing, or rather scrambling, roses, which survive largely unchanged to the present day.

Work seems to have gone ahead at an almost unseemly pace. The main perimeter hedges were planted with hornbeam, not only three deep (ever a challenge!) but also as two hedges separated by a narrow gap. The largest lawn in front of the house was flanked by pleached hornbeam trained on posts and wires. To either side a consecutive series of 'rooms', not unlike those in the gardens at Sissinghurst Castle or Hidcote, were made. Each 'room' had a purpose.

It seems to me, having lived in the house for ten years now, that the garden was planned in a perfectly logical sequence to follow the seasons. The earliest bulbs and shrubs come out in January around the main gate and the front entrance. As the year progresses, month by month the walk around those plants in bloom extends, until by late June the unwary visitor is beguiled into a walk around the lake!

The evolution of the garden became slowly apparent after many hours of talking to Lady Redgrave and to David Stenning, the head Garden Boy until after John Fowler's death. As the years went by, the garden was elaborated and replanned, but always within the bounds of the original layout. There is no definite drawing for that; on an old envelope I discovered in a drawer here is probably the only plan that ever existed.

The garden was to be a 'stage set' for the 1740 folly. The house was given a simple brick terrace facing south south east, which catches almost every ray of sun, year round. The long view is across the small lake, recreated by Lady Redgrave just after the last war out of a sapling-infested swamp. On the far side of the lake a great belt of oak, ash and beech masks the Basingstoke Canal. The view is punctuated just off the main axis by a single Lombardy poplar. This poplar leads one to conjecture that not only Sissinghurst and Hidcote were the basis for the theme of the layout. Perhaps the France of the eighteenth century beckons, in the masterly layout of the young Louis XIV's early days at Versailles? A formal axis, a grass ride, a piece of water and of course the poplars. No one will ever know for sure, but John Fowler was most certainly influenced by French architecture and decoration of the seventeenth and eighteenth centuries, as indeed who could not have been? In terms of his decorating it merged into the mainstream of his work, culminating with the long series of jobs for the National Trust at Clandon, etc. The early pictures of the interior always show pride

of place given to items like a wonderful French commode and a large
marble plaque of the Sun King's emblem.

Later, it seems that the garden plan was elaborated – more
borders were added, more hedges, a small box-edged herb garden.
But always the planting remained essentially the same. There was a
mixture of old-fashioned roses, herbs, hardy perennials, cherry trees
and lilacs, and slowly more and more garden ornaments were added
in the form of the two pavilions and the large Garden Room with
its view down to the lake. There are Coade stone statues, gothick
garden furniture, and ever more tubs and large terracotta pots. At
my last count there were forty-two of these. All in a garden which
is under an acre in size.

Yet there never seems to have been too much of anything. Some
trees grew too fast for the 'plan' – they had to go! But the general
feel of the garden in mid-summer is of order, in the shape of hedges
and lawns and the profusion of borders with alchemilla tumbling

over the edges. The four main herbaceous borders flanking gravel paths were planned to be over head height in June, despite being only four feet wide. Each is punctuated with box pyramids, cones and balls. Just beyond, the eye is led on by more box in tubs. And so it goes. Each square yard is packed with neatly restrained detail.

John Cornforth has described The Hunting Lodge, with its garden and garden buildings, as John Fowler's Trianon. This is perhaps a little excessive, but certainly he expended every ounce of his energy, spare time and money, on making it work. To achieve. this he seems to have instituted a sort of 'reign of terror' every weekend. When I finally replaced the antiquated central heating system the old coal bunkers were demolished, and behind those I found a list of 'jobs to do' for one Saturday. No guest was left undisturbed! The list begins with fill and clean out the boiler, goes on through sweep the rear doorstep (which one? there are three) and ends up with clear the ditches of leaves.

A lot of this of course was done by the Garden Boys, but the guests had to tick part of the list! In between they were given

splendid meals, and I'm sure they partook of fine wines; even so, someone had to weed the terrace, and sweep out the dining room. The trouble with a house like this is that, small as it is, there never seem to be enough hours in the day to devote to it.

Other than at The Hunting Lodge, John Fowler did not ever create fully another garden. He collaborated on many – for friends mainly, and with his cousin Barbara Oakley. I think the truth is that he lent advice and ideas: the pyramidal-topped, white-painted gate posts seem to turn up in the most unlikely places, closely followed by the tubs of box and pelargoniums! But really there are only two gardens other than this one in which he appears to have been closely involved. One of course was literally next door to The Hunting Lodge, Lady Redgrave's garden at Wilk's Water by the lake (now the home of Mr and Mrs Robin d'Abo). As one wanders around there one sees the same favoured plants – the amelanchiers, yew hedges, alchemilla, the early tulips, etc. The second garden is just around the next bend on the old road back to London where John Fowler helped Mrs Peter Adams create a marvellous informal garden with a few more punctuation marks. There is a local rumour that a lady in a nearby village telephoned Mr Fowler one day and asked him if he would just come over and plan her garden – and perhaps he did, because there are some very smart white gates. But I feel sure that if it was a Saturday he was back at his own house long before lunch, just to make sure that there were no leaves on the drive.

Gardens of some Indian Hill Stations

DAVID SAYERS

The modern tourist in India, dashing along an itinerary of temple to fort to palace to temple again, seldom thinks of escaping to a hill station. In any case the two or three weeks' tour is over all too soon and the flight home quickly gives escape from the clamour and dust. Nevertheless a facet of India is missed, those *refugia* of the British Raj from the summer heat of the plains.

Simla crowns them all: Simla, where, beginning with Lord Amherst in 1827, Governors General and Viceroys went with their retinue and administration. Other hill stations in India served the needs of those lower in the pecking order – teachers, missionaries, those who were not of sufficient social or military rank. Lower both in social elevation and topographical altitude are Mussoorie and Dehra Dun, not a great distance across the valleys from Simla.

Dehra Dun is not quite a pukka hill station and I enjoy it immensely because it lacks the pretension of 'being' a hill station. Lying at 2300 ft within a wide valley, in April it is hot during the day and the evenings are cold enough for a cardigan. It has a delightful bazaar with all manner of small shops and services one learned to do without in England more than a generation or three ago. Foreign tourists hardly ever go there; above all, it has the FRI, the Forest Research Institute and Colleges.

The FRI has a singularly impressive building with colonnades, and high ceilinged rooms for offices, labs and museums. Designed by C. G. Bloomfield and inaugurated in 1929, it covers 7 acres. The whole campus comprises some 1200 acres, and is a main centre for training, research and advice. Quite unlike nearly all government buildings in India, this property is immaculate. The smell of polished teak and other hardwoods permeates throughout and the paintwork gleams; there is rivalry between the foresters and the nearby military academy for the best-kept building.

Lighting is gloomy in the museum, but the exhibits embrace all aspects of forestry and include dioramas showing different forest management systems, the environmental consequences of forest destruction, and the current social forestry programmes. Many exhibits must date back to the 1920s. I rather enjoy them for they have a quantity of detail often lacking in present-day and necessarily cursory interpretations and, anachronisms as they mostly are, they breathe unwittingly a sense of history.

The grounds are expansive lawns beyond which are the arboretum and experimental forestry plots – a plantation of giant bamboo *Dendrocalamus* sp. is most impressive, next to an old forest of Sal, *Shorea robusta,* that immensely important timber species. We drove through managed forests of Sal as we approached Dehra Dun, the large dry fallen leaves crackling underfoot whenever we stopped the car to explore a particularly inviting glade. Stitched together the leaves make ideal picnic plates and one often finds them scattered at beauty spots, stained by turmeric and tacky with rice grains: the original biodegradables. By ravines and open places *Bauhinia variegata* produced clouds of white spring blossoms. *Clerodendron infortunatum* is a common undershrub, about waist high with large attenuated heads of white flowers with the typically exserted stamens.

Three trees particularly impressed me in the arboretum: the brilliant deep-yellow flowers of the leafless *Tecoma argentea* seen against a blue sky, the little avenues of bottle-brush trees, *Callistemon viminalis,* flowering far better than I ever saw it in its native Australia, and an exquisitely symmetrical, densely branched, wide-crowned horse chestnut smothered in white inflorescences and labelled *Aesculus assamensis.*

The herbarium and library are housed separately, close by the arboretum. The racks of journals and periodicals recently received from India and overseas impress for the intensity of their readership. Although current, they were already dog-eared, as in a dentist's waiting room, curled at the edges and blackening with the wet of many thumbs. Lengths of musty shelves hold old travel accounts of the hills and high mountains. It is just the sort of place where a travelling plantsman would dearly love to rent a villa with a cook for a month or two, and sit in the shade of a tree in the arboretum slowly reading through those treasured books.

A road that goes to nowhere but Mussoorie leads from Dehra Dun. It takes about an hour along a zig-zag route up a hellish hot south facing hillside. A few *Pinus roxburghii* survive; oaks (*Quercus incana*) pollarded for fuelwood and equally sad *Rhododendron arboreum* indicate what was and could again be the natural forest cover.

Ubiquitous on these exposed slopes is a common shrub *Adhatoda vasica,* an acanth with white flowers. Sometimes with it is the lovely blue *Caryopteris odorata. Woodfordia fruticosa* is very common, a long loosely branching shrub with showy deep brick-red flowers borne along the woody stems. Conspicuous, too, are the large buttercup-yellow flowers of *Hypericum oblongifolium,* sadly unlikely to be winter hardy in Britain. Slender stems of *Jasminum dispermum* climb between the shrubs, clusters of delicate white flowers tinged pink asserting their fragrance in the hot sun. *Jasminum humile* is also to be found here, along with *Buddleja asiatica,* and *Spiraea canescens.* On grassy slopes usually by the roadside may be found *Campanula colorata,* the blue-grey flowers and white-woolly leaves of *Salvia lanata* and large patches of *Erigeron bellidioides,* a little daisy with flowers more white than reddish.

Mussoorie is situated upon a ridge at 6500 ft, the town centre a series of shop- and hotel-lined streets which more or less follow the contours. It has a short intensive summer season when it is filled with holidaying Indians; in April the still largely empty hotels are reminiscent of our own seaside boarding houses. Suddenly one is aware of a wonderful fragrance, and there growing out of a tiny

Mussoorie houses and oak trees

courtyard is a quite splendid specimen tree of *Michelia doltsopa,* its magnolia-like flowers white against large leaves. A native of the Eastern Himalaya it is alas for our warmest gardens only (I remember seeing a young tree in the Blandy garden in Madeira and although not 10 feet tall it was covered in blossom.) I walked along the north side of the ridge to visit the old British cemetery in the hope of finding more of the past, and maybe wild flowers. The cemetery is in a lovely position with steep hillsides falling abruptly away to give fine views. The sad graves are covered by a thin mantle of brown needles from the pine trees that create a shaded but suspended tranquillity. The fencing is broken and sheep and goats maintain the grass, while tree roots and weather work fast upon the epitaphs to childhood and youth. Nearby on a shady bank in grass were a few spikes of *Notholirion thomsonianum.* What a lovely plant it is, about 12 inches tall with as many drooping tubular flowers of a lovely pink, and the most heavenly perfume. It seems it was first introduced into cultivation by Loddiges Nursery, who flowered it in 1844. Frustratingly it is not easy to keep, for the mother bulb dies after flowering and the tiny bulb spawn must be carefully nurtured. Interestingly I found it again another year in the Kulu valley as a weed in wheat fields, clearly thriving in the regularly cultivated soil. In the terraced fields out of Simla one finds *Tulipa stellata* similarly flourishing.

The drive from Dehra Dun to Simla is motoring at its best: an excellent though narrow road, very little traffic, constantly changing views of rolling hills, sharp ridges and deep valleys, with sometimes along the horizon a row of snow-capped peaks. Often forests of Long-leaved or Chir pine, *Pinus roxburghii,* scent the air with resin, little cups hanging below blazes on their trunks to catch the turpentine. Past Solan, a most important little town where Golden Eagle and other beers are brewed, and then: Simla.

Simla is set amidst deodars, *Cedrus deodara,* and as one enters the town these classic conifers dominate one's first perceptions, their dappled shade contrasting with the bright sunlight of the journey. This sister 'Queen of Hill Stations' (its pair is Darjeeling) is set at about 7200 ft upon the watershed between the Ganges and Indus rivers and, like other hill stations, is a series of narrow streets following the contours. Large private houses often of the last century occupy more or less secluded situations and public buildings of the

Simla

British administration still dominate. Simla has seen many explorers
and botanists. Among the earliest plant records are the Countess of
Dalhousie's collections made in 1830. Victor Jacquemont, a Frenchman collecting for the Jardin des Plantes, stayed in 1830/31 before
going to Kashmir. Dr Thomas Thomson and Captain (Sir Richard)
Strachey in 1847 stopped in Simla on their way to define the boundary
between India and Chinese Tibet. The outstanding soldier and
amateur botanist Colonel Sir Henry Collett was the author of *Flora
Simlensis*, first published in 1902 and still the standard reference.

Thomson describes the forests surrounding Simla in 1847: 'By
far the greater part consists of an oak (*Quercus incana*) and a rhododendron (*R. arboreum*), both small evergreen trees, rarely exceeding
thirty or forty feet, with wide-spreading arms and ragged twisted
branches'. Other common trees were *Pinus longifolia* (*P. roxburghii*),
Pieris ovalifolia, *Ilex dipyrena*, euonymus, rhamnus and cornus. In
Collett's *Flora Simlensis* there is a contribution from J. S. Gamble,
formerly Director of the Forest School, Dehra Dun, describing the
situation some 50 years later, by which time considerable changes

had taken place due to the felling of timber trees and clearance of large areas for potatoes and other crops. Gamble writes that the three spurs over which Simla is located have now been acquired by the Government down to a level of 6000 feet 'and [are] managed by a Municipal Committee who have taken great pains to preserve the forest vegetation so that the station of Simla presents a marked contrast to the country outside, which is characterised by bare grassy slopes with occasional villages and patches of cultivation wherever the slope is sufficiently easy to admit of terracing, and with patches of forest in ravines and steeper hillsides'. Gamble goes on to say that measures have been taken to restore the destroyed forests, but I wonder whether it was the introduction of those potatoes and the consequent soil erosion that accounts for the bare hillsides one still sees today.

Every botanist climbs Jakko Hill, which Thomson described as having *Pinus excelsa* common on the south face and *Cedrus deodara* common above 7000 ft, with the summit at 8130 ft a short flat ridge with the east and south faces bare and grassy or covered with scattered shrubs – salix, rosa, rubus, lonicera, viburnum, berberis, indigofera, prinsepia. Today the cedars remain, and there is oak and pine and certainly the prinsepia and berberis, but there are wide steps cut into the steep climb to the summit and the ground is much worn by visitors, domestic animals and monkeys. Through erosion the cedars on the summit had their roots bare of soil, so they appeared raised two feet above soil level like mangroves. A year later the roots had been encircled, or entombed, with concrete! There is also a temple to Hanuman, the Hindu Monkey God, and with so many tourists feeding the monkeys these have become exceedingly assertive, not to say aggressive. The little summit restaurant has been caged in with wire netting and it is an odd experience to be sitting inside eating sticky buns while monkeys climb outside the netting and look in with their arms outstretched for morsels.

On the descent I was intrigued by an imposing house with a large Victorian conservatory. The white ornamental gate to the drive was ajar, so I trespassed over the gravel to be confronted by empty staging in the conservatory and a family, presumably the gardener's, living in what was once a fine potting shed. The house was forlornly shuttered, but the view of the hills from the front lawn was splendid. It seems the house was built in 1838; in the 1870s the then-owner employed a European gardener, and the conservatory was built and the garden opened to visitors.

Another house with a once famous garden was Wildflower Hall, some six miles from Simla and one of the residences of Lord Kitchener. A keen gardener, he apparently was apt to get all his servants including grooms and table servants as well as coolies to work with him in the garden. There is little evidence now of all this intensive energy, but the myriads of tiny *Primula denticulata* wild in the turf beneath some grand old cedars were pretty to see.

The private house in which I was a paying guest typified the sense of history and the presence of ghosts one can experience in these hill stations: it was the house from which in 1838 the Governor-General Lord Auckland issued the Simla Manifesto, the fateful decision to invade Afghanistan.

Darjeeling may be Simla's sister but is not her twin, for this Queen has a different air. It is not so much a centre for holiday makers and honeymoon couples but much more a working town; with the current Gorkhaland movement it is a centre of political activity. But the famous tiny railway still sometimes runs and the

British cemetery with Darjeeling in the distance

blessed Hotel Windamere provides a wonderful respite from travel-ler's curry, with its home-made steak and kidney pie, plum pudding, and coffee in the drawing room round a log fire. The once famous Lloyds Botanical Garden founded in 1865 is obviously short of funds. Like so many gardens in India it relies upon its heritage of mature trees and plants little for the future, while the shacks of the homeless encroach upon its boundaries. *Magnolia campbellii* is what I remember, many of them, and with a range of colour forms from pure white to deep, vivid pink. The nearby bazaar is crammed closely with tiny stalls representative of many enterprises, and here one can also buy tea of different grades. True, pure Darjeeling tea is grown at the highest altitude and because little is produced it is very expensive, the best exorbitantly so.

One descends to Kalimpong driving along a grandly scenic route, the hills carpeted with green tea bushes. The Foresters have diversi-fied, and on the way in a pretty setting they run a splendid orchid garden. Mostly cymbidium hybrids, these grow in beds with lathe shading to protect them from strong sun, and very well flowered they were too, although not the newest cultivars our buyers now expect. The spikes are destined for the cut flower market in Calcutta. A tall glasshouse protects specimen cymbidiums in pots, some splendidly grown with as many as a dozen spikes from a 10 inch pot, together with a selection of local native orchid species.

After this enjoyable stop one is ready for the several orchid nurseries in Kalimpong. Lathe-shaded houses provide the growing conditions for many of the Assam species, one of the world's richest areas for orchids. Some nurseries are trying laboratory techniques for production, while another is laid out around the owner's house and charmingly integrated with the garden. Surplus plants are stuck into the many waist high azalea hedges that formally border some of the paths, and here they thrive as epiphytes – dendrobium, arachnanthe, bulbophyllum, vanda and coelogyne.

This time I stayed in the 1920s house built by David Macdonald, formerly a British Trade Agent to Tibet, which is now run as an hotel by his daughter. *Primula malacoides* was a weed invading shaded patches in the lawn. Up the hill behind, the road passes a number of sturdily built stone houses reminiscent of the wealthier parts of Surrey. Their gardens have been kept neat but not replanted, and there is now a wonderful mixture of choice things from long

One of the very English houses in Kalimpong

ago with the Indian *mali's* beloved hollyhocks and marigolds. Twelve-foot-high evergreen azaleas vie with camellias for survival and against this background sweet peas and other summer annuals are to be found in beds with schizanthus, mesembryanthemum, freesia and that most striking Assam cymbidium with its one or two large white flowers on short stiff upright stems, *C. eburneum*.

These hill stations are all Himalayan, and there are many more. There is Udagamandalam (otherwise known as Snooty Ooty) in the South, where I long to find wild *Lilium neilgherrense* but after three visits begin to despair. Above Bombay is Mahabaleshwar and in India's heartland Pachmarhi, just two more of the many hill top towns where once, with long years of service ahead to the next furlough home, attempts were made to induce a breath of English air.

Photographs by the author

The Plantsman of Baden
Maximilian Leichtlin, 1831–1910

AUDREY LE LIÈVRE

On 3 September 1910, at a time when England was beginning to accustom herself to a new King, George V, and Germany watched in awe and satisfaction the increasing size of Kaiser Wilhelm II's fleet, a small matter-of-fact notice appeared in the Baden *Tagblatt*. Max Leichtlin, aged 78, was dead. It was just over five years since he had told his English gardening friend, Ellen Willmott, that he was ready to bid adieu to this wicked world (Note 1) and now a stroke had carried him off, gently, in the night. The death announcement followed unusually briskly on the death, and the sorrowing *hinter-bliebene* – those left behind – were not listed by name, as was customary. In any case only two of them were at hand – the children of Max's elder brother, Eduard, who were only about 15 years younger than he was, and perhaps not anxious to be reminded of death.

The family's paper firm, Gebrüder Leichtlin, has long since been absorbed into Papierhaus Erhardt, and there is no longer any Leichtlin name in the local telephone directory. But lasting fame is Max Leichtlin's, and all gardeners, whether they realise it or not, owe him a debt, commemorated not only by the plants which bear his name. All over the world, in the years before 1873, when he retired from business in Carlsruhe to set up his botanic garden in Baden-Baden, and 1906 when his health began to fail, Max Leichtlin was known to explorers, plant hunters, nursery owners, customs men and missionaries, anyone in fact who found or handled new plants or seeds. He was at the end of so many trails, the centre of so many communications.

It came about like this. Maximilian Leichtlin was born on 20 October, 1831 (the last person, as it turned out, who should have been saddled with such a grand imperial name), to Heinrich Leichtlin of Carlsruhe and his wife Frederike. 'Leichtlin' is not a name associated with any one part of Germany, and certainly not with Baden: but the fact that I have not been able to trace the births of the older sons – Eduard, Carl and Hermann – in the town records does not necessarily mean that the parents arrived in Carlsruhe

Max Leichtlin, aged perhaps about 40 – still the brisk businessman as well as the knowledgeable plantsman. *Royal Botanic Gardens, Kew.*

dragging the three children by the hand and wheeling their possessions piled high on a handcart. They could simply have gravitated to the town from somewhere along the Rhine or deeper in the Black Forest. Heinrich Leichtlin (presumably with an unidentified brother) founded the firm of Gebrüder Leichtlin in 1823, when Eduard was probably about 11 and Hermann 2 or 3. We know that Carl was 5 because the announcement of his death in 1862 aged 44 is preserved amongst papers relating to the firm in the Stadtarchiv Karlsruhe (SAK) (Signatur 8/StS 13/74). From small beginnings Gebrüder Leichtlin came later to manufacture tracing paper, rice paper, sealing wax, varnish and other useful items, and to sell, both wholesale and retail, a whole range of office and artists' materials, including business books, bookbinder's canvas, photograph albums and mathematical instruments. There were also fancy goods on offer such as jewellery cases and cigar boxes. The firm supplied the Carlsruhe Polytechnic, and had a representative in London (E. Preller of Wood Street). By 1895 it was said to be the most important firm of its kind in the whole continent, and sometime previously had won awards for chemically-prepared tracing paper at the World Exhibition in Chicago, and also at Vienna. (A Memorandum concerning the firm is preserved at the Generallandesarchiv Karlsruhe (GLAK), Signatur 60/615.)

The three older brothers joined their father in the business, but Max was destined to follow a different path. From a letter which his father wrote to the authorities at the Botanic Garden when Max was 16 it is clear that the boy had a mechanical bent and originally wanted to follow it, but he had been ill in childhood and his father sought a less exacting career for him. Max had always been interested in gardens, and this seemed the ideal solution (if the authorities would only co-operate, is the letter's unwritten wish!). They did, having made it quite clear that they expected the parents to take responsibility for their son's board and lodging. Evidently they were impressed by the boy's record at the Polytechnic, which he had attended since the autumn of 1845. Reports commended his diligence and conduct in subjects including French and German, History, Religious Knowledge, and Geometry, and he was accepted for entry to the Botanic Garden as an apprentice in 1848. (GLAK Faszikel 56/5918 *Annahme von Lehrlingen bei den grossherzoglichen Hofgärtnereien*).

In view of what was to happen later, it is scarcely believable that
gardening could have been Max's second choice of occupation. But
1848 marked the beginning of a long period of learning, the order of
which differs slightly in the various obituaries. (Note 6). Following
his apprenticeship he seems to have held jobs as gardener at Boll-
weiler (near Mulhouse), at Frankfurt-am-Main, and also at Ghent.
He spent some time at the Gardeners' Training Establishment at
Potsdam. It is almost as though he were taking a modern sandwich
course. And then he began to travel, apparently all over Europe, and
finally to Brazil and the Argentine. Here, no doubt, in his very early
twenties, Max Leichtlin's taste for plant hunting was fostered.
Coming back penniless from this jaunt, he seems to have spent a
few months working at Glasnevin, Dublin, for Dr David Moore,
Curator of the Botanic Gardens. There is no evidence that he was
on the staff there, but he seems to have known the Moore family
quite well, and one explanation might perhaps be that he worked
unpaid in the Gardens in exchange for board and lodging at the
Moores' house.

The next stage was probably the most important of all. Every
biographical source credits Leichtlin with having spent two years
with the firm of Louis van Houtte, from about 1856 to 1858. Van
Houtte was an interesting and enterprising man, just the sort to
appeal to the energetic and rapidly learning young man. Le Texnier,
in his *Notices sur les Jardiniers célèbres et les Amateurs des Jardins* (1907),
tells us that at the age of 22 van Houtte founded the magazine
L'Horticulture belge and set up a business selling gardening sundries
in Brussels; but on the death of his young wife in 1833 he threw all
this up and accepted the offer of a plant hunting trip to South
America with commissions to find *Orchidaceae* for de Von, the
Brussels Botanic Garden and Prince Léopold. He returned to Belgium
in 1836 and eventually set up a nursery in Ghent in 1839 – a nursery
which became famous all over Europe, and sent vast quantities of
plants overseas. It is possible that, during the first period when he
was alleged to be working in Ghent, Leichtlin attended the Ecole
pratique et théoretique d'Horticulture, which van Houtte established
in 1848. If so, one might speculate that his later South American visit
might have been directly inspired by the nurseryman. What is
certain is that Leichtlin must have met the Czech Benedict Roezl at
the van Houtte nursery, for Roezl trained there, becoming *chef de*

culture until he moved on in 1853 or thereabouts. His later plant hunting activities in Mexico and on the west coast of the United States gave Leichtlin some of his more startling novelties.

Did Max Leichtlin perhaps think of making a career in the stimulating atmosphere of van Houtte's? If so, his plans were halted abruptly, presumably by a family summons. About 1857 Max's brother Eduard died, and evidently it was thought high time for Max to shoulder his share of family responsibility in their large and thriving concern. So he went home to Carlsruhe and for 13 years laboured away in the office and the tracing paper factory. Eduard's sons Camill Ludwig Frederich and Rudolf Frederich Emil, whose births are recorded in the Birth Registers (GLAK) as 20 November 1845 and 20 February 1848 respectively, were in 1858 13 and 10 years old. It may well have been that Max set a limit to his efforts, agreeing to bridge the gap until the boys were ready for work and Camill, a clever youth, had taken his degree in Chemistry at Leipzig University. (Camill's inventive turn of mind later benefited the firm.) (GLAK Signatur 60/615).

Carl and Hermann, as well as Eduard, had married, only Carl being childless. I like to imagine the families living, if not exactly hugger-mugger in a flat above the business (which started in Zähringerstrasse 73), then in adjacent streets all close to the Market Place, right in the middle of the town. (GLAK *Adressbucher*) Heinrich, father of the four boys, survived until 1861 (SAK Signatur 8/StS 13/74) and Frederike for at least a further 14 years. (Kew: 4 May 1875). Max Leichtlin mentions his mother still living in Carlsruhe in that year, but as she does not appear as a householder she presumably lived with one of her sons. Max, who did not marry, lived at No 73, and acquired a separate garden, where he developed the prototype of his highly-organised establishment of later years. Entry No 352 (22 December 1871) in the *Grundbuch* (Land Register) (SAK) shows its area as $2\frac{1}{2}$ Ruthes, but since this measure differed from one state to another the most we can say is that the maximum possible size of the garden would have been 900 sq ft. But Max seems to have had a gift for organising himself within a very small space, and an even bigger gift for ensuring that its distance from the family was just great enough to let him pursue his gardening in peace. The garden lay in the Ettlinger Strasse, and was shielded by the factory, about $\frac{1}{4}$ mile away, from the office and family territory on the far side of the Ettlinger Tor. Opposite lay the Town Garden, and an innkeeper lived next door. It seemed ideal. But making a garden is slow work if it is done in one's spare time only, and it was not until 1865 that Leichtlin considered himself in a position to furnish material to science.

In character, Max Leichtlin seems to have been a diffident man, and every account of his life represents him as shy and retiring. Unusually, no one ever has an ill word to say of him, and this ought to make him dull, but he wasn't, and here his picturesque English helps. In some ways he was courageous, not to say pushy, and the earliest evidence of this comes in a letter which he wrote to Joseph (late Sir Joseph) Hooker (27 November 1865) in which he describes himself as a private amateur cultivating and collecting *Primulaceae* and *Liliaceae*, especially the genus *Lilium*. While foraging round on a visit to Kew he had, it seems, come upon some seedlings in a pit: they were *Lilium* species from Japan, unnamed and new to him. He at once wrote to request a small offset or bulb of these, and before he wrote had already sent off five lily bulbs. This approach required some nerve, but was effective. In a very short time the unknown German, despite his modest disclaimer – 'still a beginner on lilies' – was on easy terms with the Director, and plied him successfully with plants. 'At such occasions like, merry Christmas', he wrote (25 December 1867), 'I beg leave to sollicit as a special favour from you the kind acceptance of a sending I have made to you yesterday.' Leichtlin's singlemindedness and grasp of his subject obviously made their mark, and when later, all unaware of irony, he wrote 'an *occasional* answer will oblige' (12 March 1871), the foreigner was forgiven.

For a long time I wondered how Leichtlin had come to specialise in lilies, and I still do not know for certain. But on the shelves of the Lindley Library in the Royal Horticultural Society Offices, in Vincent Square, London, there is a copy of Spae's *Mémoire sur les espèces du Genre Lis*, published in Ghent in 1847, and on the flyleaf are the words 'With the Krelage Sale Catalogue 21/–' (the *Mémoire* is not listed in this 1948 *Sale Catalogue*). The volume is interleaved with blank pages, and notes have been made there by two distinct hands, both writing in German. One of these is an old-style hand using the long 's' and 'h' – but the other could very well be Leichtlin's, though the use of standard copperplate capitals makes it difficult to decide. If the book belonged to him, how could it have got amongst the catalogues? Perhaps the volume was sold on Leichtlin's death, and bought by someone in Krelage's Frankfurt establishment. Perhaps Max himself bought it in Ghent on his first, or second, stay there. Even if the handwriting is not his, it suggests that the Krelage/van Houtte/Leichtlin association could have inspired the young man to specialise in a genus already of great interest to the two nurserymen. J. H. Krelage was credited both by H. J. Elwes in his *Monograph of the Genus Lilium* (1880) (P v) and by Arthur Grove in *The Lily Year Book* (1932) (p 6) as having an excellent stock in his nursery, and he also published *Notice sur quelques espèces et variétés de Lis*.

When in 1870 Professor Duchartre of the Sorbonne published his *Observations sur le Genre Lis*, based on the catalogue of Max Leichtlin's collection in Carlsruhe, he remarked that Leichtlin had spent many years in bringing together species and varieties, and to do this had used his commercial connections as well as having corresponded with amateurs, travellers and plant collectors. Kew and St Petersburg gave him unpublished material, but he paid large sums to buy rarities. Duchartre (who had himself just lost his own collection in the Siege of Paris – one supposes either in the bombardment or eaten by the starving citizens) said that Leichtlin's was by far the richest collection in existence and that, besides undertaking serious study himself, he had found time to help other interested amateurs. It is clear that Duchartre and Leichtlin were in close communication for a long time before the *Observations* appeared.

Leichtlin was particularly interested in American and Japanese lilies, and in 1867 his increasing fame and status was recognised when Joseph Hooker named *Lilium leichtlinii* after him. This was a chance seedling of *Lilium auratum* noticed by Mr J. H. Veitch, and was a fine yellow spotted lily in the martagon class. It was not easy to grow, and comments on this vary from Leichtlin's gentle '. . . she needs a little more attention than her sisters of Japan . . .' (Arthur Grove *Lilies* (1911) (p 93)) to the more downright 'the man who can grow *Lilium leichtlinii* can grow anything.' (A. Grove on H. J. Elwes in *Lily Year Book* (1940) (pp 4–6)).

Duchartre lists the whole collection as containing 251 species and varieties from all over the world. To cram all these, with their progeny, into a space of not more than 900 sq ft (including pathways), where some room had to be left for other genera, was an achievement. The garden also contained trellises, presumably portable, which were positioned to give the lilies the dappled shade which most of them needed in order to flourish. The naming of some of these (described in Patrick Synge's book *Lilies* (1980)) is interesting. *Lilium humboldtii*, for example, was discovered by Benedict Roezl in California on the 100th birthday anniversary of Baron Alexander von Humboldt. Roezl and Leichtlin joined in naming the lily, said to have flowered for the first time in the latter's garden in 1870, in celebration of the great traveller.

Lilium tigrinum var. *splendens* came from a single bulb recognised as superior in a consignment sent to the nurseryman Jean Linden in Brussels in 1867. He divided it up with Leichtlin, who raised a large stock from which he compensated the Belgian, who had lost his half of the original bulb.

Lilium hansonii came from Japan. A few bulbs were sent to the garden of the late Dr Philipp von Siebold in Leiden and were purchased by Leichtlin, who was quick to recognise a new species, naming it after Peter Hanson of Brooklyn, New York, an amateur grower with an admirable collection of lilies, and a valued correspondent (perhaps the correspondent from whom Leichtlin was able to obtain lilies from any quarter of the United States?) (Kew: 14 November 1869)

His lily interests brought him one very spectacular piece of travelling. He wrote to Hooker on 23 February 1869 'Extremely pleased I was to hear that we shall probably meet at St Petersburg'. This occasion was the International Horticultural Exhibition under the patronage of the Tsar and Tsarina (reported in *Gartenflora* Vol 18 (1869) pp 188–92), at which both Hooker and Leichtlin were listed among the 'best-known guests'. Hooker presided over the second session of the congress, and Leichtlin served on the panel of judges for the lily exhibits. The guests saw the wonderful gardens of the area at their best in May, and were most royally entertained: rivers of champagne flowed on every possible occasion.

In July 1870 the war which the Germans are annoyed to find us calling the Franco-Prussian War (since not only Prussia was involved) broke out, upsetting Leichtlin's gardening because he took on the patriotic task of managing a hospital for war wounded. It did not last long, and by September 1870 things had taken a turn for the better and he could attend to his plants again: but the interlude may have contributed to a growing restlessness.

He had already, on 3 October 1868, sent Hooker some *Aethionema grandiflorum* Boiss, brought from Kurdistan by Dr Kotschky, and a letter which he wrote to J. H. Balfour at Edinburgh on 20 March 1870 shows that his interests already extended to *Fritillaria, Iris, Cyclamen* and *Lachenalia*. He followed this up, in a letter of 28 October 1870, by saying specifically that he is now going on to irises and unusual and rare perennials. Perhaps he was already beginning to feel irked by the restrictions of his little plot.

On 24 November 1871 Leichtlin wrote to Hooker to say that his garden was to be expropriated, adding that he is about to buy a nice little cottage at Baden-Baden with a few acres of ground, and would transport his collections there during the following year. The letter finishes 'No No I shall not give up!!' This is all very puzzling, because the *Grundbuch* makes it quite clear that the garden was *not* expropriated, but sold to a certain Leopold Weiss, a manufacturer, for the sum of 112 gulden 30 kroner (very roughly about £380).

The end of Max's papermaking career was in any event approaching, as Camill and Rudolf were ready to join the firm. Both of them appear in the Carlsruhe *Adressbuch* of 1873 (GLAK) as 'businessmen', living in the Sophienstrasse with their widowed mother. In this year Max appears for the last time in the Zähringerstrasse. Having now, at 40, reached the happy stage of being able to please himself, he sensibly decided to move far enough away to avoid embroilment in the affairs of Carlsruhe.

He seems to have taken his plants over piecemeal, to survive during the week without him, when visiting his 'Baden den' on Sundays before the move. (Kew: 16 January 1873). This was just as well, as the mind recoils from the horrors of a train journey with the luggage van, if there was one, crammed with plants: though Haus Leichtlin (No 1, Göttengasse), was in fact quite close to the station with its grand concourse. It was a pleasant house which has now been to an extent modified, on the hill above the great mansions of the Lange Strasse. Max Leichtlin's 112 gulden must have gone into this purchase.

On the opposite side of the Göttengasse, also on a steep slope and facing more or less south-west, lay the botanic garden. Unfortunately there is no one left who remembers it as a garden. The land belonged

and still belongs to the Convent of the Holy Sepulchre, and must
have been leased to Leichtlin, as such land is not normally sold. Its
name, Pflutterloch, means marshy land in the Baden dialect, and
certainly there is still a stream at the bottom of the hill, but the slope
itself seems well-drained. Perhaps the nuns already had a garden
there, but it seems more likely that Max himself terraced the area
to suit his needs, and there are still traces of terracing there. The
garden was not large, perhaps two acres, and is believed to have
been reduced to about half an acre towards the end of Max's life.
(Note 6f). It is a most genial spot, open and sunny, tranquil even
today, and the surrounding hillsides are covered with trees. I like
to think of Max Leichtlin as visitors have described him (Note 6f),
working bareheaded in his shirtsleeves in his garden in the afternoon
sunlight, stopping to pass the time of day with people hurrying
along the Göttengasse up to the town or to the Neues Schloss, which
from a height and a short distance looks down on Haus Leichtlin
and its botanic garden (the grand name for which, after two changes
in the Latin, became Hortus Botanicus Aquis-Aureliis – the Roman
name for Baden-Baden: the everyday name, which appeared on the
bills, was the Leichtlin'schen Garten).

Baden-Baden: Augusta-Platz. *A. le Lièvre.*

The first letter which Max wrote to Hooker from Baden-Baden is dated 13 December 1874, but before leaving Carlsruhe he wrote, on 19 November 1873, clearly looking forward to his new life: 'Of course I must stick to certain classes of Plants in order to do these well, and there is certainly a vast deal to do in keeping up a good collection of fine old and new out-of-door plants. I shall mostly care for these; but with bulbs I cultivate also such as come from temperate regions, from the Cape etc. Any time when your gardens receive sendings from Japan, China, Australia, Cape California, the plains of the Andes, Mexico, Himalaya etc. *such* ones as you can conveniently spare will be acceptable. I shall *not* cultivate tropical ones . . .'

There is no doubt that his plan for the garden was coming sharply into focus, and he set out to develop the kind of enterprise which suited his talents and circumstances. At its heart stood his determination to seek out, acquire, propagate and distribute plants of real garden worth and, where he felt that circumstances demanded it, to hybridise and select to improve the breed. He must have worked with the vision of gardens filled with gorgeous flowers perpetually in front of him, for though his plan could and did contribute powerfully to science because of the observations he was able to make, its primary purpose was to give pleasure – and, I think, to give his plants the opportunity to realise their full potential – aims which never left him.

It was often said that lilies did not grow happily in the Baden-Baden garden. I wonder whether this can have been true. There is nothing in Max's letters to suggest any difficulties. Although the publication of Duchartre's *Observations* must have constituted the high point of his lily work at Carlsruhe, and though lilies formed a smaller percentage of the total plant population at Baden-Baden, he still grew them and still worked on them. Especially was this so because, in the mid-1870s, he was introduced (perhaps by Hooker) to a towering, bearded, restless landowner from Gloucestershire, H. J. Elwes, footloose and bursting with energy, who in 1872 took to the pursuit of gardening so eagerly that by 1876 he was ready to embark, with enormous enthusiasm, on his *Monograph of the Genus Lilium*, which was published in 1880 and remained definitive, with supplements but without major revision, for almost 100 years. Helping Elwes meant a lot more work on lilies.

Luckily, several accounts survive of the Leichtlin'schen Garten in its heyday. (Note 4). The garden had narrow terraces, which provided deep soil, good drainage and maximum heat retention: the stones with which they were faced were smothered with aubrietia in the spring, and climbing plants thereafter. There were borders and flower beds, frames and stone troughs and seed-pans: there were various small greenhouses, one at least of which was sunk in the ground, with lights removable in summer. There were also portable lights which were used to ripen iris rhizomes after flowering. Leichtlin did not generally grow plants proved to be genuinely half-hardy or tender, preferring those which could winter out-of-doors (*winterhart* – a good self-explanatory word – was his favourite epithet): but he did test potential hardiness to the full. Baden-Baden has a warmer spring and a hotter and sunnier summer than does England, but it also has a colder winter (—22°C in the winter of 1879/80, but that was an exceptionally bad winter everywhere). In all his correspondence Leichtlin complains about the weather just like an Englishman, mostly about excessive rain or the reverse. The garden was too small to take many large shrubs and trees, even had he wanted to grow them, which probably he didn't.

He already had a network of correspondents all over the world from whom he could obtain all the raw material of plants which he wanted. In previous years he must have spent untold hours sitting at the family table in the Zähringerstrasse labouring away at his letters, and now these efforts were paying off handsomely. From time to time he would lose one of his contacts and have trouble in finding a replacement, and every now and then – during the Boer War, for example – a country would be closed to collectors. But only towards the end of his life, when problems arose simultaneously in Russia, Japan and India, did they really disturb him. (EW: 8 February 1906). The restrictions imposed by the outbreak of phylloxera in 1883 (Kew: *Misc Reports* 1.27, p 253 + letters) were clearly a trial, but they had their ridiculous and amusing aspects. Live plants could not be imported by post (save in 8oz sample packets from England) lest they speed the deadly louse on its way to the vineyards, but, as Max Leichtlin said 'asinine and immoral subjects do our best to transgress it [the law] wherever we can' and in any case live plants could be imported by individual travellers. He himself brought in boxes of plants by the simple means of travelling back to Baden-Baden from Vienna by the Orient Express.

The Leichtlin'schen Garten was essentially a one-man operation. Despite his undoubted geniality with friends, Max Leichtlin was a loner, and liked it. He enjoyed communing with his plants, and to read his letters is to be aware of a man who spent his days studying their ways. His written instructions for planting and cultivating are detailed and given with an authority that he otherwise did not display in ordinary life. (EW, Kew, Edin: *passim*). He told Ellen Willmott that he would pass by a plant 5 or 6 times a day to watch its development and admire its colours. (EW: 15 September 1897)

He liked an intelligent correspondent who loved plants and was ready to learn, and took endless trouble with Ellen Willmott – in 1898 still early in her horticultural experience – as she fitted this specification exactly. He put up bravely with her machinations to be the first to acquire his newest rarities, often slipping a few extra bulbs into her order 'for your kind acceptance'. He felt presumably that so supportive a client should be allowed a few idiosyncrasies. Her orders had preference over all others, he told her – and how delighted she must have been to learn that she was the sole possessor in Europe of that delightful lemony crown imperial, *Fritillaria raddeana*. (EW: 29 June 1899).

Leichtlin had a gardener to help him whom he described as a well-drilled excellent machine (EW: 20 March 1900) but without understanding of the needs of plants (nevertheless, he was found to be irreplaceable when in 1905 he broke his leg and shortly afterwards died). (EW: 23 June 1905). There may also have been a labourer. But all the skilled work was Leichtlin's, and as a result he could not afford to leave the garden for long, since seeds, young plants and hybridising all needed his personal attention. He told Ellen Willmott ruefully (18 June 1897) 'I only live in hopes to see again the chalky rocks of Dover'.

There were, of course, a multitude of ordinary jobs to be tackled – the lifting and packing of plants (I hope Max had commandeered an adequate supply of packing material from the stores of Gebrüder Leichtlin), and the routine of orders and accounts. All the latter was conducted in his large, clear, black handwriting (very probably his experience in the family firm was of great use to him) and in his good but idiosyncratic English. (It is interesting, as a diversion, to trace the influences at work in his use of that language, which include the Bible, business practice, and the kind of English which he must have learnt as a gardener – a Christmas present, for instance, was always a 'Christmas box' to him.)

He must early have had to make decisions about money. He told Ellen Willmott that he lived on a 'rent' (pension) 'which allows me a modest comfortable existence but all my dealings and doings in plants must be paid by the garden that is derived from the sale of my plants'. (EW: 23 March 1900).

Sensibly, he kept the expenses of household and garden separate, and the decision to make his garden pay for itself dictated the lines on which the business was run. He settled each year's accounts at the end of December, after which he could see what funds would be available for helping to finance collectors, and so fill his garden, for the coming year.

To further sales he sent out lists, apparently at rather haphazard intervals to begin with, but for the years 1900–06 copies are extant (Lindley Library (all): EW, Edin (some)) and make interesting reading. Originally intended for a few nurserymen, they later went to private customers, of whom by 1902 he had 80. (Edin: 10 October 1902) These arrangements had been developed at the request of friends who did not always have suitable stock with which to respond to Max's generous gifts.

In a letter of 7 December 1891 he told Thiselton-Dyer that he could not afford to subsidise collectors without recouping costs: as a result, Kew successfully negotiated to give up the exchange of plants and share in Leichtlin's novelties on the same terms as the nursery trade. (Kew: 17 December 1891). In 1902 Isaac Bayley Balfour found out about the trade list, and he too transferred on to business terms. (Edin: 8 October 1902)

Max Leichtlin, I think, didn't care in principle whether he sold, swopped or gave, so long as his enterprise flourished. And it did. With the steady trade income, and the prodigally large orders placed by Miss Willmott (£119. 19s. 6d. in the autumn of 1897, for instance – a large sum) he was able to cover his costs and to support expeditions to Armenia, Persia and many other countries. (EW, Kew, Edin: *passim*) And he could indulge his naturally generous bent, digging up precious bulbs to share with his visitors (not only on the prudent principle that what you give away is there to come back to you at need, but simply because he liked doing it).

Though Elwes (Note 4g) regarded the little garden as too small for all the work it was required to do, it was already almost a production line, and every year, in a relentless purge, Leichtlin threw away 'many plants which would be highly prized by less intelligent collectors'. He was clearly regarded as someone who liked a challenge and, as Arthur Grove said in *Lilies* (1911) (p 93) 'his were the hands to which so many collectors sent their finds, sure in the knowledge that if he couldn't manage the plants no one could do anything with them'. As the Rev. Henry Ewbank, visiting him after a gap of four years, rightly remarked, the hallmark of the Leichtlin'schen Garten was novelty, for he found that plants which he remembered had long since been proved, multiplied, sent on their way and replaced by a fresh batch of marvels. He noted with approval *Onosma albo-roseum* from Armenia, and *Rheum riwas* from Persia, with its young leaves resembling a toad. (Note 4d).

Max Leichtlin took the risk of getting plants from Japan, despite the perils of the long sea journey: he was involved with Persian plant hunting, possibly through Dr Otto Stapf, of Vienna and later of Kew. Seeds arrived from Tokyo, 'a few splendid novelties' from Armenia, *Kniphofia* species were collected by Schimper in Abyssinia and found their way to Baden-Baden, sometimes via the Berlin Botanic Garden: and Kotschky's findings were brought from Kurdistan. (EW, Kew, Edin: *passim*)

He was in constant touch with Dr Eduard Regel at the St Petersburg Botanical Garden, and won himself various mentions in the plant hunter Olga Fedtschenko's survey of the genus *Eremurus*, published in 1909. Elwes, in his Notes from a Cotswold Garden (*Gardeners' Chronicle* Vol 59 (1916) pp 193–94) mentions a crown imperial called 'gigantea' which he received from Leichtlin around 1900, and which the latter had obtained from a Russian friend in Turkestan: he also maintained that Leichtlin knew Russian officers who came to Baden-Baden. Certainly there were many Russians living in the town – enough to justify building a Russian Orthodox Church there in 1882. Tsar Alexander I, when heir to the throne had married Princess Luise of Baden, and a Russian Embassy was set up in Carlsruhe near to the Grand Ducal seat, to which Alexander succeeded after the overthrow of Napoleon. After this many Russians flocked to the area – including the writers Gogol, Turgenev (who lived in Baden-Baden for several years) and Tolstoy. Many diplomats, officers and industrialists moved to Baden-Baden, building splendid villas or living in hotels. (See *100 Jahre Russische-Orthodoxe Kirche in Baden-Baden*, Dr W. Günther (1982)). But Max Leichtlin in his quiet house, probably spending most of his evenings writing, seems to have been singularly untouched by the elegant social and literary life taking place so close to him, and my own guess would be that his Russian contacts were chiefly made, and sustained, by letter.

I mention that he must have spent his evenings writing because he had not only a huge correspondence to keep up, but also bills to prepare and new lists to draft. Furthermore, in the 1880s and '90s especially, when he was at his most productive, he wrote numerous short notes for *Gartenflora*, *The Garden* and *Garden and Forest* (this latter was edited by Professor C. S. Sargent, tree man and Director of the Arnold Arboretum at Harvard. Leichtlin seems to have felt a great affinity with America and Americans, though he never left Europe). Some of these notes described a single plant, some gave invaluable guidance on cultivation of unusual bulbs and perennials, and some (Notes from Baden-Baden) told the reader what was to be seen of special interest in his garden at the time of writing. A few raised subjects not usually connected with Leichtlin's interests, such as the need for a good graded colour chart to describe flower colours: and they reveal, in passing, how he must have pored over periodicals and learned journals (even *The Proceedings of the Californian Academy of Natural Sciences* is mentioned when writing to J. H. Balfour on 20 March 1870). Most of them, however, give the reader the benefit of his long experience of growing plants, which formed the basis of all his writing. When he contributed to (but apparently did not attend) the Royal Horticultural Society's International Conference on Hybridisation in July 1899 (the fateful Conference which led to the re-discovery of Mendel's famous paper) he did not send in a formal paper, but a list of five points headed *The Principles of Hybridising holding good in the Majority of Cases* – no more than 100 words in all, but every word with years of experience behind it. Similarly, when he read a paper to the Royal Horticultural Society in 1901 on *The Cultivation of Hardy Plants and Shrubs*, it was a meaty statement, severely practical in tone and content.

But all these activities were peripheral to the main purpose of his life – keeping his garden perpetually full of worthwhile plants. He did some plant hunting himself, but could rarely spare the time.

However, *Lilium martagon* var. *dalmaticum* was one of his quarries. He told Hooker on 19 November 1873 that his expedition to Montenegro in search of *Lilium albanum* Grieseb. and *Lilium martagon* var. *dalmaticum* had failed. Whether this was a personal attempt is not clear, but in any case a year later success was reported by letter to Elwes, who includes a quotation in *Monograph of the Genus Lilium* (Intro p. v). The lily was found in wild country on the frontiers of Turkey, growing in calcareous gravelly soil lodged on the sides of crevasses. *Jankaea heldreichii* was found under the protection of a company of soldiers, on Mount Olympus near a bandits' lair, (Note 4d). But was Leichtlin himself there? All the sources are silent. He mentions casually to Hooker that he has been plant hunting in Vienna and the Tyrol (Kew: 7 May 1879), but apart from this, there is no direct evidence of further plant hunting.

We now arrive at an area of great difficulty. Max Leichtlin was justly proud of the plants which he considered himself to have introduced, and often used the phrase 'introduced by me' in his Notes. But there are problems about defining the introducer of any given plant. Many people would say that the collector is the introducer, and leave it at that. Others would assert that the commissioner and paymaster of the collector or expedition; or the botanist who describes the plant; or the horticulturist/nurseryman who raises it, shows it or stocks it, should receive the credit. In all of these possibilities anomalies arise.

As far as Leichtlin was concerned, he sometimes, but not always, commissioned and paid the collector – though there were many occasions when collectors and correspondents sent him their rare plants without being specifically asked, knowing that chances of survival would thereby be much improved. He certainly supervised and stage-managed the entry into European gardens of numerous species from plants propagated or seeds sown by him, sometimes via his own list. It would therefore seem fair to credit him with the introduction of such plants, even though the difficulty of defining a role such as his for universal application would be extreme.

All this amounts to the fact that the lists which I have given at Appendix A should be treated with caution. My own feeling is that the list of introductions attributed to Max Leichtlin, which contains only those species the introduction of which is clear from *The Botanical Magazine*, is probably shorter than it ought to be, and that many of the 'possible' list in fact belong there. *The Botanical Magazine* has thus been taken as baseline, but unfortunately there are many cases where, though we are told that the plant described and figured has been supplied by 'that admirable cultivator' or that 'indefatigable correspondent' Max Leichtlin, we are not told whether he was responsible for its introduction to Europe. Which is tantalising. Nevertheless, these lists are a start.

Novelties could, however, arise as well from the garden itself as from overseas. Leichtlin's Notes from Baden-Baden perhaps best reveal that, particularly during the period 1880 to 1900, he worked steadily on hybridising very many species and improving them by selection, the two processes often interacting. He worked on some genera for the whole of this period and sometimes beyond. *Kniphofia* was one of these, *Aubrieta* another. Each July kniphofias began to bloom in his garden, and by careful placing he was able to bring about a number of new crosses ranging in colour from pale sulphur yellow to dark red. *K. natalensis*, for example, which others thought to be useless, was capable of producing very good hybrids, as it was a variable species. (*Garden and Forest* Vol 6 (1893) p 446). Most of Leichtlin's species seem to have been obtained from Abyssinia. Every visitor to the Leichtlin'schen Garten commented on the richness of the *Kniphofia* range (see especially Note 4a).

Leichtlin's work on *Aubrieta* is well known. About 1882 he set to work at the instigation of his friend William Ingram (gardener at Belvoir Castle) to produce a crimson aubrietia. Five years later, using *A. hendersonii*, he had achieved this (*Aubrieta leichtlinii*). Immediately afterwards he started work on a different strain, producing first the double bloom 'Beauty of Baden' and then the so-called 'Leichtlin's varieties' of *A. deltoidea*, in lavender, rose, rosy lilac, violet and red lake. In 1903 a white seedling made its appearance – in fact he always had an eye open for albinos, enjoining Ellen Willmott (EW: *passim*) to do likewise. Finally, in 1907, he recommended planting *Physotychus guavalodes* – a very similar flower, but with greyer leaves and citron yellow flowers – among aubrietia, to set off its colours. (*The Garden* Vol 71 (1907) p 222)).

Other species received his attention for varying lengths of time. In 1883 he became a Foreign Member of the Royal Horticultural Society, and then from 1900 to his death in 1910 an Honorary and Corresponding Member; while from about 1894 he served as a

Member of the Narcissus (later Narcissus and Tulip) Committee. He had earlier worked on daffodils, and Peter Barr's *Supplementary Catalogue* to the *Catalogue* of the important Daffodil Conference (1884) showed six new daffodils attributed to him – 'Cupid', 'Daisy', 'Herbert von Bismarck', 'Prince Bismarck', 'Mabel Cowan' and 'Margaret Jones'. Mabel Cowan was probably the wife or daughter of the English daffodil specialist, but one pauses briefly to wonder who 'Margaret Jones' might have been – for Leichtlin was so very much a bachelor all his life. *Nerine* was also a favourite in the 1880s, but may not have proved hardy enough for his liking, for after raising many new hybrids from crossing selected plants of the best species, he disposed of his collections in July 1886 to Kew (Kew: 14 July 1886), and in 1890 to H. J. Elwes (*Gardeners' Chronicle*, Elwes Obituary Vol 72 (1922) pp 319–20). The latter continued with hybridisation and went on to win many awards at Royal Horticultural Society Shows.

Max Leichtlin is often credited with the raising of gladiolus hybrid 'Princeps' and indeed he seems to have named it. But its story (detailed by Leichtlin himself in *Gartenflora* Vol 52 (1903) pp 138–39) shows one of his rare failures. In 1872 he obtained from Mr W. Wilson-Saunders in Reigate, Surrey, a bulb of *Gladiolus saundersi*. He failed to get a good form through hybridising with *G. gandavensis*, and eventually gave up the work and disposed of the collection to a French firm, who after an exhibition in Paris sold it to Messrs Childs in America. This firm undertook further work, and marketed the race produced as *G. childsii*. In 1869 *G. cruentus* was introduced by William Bull in London, and later a second variety introduced by the same firm. Leichtlin worked on both of these without success. In 1895, however, he was asked by Dr van Feet (surely this must have been van Fleet of rose fame?) to send him all the available *Gladiolus* hybrids. From these – it is thought using *G. childsii* as the pollen parent – hybrid 'Princeps' was produced. It was, as Leichtlin says in his list, 'the most magnificent Gladiolus hitherto raised – Beautifully shaped, rather flat, bright deep scarlet adorned by white feathers – the first of a novel strain of Gladioli'. Other 'Princeps' hybrids subsequently appeared in the Lists, but who produced them is unclear.

Countless species of *Fritillaria* grew in the Leichtlin'schen Garten. He comments 'I am wondering what a new species will turn out from the Black Mountains of India' (*Garden and Forest* Vol 7 (1894) p 176). In 1890 he is enthusiastic about *Iris gatesii* and *I. bakeriana*, and reports 'other novelties coming on'. (*Garden and Forest* Vol 3 (1890) p 80 and p 253). He did much work on the hybridisation of *I. reticulata* (*Garden and Forest* Vol 4 (1891) p 438), and later undertook experiments on planting irises at varying depths. He reports (*Garden and Forest* Vol 5 (1892) p 224) on *Tulipa leichtlinii* 'introduced by myself from Cashmere', saying that very many new species are being brought in from Armenia and Persia, so that a vast field is now open for systematic crossing of species, or species and forms.

He reports sudden triumphs, the result of efforts over a long period – how, for example, after persevering for many years on sowing and selecting *Scabiosa caucasica* var. *connata*, even though variations were slight, he at last achieved a plant with bright deep ultramarine flowers, and another with pure white flowers. (*Garden and Forest* Vol 10 (1897) p 424). In *Clematis*, he was also successful: with *Clematis coccinea*, after repeated sowings, he finally produced a seedling of strong rosy scarlet, with flowers three times the size of the wild plant. He also had his eye on *C. tangutica*, which he thought might perhaps be very useful for hybridising. (*The Garden* Vol 64 (1903) p 90 and p 232). After 25 years of work on improving blue primroses he at last, in 1905, obtained 'Advance', with large leaves and bright ultramarine flowers. (*The Garden* Vol 71 (1907) p 186). For many years he raised Moutan peonies and at last, in 1900, he was successful in producing a fine cross of 'Gloria Belgarum' and a deep red single-flowered Japanese variety. Even the perfectionist Leichtlin admitted that the result was perfect in shape and outline. The flower was deep magenta red with a touch of violet, and he called it 'Isis'. (*The Garden* Vol 57 (1900) p 475).

These extracts represent only a tiny portion of Leichtlin's achievements. I am certain that, had he not been so unceasing in his efforts, looking over his plants with an eagle eye several times a day, noting variations in colour, shape and markings in each flower, relentlessly disposing of all material he could not use, he would never have accomplished so much. The simple fact was that he was bored by easy work, and would undertake nothing that an ordinary cultivator could deal with. For him were the new, rare and difficult plants, sulky, unwilling to be managed and hard to satisfy. Then he was on his mettle and would pacify, coax and bully until the plant yielded to his ministrations and gave of its best. He was also endlessly patient: among hundreds of *Tulipa batalinii* which went through his hands, all were sulphurous and ochraceous in colour bar one – of wonderful soft crimson tone – and this one he propagated and offered on his list of 1905 (only two bulbs!). (*The Garden* Vol 65 (1904) p 406).

Max Leichtlin usually worked in his garden from morning till evening, because work was his favourite occupation. But that did not mean he had nothing else to do. Dr Wittmack of Berlin held that he was as welcome a judge as he was an exhibitor at International Shows. (Note 6b). This may well have been true, but I have found only one instance of his acting as a judge (at St Petersburg, *vide* p 16 above) and one of his attendance at the 50th anniversary Show at Vienna in 1877. There must have been others. For many years he served as a Stadtrat (Town Councillor) in Baden-Baden, which meant much work.

Living alone and simply, he seems to have done no cooking. He took his meals at the St Petersburg Hotel (the building is still there, but only just recognisable as once a hotel); and when he felt like it, spent time in the Süsser Lockel, a bar in the Hotel Stadt Paris. The Süsser Löckel is still there too, but not in a form which Leichtlin would recognise. Each outing meant a brisk pleasant walk along the Schlossstrasse, pursuing divergent bee lines down the many steps and passages of the old town. Elwes thought him an open-handed and sociable man, and wrote (Note 6e) that on drives through the forest he would stop at his friends' houses to taste the best wine, of which he was very fond, though a sober man. 'Hail fellow well met' with everyone, he would stop to exchange jokes with innkeepers and coachmen in the Baden dialect.

To such a modest and simple man, rewards when they came were clearly a surprise. The first to appreciate the quality of his contribution was Joseph Hooker in his *Botanical Magazine* dedication of 1883, made after the little garden at Baden-Baden had been in full swing for 10 years and its worth had been fully proved. It came, Hooker said 'in recognition of your eminent services to Horticulture, and as a slight mark of that esteem which I, in common with the intelligent gardening world of Europe, entertain for your knowledge, skill and enthusiasm – and for the liberality with which the treasures of your garden are distributed amongst your fellow-horticulturists'. No one could have put it better or more succinctly, and Leichtlin was quite overcome. 'I never expected that once such an honouring mention would be made of this by your authority and also in such kind terms.' (Kew: 12 December 1883) In 1892 *The Garden*, edited at that time by William Robinson, followed suit. A good deal less elegantly phrased, it yet contained the earliest account of Max Leichtlin's life available, and seems to have been correct as far as it goes. (One wonders where Robinson got the information.) When in the following year a similar piece appeared in *Dr Neubert's Deutsches Garten-Magazin* (Vol 46 pp 243–44), for no especial reason, a photograph was included with a caption in Leichtlin's own handwriting. In cheerful mood, he wrote (I translate) 'This is me, aged 61, full of enterprise and enthusiasm, and young in heart'.

Four years later he was awarded a Veitch Memorial Medal (some would have thought he qualified for a Victoria Medal of Honour) for his services to horticulture, and here again, the citation manages exactly to convey the essence of what he sought to achieve. 'He occupies a unique place among the horticulturists of the present day ... In this remarkable garden, scarcely half an acre in extent, Max Leichtlin has worked for upwards of 40 [this should be 25] years ... During this period, remote corners of the earth have been searched for plant rarities, and when once these treasures have found a home in the little garden at Baden-Baden, the skill of the owner has rarely failed to make them available for the gardens of Europe ...' Unique was certainly the right word. For though Leichtlin might well have been inspired by the charismatic van Houtte and his large-scale operation at Ghent, he did not attempt to imitate it. He knew just what he wanted, which was to have every last piece of work under his own control.

Finally, he was honoured in celebration of his 70th birthday in 1901 by the presentation of the silver-gilt medal of the *Verein zür Beförderung des Gartenbaues in den preussischen Staaten,* again in recognition of his services to horticulture. He had been elected a corresponding member of the Society in 1879. The *Tagblatt* (Note 6h) also refers vaguely to honours from Russia, but there is no other sign of these.

Naturally, work was not interrupted by these events. And trouble, when it came, had nothing to do with Max Leichtlin's reputation nor with the quality of his work. It merely showed the natural tendency of difficulties to happen all at once. Thus in June 1905 he suffered a severe attack of shingles which, combined with rapidly worsening rheumatism, caused him severe pain and impeded his movements. He became very depressed. At the same time, he mentioned some financial difficulties to Ellen Willmott (who wrote back very promptly and sympathetically, being about to plunge into deep financial trouble herself). He said that the problem was of a temporary nature, but his was a naturally optimistic temperament, and it seems more likely that they had come to stay. (EW: 15 June 1905) It is certainly true that in the following year he added some of his cherished books to his list, including his set of *The Botanical Magazine*, which was priced at £150, 23 volumes of *Flore des Serres et des Jardins de l'Europe* at £14, and Elwes's *Monograph of the Genus Lilium* (minus one part) rather under-priced at £3. They did not reappear on the 1906 *Last List of Plants*, so presumably Max's limited financial acumen had made bargains of them all, quickly grabbed.

The final blow lay in the death of his old gardener – the well-trained machine – whom he could not replace.

As early as 1899 Max Leichtlin had remarked 'I am by and by becoming old [he was then 68] and wish to make my plant collection less burdensome'. (EW: 18 July 1899) This was a preliminary to offering Ellen Willmott a number of 'fancy' bulbs (strange how he could not rid himself of this word, dating back to the days of his dealings in 'fancy goods') available in small quantities. The outcome of this is not recorded. In 1905, however, things were serious. He had to face squarely the problems of a man accustomed to doing everything for himself, who suddenly felt tired and ill. So he tried to sell his house, estate and collections (which latter he valued at £200, which *must* have been far too little) complete. (EW: 23 June 1905) But if the nurseryman who had enquired eventually made an offer it was not accepted, and by the end of 1906 Leichtlin must have been feeling rather better, as health is not mentioned, and he was still distributing plants. But gradually his undertaking was slowing down and closing, as his hands grew slack on the reins. 1907 is the year after which the Notes from Baden-Baden in *The Garden* cease. During that year they are a little thinner than usual, but still contain valuable information. It must have been at about this time that he wrote to the editor to say that he had had to dispose of most of his plants, for he could not carry on. (Note 6e) (At the time there was a landscaping nursery in Baden-Baden, and it is possible that he sold to them.)

But he continued to take a close interest in plants, and it is hard to imagine him giving up his correspondence. The *Tagblatt* obituary implies that he stayed where he was, in the Göttengasse, becoming almost a recluse: but sometimes he would find his way to the Süsser Löckel and, with a glass of Baden wine in his hand, recapture his old form and, as the paper puts it 'spend freely from his rich treasury of recollections'. Perhaps he remembered occasionally his words to Hooker (Kew: 12 December 1883) 'whenever my energies tend to give way or when difficulties come upon me I shall with grateful feelings remember that dedication and take fresh courage'.

Many of his old horticultural friends were by this time dead, but I hope that some of his Baden acquaintances came to visit him – perhaps a fellow retired Stadtrat – and that his nephew Camill, now Konsul Camill (an honorary title) had time to come over from Carlsruhe to see him (but Camill himself was to die in 1914 and his brother Rudolf in 1915). For the last four years of his life Dr Emil Klein, described as 'an American dentist' shared Haus Leichtlin, perhaps practising there. It was he who registered Max's death.

But whether or no he was lonely, Max Leichtlin had so many achievements to savour. At the height of his powers he was asked if he could write a book in which he would record all the secrets of his work. 'I am only an apprentice' he replied. (Note 4d) Apprentice or no, because of his work the red *Clematis coccinea* has become the parent of countless others: the red aubrietia finds its place in spring among the mauve and white on the terrace walls, and the late summer borders are full of kniphofia in a great range of yellow, orange and red. Enjoying these feasts of colour, it is good sometimes to think of that small control tower of the world's garden plants on the hill at Baden-Baden.

APPENDIX A

This list does not include hybrids raised by Max Leichtlin

SPECIES INTRODUCED TO EUROPE BY MAX LEICHTLIN (confirmed by *The Botanical Magazine*)

Agave (Leichtlinia)		*Iris sindjarensis*	(t 7145)
protuberans	(t 8429)	*Kniphofia rufa*	(t 7706)
Carpenteria californica	(t 6911)	*Kniphofia tuckii*	(t 7644)
Crocus alexandri	(t 7740)	*Milla leichtlinii*	(t 6236)
Fritillaria aurea	(t 7374)	*Milla porrifolia*	(t 5977)
Fritillaria nobilis	(t 7500)	*Pasithea coerulea*	(t 7249)
Iris gatesii	(t 7867)	*Tulipa sintenisii*	(t 7193)
Iris hookeriana	(t 7276)	*Tulipa violacea*	(t 7440)

SPECIES RE-INTRODUCED TO EUROPE BY MAX LEICHTLIN (confirmed by *The Botanical Magazine*)

Campanula mirabilis	(t 7714)
Calochortus elegans	(t 5976)
Calochortus leichtlinii	(t 5862)

SPECIES CLAIMED BY MAX LEICHTLIN AS INTRODUCED BY HIM, but *The Botanical Magazine* either does not substantiate or does not describe at all

Anemone blanda var. *scythinica*		*Iris sophenensis*
Crocosmia aurea var. *imperialis*		*Papaver glaucum*
Crocosmia aurea var. *maculata*		*Tecophilaea cyanocrocus*
Iris bakeriana	(t 7084)	*Tulipa leichtlinii*
Iris germanica var. *macrantha*		

LIST OF POSSIBLE INTRODUCTIONS TO EUROPE BY MAX LEICHTLIN (*The Botanical Magazine* is either unclear or does not describe at all)

Aconitum fischeri	(t 7130)	*Decaisnea insignis*	(t 6731)
Agapanthus weillighii	(t 9621)	*Haberlea rhodopensis*	(t 6651)
Allium giganteum (part)	(t 6828)	*Hydrangea petiolaris*	(t 6788)
Anemone cernua	(t 7858)	*Incarvillea delavayi*	(t 7462)
Arctotis aureola	(t 6835)	*Iris korolkowi*	(t 7025)
Beochornerea decosteriana	(t 6768)	*Iris sari* var. *lurida*	(t 6960)
Bongardia rauwolfii	(t 6244)	*Iris suwarowi*	(t 7029)
Celmisia lindsayi	(t 7134)	*Kniphofia leichtlinii*	(t 6716)
Clematis coccinea	(t 6594)	*Kniphofia breviflora*	(t 7570)
Codonopsis convolvulacea	(t 8178)	*Kniphofia multiflora*	(t 7832)
Colchicum sibthorpii	(t 7181)	*Kniphofia uvaria* var.	
Crocus veluchensis	(t 6197)	maxima	(t 6553)

Lilium parryi	(t 6650)	*Muscari szovitsianum*	(t 6855)
Lycoris squamigera	(t 7547)	*Scilla messeniaca*	(t 8035)

NOTES

1 Letters from Max Leichtlin to Ellen Willmott are held at Spetchley Park, Worcs. (This one is dated 23 June 1905). (*Abbreviation*: EW)

2 Letters from Max Leichtlin to J. D. (1877 Sir Joseph) Hooker (Director, Royal Botanic Gardens, Kew, 1865–85) and to W. (1899 Sir William) Thiselton-Dyer (Director 1885–1905) are held in the Kew Archives – unless otherwise stated, in *Directors' Correspondence* Vol 140 pp 721–834. (*Abbreviation*: Kew)

3 Correspondence between Max Leichtlin and J. H. Balfour (Regius Keeper of Royal Botanic Garden, Edinburgh 1845–80) and Isaac (1920 Sir Isaac) Bayley Balfour (Regius Keeper 1888–1922) is held in the Archives at the Royal Botanic Garden, Edinburgh. (*Abbreviation*: Edin)

4 Accounts of Leichtlin's garden at Baden-Baden:

a.	*Gartenflora*	Vol 30 (1880) pp 369–75 (Dr E. Regel)
b.		Vol 38 (1889) pp 266–69 (Max Leichtlin)
c.		Vol 41 (1892) pp 607–08 (L. Beissner)
d.	*The Garden*	Vol 37 (1890) pp 546–47 (Rev. Henry Ewbank)
e.	*The Gardeners' Chronicle*	Vol 8 (1890) (3rd Series) pp 5–7 (repeat of d)
f.		Vol 20 (1896) (3rd Series) pp 391–92 (Rev. Henry Ewbank)
g.	*Garden and Forest*	Vol 3 (1890) pp 523–24 (H. J. Elwes)

5 Notes from Baden-Baden:

The Garden	1883–1907 *passim* (see Volume Indices)
Garden and Forest	1888–1897 *passim* (see Volume Indices)

6 Obituaries:

a.	*Tagblatt*	4 September 1910
b.	*Gartenflora*	Vol 59 (1910) pp 510–11 (Dr L. Wittmack)
c.	*Revue Horticole*	Vol 10 (1910) p 445 (New Series)
d.	*Deutsche Obstbauzeitung*	Vol 56 (1910) p 356
e.	*The Garden*	Vol 74 (1910) p x (17 September 1910)
f.	*The Gardeners' Chronicle*	Vol 48 (1910) pp 238–39 (H. J. Elwes) with letters from R. W. Wallace (p 249) and A. Grove (p 286)
g.	*The Gardeners' Magazine*	Vol 53 (1910) p 738
h.	*Journal of Horticulture*	Vol 61 (1910) p 261 (3rd Series)

The author would like to express her thanks to John Berkeley Esq. of Spetchley Park, Worcs.; to the Director of the Royal Botanic Gardens, Kew; and to the Regius Keeper, The Royal Botanic Garden, Edinburgh, for permission to use and to quote from letters in their possession (see Notes 1–3). Thanks are also due, for much patient help and useful information, to the following: the staff of the Lindley Library, and of the Royal Botanic Gardens, Kew; Royal Botanic Garden, Edinburgh; Generallandesarchiv, Karlsruhe; Stadtarchiv, Karlsruhe; Stadtarchiv, Baden-Baden; Deutsche Gartenbau Gesellschaft (including the library in Berlin); Gartenamt, Baden-Baden; and also to Dr E. C. Nelson, of the National Botanic Gardens of Ireland, Glasnevin; Herr Rolf Kohler, Frau Margot Lutze and Dr M. J. Tooley of the University of Durham.

Fully dressed. The retaining walls are used to great effect. Here a yellow
banksia rose and white *Abutilon vitifolium* reach for the balustrading

The Powis Treatment

ANNA PAVORD *vists the outstanding garden on the border of England and Wales*

Powis Castle, in the eighteenth century, was not a place that you would have gone out of your way to see. A traveller in 1784 remarked on the gardens 'laid out in the wretched taste of steps, statues and pavilions' where 'not even the fruit is attended to; the balustrades and terraces are falling down and the horses graze on the parterres.' Paradoxically that neglect was Powis's salvation, for while the most important of the country's landowners were busy modernising their parks and gardens under the stern eye of 'Capability' Brown and his landscape men, Powis mouldered gently on, its Italianate terraces untouched, its untended yews bulging into ever more fantastical shapes against the castle walls.

By the time its owners started taking notice of it again, the danger of a back-to-nature purge was over and the terraces, laid out possibly by William Winde around 1700 for William Herbert, Earl, Marquess and finally Duke of Powis, are recognised today as one of the finest surviving examples of late seventeenth-century taste.

The garden has many natural advantages. The steeply sloping site around the castle is dramatic and the terraces face south-east. The limestone soil drains well and the high walls provide sheltered homes for many rare and tender shrubs.

The ridge opposite the castle is covered in woodland, an eighteenth-century wilderness in sharp contrast to the formal terraces. The soil here is different too, acid loam, perfect for the species planted during the rhododendron craze of the Victorian age. Hidden in the wood is the Ladies' Bath, a rather murky bathing pool fringed with ferns. Great oaks grow in the woodland, as they do throughout the park. In the eighteenth century, Powis oak was in great demand for shipbuilding. Admiral Rodney would have no other for the ships he commissioned for the Royal Navy.

Powis, which now belongs to the National Trust, also has an important unnatural advantage: an opinionated, dedicated and quite brilliant head gardener, Jimmy Hancock, who is as proud and as possessive of his showpiece as any Cicerone. He has an unrivalled eye for a good plant and since the planting here is unencumbered by

Looking out from The Orangery which now houses ferns, ivies and busts of
Caesars

End of April and the box-edged terrace beds are full with emerging perennials
which will display themselves profusely until the autumn frosts

A sheltered seat at the end of the Vine Walk in the Old Kitchen Garden

Late summer and the box-edged beds show no sign of giving up

the ancestor-worship that hangs over other Trust gardens such as Sissinghurst and Hidcote, you will always see something fresh and intriguing. This summer *Salvia guaranitica* with dark leaves and brilliant blue flowers flourished on the lowest terrace. *Dicentra* 'Stuart Boothman' with grey ferny foliage partnered fine variegated sedum. The tender honeysuckle *Lonicera splendens* scrambled up the retaining wall, grey leaves with soft cream flowers.

The most extraordinary thing about Powis, almost a conjuring trick, is that whatever season of the year you choose for your visit, the garden seems to be at its peak. There are none of those gaping holes in the borders that you suppose must have been nice last month, or perhaps will look good next. You can visit from April to October and it will never be anything but stunning.

This sort of non-stop but ever-changing performance demands expert planning and a goodish reserve of plants which can be brought on behind the scenes until they are ready to star. Nothing is put out in the borders until it is a pleasure to look at. Hancock is a perfectionist and it shows, not only in the quality and staggering

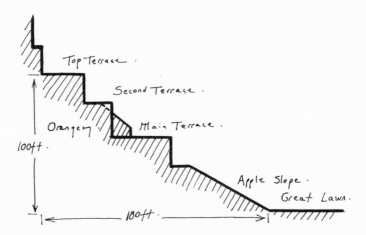

Powis Castle: cross-section drawing by Simon Dorrell. 'From the base of the Castle to the level stretch of lawns below there is a fall of 100 feet, of so rapid a nature that the impression given is of terraces narrower than the height of their retaining walls, although in reality their width is not so inconsiderable.' (Christopher Hussey: *English Gardens and Landscapes 1700–1750*, Country Life, 1967.)

range of the plants he grows, but also in the way that they are staked and pruned and trained.

There are four terraces spilling down the hill on which the castle stands. They appear narrow because of their great length (approaching two hundred yards) but the top terrace is almost 50 ft wide, with views over the great lawn to the Breidden Hills beyond.

The general principle behind the planting has been to group strong colours at the eastern end of the terraces, where they are thrown into relief against the dark bulk of the great yew hedges. Softer colours are used at the western end of the borders.

Though this overall thread continues through the four terraces, each has its own particular character. The top terrace is planted to give a sub-tropical effect: glaucous melianthus with purple hebe, variegated aralia with leaves as long as your arm, exotic spiky phormiums and the slightly sinister *Salvia discolor* with sticky stems and a hooded black flower surmounted by a cap of grey-green. Mounds of the filigree *Artemisia* 'Powis Castle' light up the feet of the yew trees.

Steps lead down one side of the old aviary to a second terrace, where

Lead statues of shepherds and shepherdesses add vitality to the balustrading over The Orangery

the main borders are given over to plants that thrive in dry, sunny conditions. To the west the planting is in soft pink, mauve, pale blue and white. Furry *Phlomis italica* with pale pink flowers partners the rare *Fabiana imbricata* with purple tubes of flowers at the very tips of each growth. *Rosa glauca* is underplanted with perennial pale purple wallflowers and the lime green heads of *Euphorbia niciciana*. Statues of eighteenth-century shepherds and shepherdesses decorate the stone balustrade.

From there, steps lead down to the orangery terrace, where in late May a magnificent Banksian rose will be in full yellow flower. The orangery itself is fine and formal, its cool interior dressed with holly ferns, evergreens and some frowning busts of the Caesars. Outside, the herbaceous borders edged with box are packed with perennials primed to come to their peak at midsummer. The plants chosen are lush and leafy, in contrast to the hot Mediterranean character of the plants on the aviary terrace above. There is a pink cow parsley, *Pimpinella major rosea*; statuesque acanthus and crambe; and greeny-yellow *Thalictrum flavum* growing together with the tall creamy spires of cimicifuga and huge hands of rodgersia, here the pink flowered *R. pinnata*.

The final descent is by way of a grand double staircase to the apple slope terrace. The border east of the steps has been planned for a May-June display, with buddleias giving colour later in the summer. To the west is an autumn border which blazes away through September with hibiscus, the orange *Buddleia globosa* and the variegated buddleia 'Harlequin'. Fuchsias are favourites here and also some rich, lush dahlias such as 'Bishop of Llandaff' and *D. laciniata purpurea*.

In the 1880s and 1890s, the garden was featured several times in the widely-read *Gardeners' Chronicle*. The planting on the terraces was then quite different. Each had a predominant colour theme, the lowest terrace white, the middle yellow and the highest one purple. Praise was lavished on Powis's 'noble drive' through the parkland approaching the castle, 'so unlike the dark inartistic avenue which spoils so many places.'

Special commendation was given to the huge balloons of *Clematis jackmanii* trained over supports seven feet high and five feet wide, which used to dominate the top terrace together with stands of pampas, then hugely popular in gardens. There was a border of

Pyramid apple and pear trees dating from the 1890s in the Old Kitchen
Garden. Each tree stands in its own circular bed with one kind of groundcover plant – examples being golden marjoram and *Stachys lanata*

The elegant brick retaining wall at the foot of the stone-built Castle.
Artemisia 'Powis Castle' at home beneath the great domed yews

carnations and picotees more than two hundred feet long and six feet wide. These were one of the specialities of John Lambert, head gardener at the time, who used to contribute occasional columns to *The Garden*, another popular gardening periodical of the late Victorian age.

The apples that gave the lowest terrace its name have long since gone and have been replaced with a collection of shrubs: *Cornus kousa chinensis*, liquidambar, stranvaesia, magnolias and maples. The apples planted in the old kitchen garden around 1890 still survive and are trained in neat pyramids with wide pools of creeping plants around their feet. The rest of the kitchen garden was transformed by the Countess of Powis into a formal flower garden at the turn of the century. There is a hooped vine walk leading to a seat in an arbour and huge beds of floribunda, shrub and hybrid musk roses.

Though famed for its pineapples, the kitchen garden was never one of Powis's strengths. The *Gardeners' Chronicle* found it disappointingly provided for, having 'only' three vineries, a peach house and seven other span-roofed houses and pits for pines, stove and greenhouse plants, cucumbers and melons. Two further south-facing houses were used for pot vines, early strawberries and beans.

Fuchsias and pelargoniums were always favourites at Powis and still are with Jimmy Hancock, who uses them in quantity when planting up the superb pots, urns, troughs and cisterns with which this garden is so lavishly endowed. Some of the basketwork terracotta pots from the orangery terrace are planted up in spring inside the large greenhouses hidden away alongside the entrance drive. When they are set out in May after the danger of frost has gone, they are already well established. Fuchsias and geraniums respond particularly well to this sort of gentle forcing and they are the mainstay of the planting schemes for the containers. Both are what he calls 'good doers' and both can be relied on to give a long performance. In a garden that is open to the public for seven months of the year, this is an important consideration. The fuchsias are woven round with helichrysum, felicias both variegated and plain, pale lobelia, or diascia.

Fine-leaved pelargoniums are mixed with the small-leaved *Helichrysum microphylla*, a less enthusiastic coloniser than its bossy cousin *H. petiolare*. Heliotrope looks well with grey-leaved plants. So does *Plumbago capensis*. One of the pots was planted up for a shady corner with small cuttings taken from the golden cut-leaved elder *Sambucus racemosa* 'Plumosa Aurea' which has very finely fringed leaves of pale yellow. Its companions were the blue lance-shaped leaves of hosta and a lime-coloured helichrysum.

The terraces, blasted out of the rocky outcrop, have survived as an unaltered part of the original garden layout but other areas on flatter terrain where there was more room for manoeuvre have been through several transformations. Adrian Duval, a Frenchman who was in the retinue of the Countess of Powis when she returned from her Dutch exile in 1703, seems to have been involved in designing water gardens for the ground below the terraces. The lead statue of Fame, now standing in the forecourt of the castle, was originally made for the water garden. So was the impressive group of Hercules and the Hydra, now at the end of the top terrace.

William Emes, who was responsible for much of the tree planting in the park, swept away the whole of the waterworks in the 1770s and laid out the great lawn in their place. It is an awe-inspiring stretch of turf and, with a masterly stroke of showmanship, Jimmy Hancock had fourteen of the gardening staff at Powis working in a great line raking it on the day this summer that the head gardeners' club, the Professional Gardeners' Guild, happened to be meeting at Powis and happened to be looking out over the lawn from the terraces above. Since most of them have to make do with a quarter of Powis's staff they were greener than the grass with envy.

It was Violet, a later Countess of Powis, wife of the Fourth Earl, who began to enrich the planting of the terraces in the early years of this century. She also laid out the small fountain garden that lies in the east corner of the grounds. Recently the gardeners undertook the massive job of cutting back all the bulky yew hedges around this garden, reducing their width by half, taking the side branches right back to the main trunks of the trees. New growth is already greening up the skeleton framework and when this is well established, the outer faces of the hedge will be given 'the Powis treatment'. This is one of Hancock's favourite phrases. If you admire a particularly good stand of plants, be it *Nepeta sibirica*, *Aconitum carneum* or *Morinia longifolia*, he will smile and say 'Ah – given the Powis treatment you see'.

The huge gates that mark the end of the vista in the fountain garden carry the coat of arms of the Powis family and were copied

Back stage. Two of the glass-houses and a range of cold frames where 'the Powis Treatment' is practiced. Plants are raised here for the garden and a few are always on sale to visitors in the stable block near the garden entrance

from the gates which used to stand in front of Powis House in London. They were put up in 1912, a powerful embodiment of the garden's twentieth-century renaissance. Now, under the careful guardianship of the National Trust, there is every reason to hope that it will never languish again.

Powis Castle is situated off the A483 1 mile south of Welshpool. Consult the National Trust Handbook *for opening times.*

Major surgery. To reduce the width of the ageing hedges around the Old Kitchen Garden the yews were cut back to the main stem. This seemingly-drastic measure must only be undertaken in the spring and to one side of the hedge only. When satisfactory re-growth has been achieved in the following or second year the other side could be similarly treated

Photographs by David Wheeler

A Tribute to Robin Tanner *1904-1988*

DAVID WHEELER

ONE OF THIS century's great recorders of native plants (the term 'botanical illustrator' seems inappropriate) died on 19th May just a few days before a broad exhibition of his work opened at The Old School Gallery in Bleddfa, Powys.

Robin Tanner, born in 1904, was primarily an etcher; the plates and drawings for *Wiltshire Village* which illustrate both the real and an idealised way of life in his dearly-held home county are perhaps the final witness to the last days of a rural existence before mighty machines and 'the folly of greedy prairie farming' changed England forever. *Wiltshire Village*, written with his wife Heather, was first published in 1939 on the eve of another event which was to impose its own devastating changes.

During those war years Robin Tanner began a series of pen and ink drawings for another book in collaboration with his wife: *Woodland Plants* (first published by Robin Garton in 1981 and then by Impact Books in 1987). Heather Tanner, who has kindly given permission for some drawings from that book to be included in this issue of HORTUS as part of our tribute to her late husband, wrote the text which accompanies the numerous drawings contained in that volume. With this journal's own manner of showing plants and gardens in monochromatic tones it is worth repeating what the artist said in this context: ". . . in a world of black and white only [I was] trying to compensate for the absence of colour by emphasising the variety of textures and tones and the characteristic forms of stalks and leaves and flowers and fruits."

Many of the native species shown in *Woodland Plants* have found a secure place in our gardens: snowdrops, winter aconites, foxgloves, monkshood, daffodils and martagon lilies are just a few. With these drawings to hand it is an easy task to nominate others for domestic cultivation, propagated by *seed*, of course. Many people will have encountered these plants only in a garden setting which is in itself a further comment upon what has already been lost. Those who champion what we call now "wild-flower gardening" will find much in this book to further their exciting cause. By concentrating on 'textures and tones and the characteristic forms' Robin Tanner demonstrated, perhaps better than any man, the startling beauty of our native flora which, especially when seen in natural terrain, is so often taken for granted. These drawings are not dry botanical renderings fit only for the herbarium, but powerful creative statements of importance and beauty – as much Art as anything else.

By many accounts Robin Tanner was a generous man – generous with his time, with his work and with his knowledge. In *Double Harness* (Impact Books, 1987) he gives prominence to his life-long devotion to education and the encouragement of youngsters in the book's subtitle: 'an autobiography [by] a teacher and etcher.'

Knowing that he would be too ill to travel from his home in Wiltshire to the Welsh border for his exhibition in Bleddfa in May Robin Tanner made a short tape recording to be played at the opening. In just a few minutes of speech it seems that he was able to define most accurately the impetus which drove him throughout his long life and which enabled him to work almost right up to the moment of his death:

"*. . . It is my firm belief that we all come to this world with the attributes and gifts of the artist and craftsman, and because we human beings are so made, and the planet we inhabit for a few decades is so made, we have in-*

Columbine, *Aquilegia vulgaris*. Drawing by Robin Tanner for
Woodland Plants.

evitably through the ages, been impelled to find some transfiguring language of the imagination with which to make articulate our deepest feelings and responses. We draw out of life all that we have the urge and capacity to take, thus reaching that state of rightness and potency which impels us to give back to life something that is our very best and uniquely our own; our experience has been so enriching that we are moved to do something about it, and this language we call The Arts. They are therefore at the very core, the centre of life. If the proper dignity and the essential creativeness of every individual is respected he comes, through the arts, into his full inheritance and life is simple and uncluttered, courageous, full of hope, and certainly happy. I am convinced that that is as it is meant to be . . .

"Certainly in my long life nothing has withheld me from doing the work I was born to do, and that surely has been my enormous good fortune. As a boy I had two great abiding passions: to be a teacher and to be an artist. They have never left me. It has been my great good fortune to live two long happy lives, in art and in education, and the one has never stifled or hindered the other. So etching is only part of me. I have no high opinion of my work. If I have a talent, it is a minor one. I regard what I have etched as a natural overflow of my deep love of the Wiltshire counrtyside where most of my life has been spent. North-west Wiltshire, not far from the Gloucestershire broder; Cotswold with a Wiltshire difference: less precious and less self-conscious, more earthy and in feeling much more ancient . . .

"But why did I choose the complicated craft of etching? I love to paint, but etching speaks to my condition absolutely. When I first held in my hands the incomparable etchings of Rembrandt I was astonished at their vast range of tones, of dazzling white, tender silvery greys, deep rich velvety blacks. It amazed me that with a needle and a sheet of copper this extraordinary man could convey his deepest feelings for human tragedy and ecstasy, for the poignant beauty of the natural world and of the human head, and with it all a celebration of light and darkness . . . In the hands of a great genius, etching can say all. We have learnt little since Rembrandt . . .

"I think it must be clear to anyone seeing my work for the first time that I am not a topographical artist, I depend on hundreds of studies which I make from nature but I use them in my own way . . .

"The limited edition has never appealed to me, and I never cancel a plate. As long as it will yield good impressions I like it to be used. If we have not, by our own wanton wickedness, destroyed the world before the dawn of the twenty-first century, I hope a few people will still care to print with them to see what pleasure I took in trying to record the life I knew . . ."

Gardens in Fiction

The Haunted Gardens of M. R. James

HERMIA OLIVER

Who, alone, in the small hours, has not experienced a delicious terror when some macabre sound or inexplicable movement must surely be supernatural? Hence the lure of haunted houses. A writer of splendid ghost stories, Montague Rhodes James (1862–1936), has three gardens in his tales. They are not gardens inspired by ones he knew best, the Cambridge college gardens or the Eton garden created by and named after his tutor there, H. E. Luxmoore. James had other fish to fry. His ghosts are remote from commonplace apparitions or melancholy nuns. They are extremely malevolent or intent on revenge. They become so real because their histories are so convincing. Thus the person with an intensely horrible face in 'Oh, Whistle, and I'll Come to You, My Lad' who, but for the intervention of a friend, would have pushed Professor Parkins backwards through a window, was the ghost of a man foully murdered in an East Anglian preceptory of the Knights Templar, while the exquisitely modelled figure of a crouching cat in 'The Stalls of Barchester Cathedral' was carved from the timber of a hanging oak in a neighbouring grove. James's gardens are unforgettable for other than horticultural reasons.

Monty James was the son of a devout evangelical curate who inherited a 17th-century house near Bury St Edmunds, Suffolk. Even as a schoolboy he was exploring churches and collecting such writings as early Christian texts of too doubtful authenticity to be included in the Bible. His detailed knowledge of East Anglia appears in his *Suffolk and Norfolk*, published in 1930. He was a scholar, and while a don and later Provost of King's College, he catalogued all the historical manuscripts in Cambridge – one of the illuminated MSS appears memorably in 'Canon Alberic's Scrap-book'. As soon as the pneumatic tyre was patented (1888), he spent holidays year after year cycling in Europe – holidays which provided the realistic background of St Bertrand de Comminges in 'Canon Alberic's Scrap-book' and of Jutland in 'Number 13' and 'Count Magnus'. He was Provost of King's from 1905 till 1918 and then Provost of

Eton until his death. His knowledge of medieval and biblical history included the spellings and language of the period, which he sometimes parodied. Part of his fascination is that he makes very ordinary people belonging to the pre-World War I era, with their domestic servants, gardeners and chauffeurs, become beset by powers of darkness.

In 'The Rose Garden' (*More Ghost Stories of an Antiquary*, 1911), Mrs Anstruther, of Westfield Hall, Essex, 'a stately dame of some fifty summers', demanded that her husband George, who was longing to play golf that morning, should take the gardener, Collins, to the site of her new rose garden – a small dank clearing, overshadowed by box bushes, laurels and other evergreens just off the shrubbery path to the church. When he asked if there was enough sun there Mrs Anstruther, who described herself as 'a great gardener', crushingly replied 'My dear George, do allow me *some* common sense.' There would be plenty of sun when they had got rid of some of the bushes. She wanted Collins to clear away the remains of rustic seats and an old post in the middle of the site before she came out in an hour's time.

George, who obviously believed in peace at any price, obeyed. Displaying no 'enthusiasm', Collins said he could clear away 'them seats' soon enough but, after shaking the post, said it was firm in the ground and doubted he 'shan't get that up not quite so soon as what I can do with them seats.' It would take him till after tea-time, and he added 'If you'll pardon me, sir, this ain't the place I should have picked out for no rose garden myself.'

Mrs Anstruther received George's report with some displeasure. By 4 p.m. she had dismissed him to his golf, dealt with Collins and other duties and had just settled down to continue a sketch of the church when a maid announced Miss Wilkins, 'a person of mature years' who was one of the few remaining members of the family from whom the Anstruthers had bought the estate. This was a farewell visit. When Mrs Anstruther showed her the site of her rose garden, Miss Wilkins described seeing her brother Frank asleep on a bench in the old summer-house one day 'but with such a dreadful look on his face' she 'thought he must be ill or even dead.' When she shook him he woke up with a scream and was in a terrible state all evening. For days she couldn't get any explanation from him but at last he described a dream in which he was standing in a large room with a number of people in it. Someone very powerful opposite him was asking questions. When he answered, that person or another in the room seemed to be making up something against him. The dream ended by his being taken up some creaking wooden steps and stood on a sort of platform. A small fire was burning somewhere near him. Then he was in a worse fright than ever and if she hadn't woken him up, he didn't know what would have become of him. Later in the year, when Miss Wilkins was alone in the arbour, she heard a whispering sounding like 'Pull, pull. I'll push, you pull.' The voice was hoarse and angry and seemed a long way off though it was strongest when she put her ear to an old post at the end of the seat. When her father knew of the fright both of them had had, he had the arbour pulled down.

But Mrs Anstruther must have taken a 'common sense' view and dismissed Miss Wilkins's tale as the maundering of an old woman. One feels that if she had actually made her rose garden, it would have been horribly regimented and interplanted with calceolaria or scarlet salvia. By the evening the seats were cleared and the post was uprooted.

That night Mrs Anstruther was sure that roughs had got in to the plantation and commanded George to tell Collins to do something about the owls – she was positive that a very large one perched somewhere just outside their window. George then told her of a nightmare he had had which was almost identical with Frank Wilkins's.

In the afternoon Mrs Anstruther returned to her sketch again until the light faded. On her way back to the house she saw a horrible face, 'large, smooth, and pink', with an open mouth showing a single tooth, peeping out among the branches of a box bush.

After the Anstruthers had spent a week recovering in Brighton, a letter came from the Essex Archaeological Society asking whether they possessed the original of an engraving representing 'Sir ———— ————', Lord Chief Justice under Charles II, who had returned to Westfield after his disgrace and was supposed to have died of remorse there. The rector had summoned parsons from neighbouring parishes to lay his ghost. An entry in a parish register said that the stake was in a field adjoining Westfield churchyard. Mrs Anstruther's shock on receiving this news made her decide to spend the winter abroad.

Though James does not identify 'Sir ———— ————', he was probably Sir William Scroggs, Lord Chief Justice from 1678, who presided over the trials of several victims of the Titus Oates plot. Those found guilty of treason were barbarically sentenced to be hanged, drawn and quartered. The fire disposed of the entrails. Scroggs is believed to have compared unfavourably with Judge Jeffreys. However, James's sources seem to have misled him in one respect. Scroggs was impeached and demoted in 1681 but was granted a pension. He retired to his manor of South Weald, Essex, but, according to the *Dictionary of National Biography*, died at his town house. There is no mention of remorse.

The outstanding feature of the garden in 'Mr Humphreys and his Inheritance' (*More Ghost Stories of an Antiquary*, 1911) is a circular yew maze surrounded by a high wall. It had been totally neglected for three or four decades so that the overgrown hedges, nettles and brambles had made it all but impassable. Over the padlocked gate at the entrance was a motto in Latin, 'My secret is for me and for the sons of my house.' Near the maze was a Temple of Friendship, a smaller version of the Temple of the Sibyl at Tivoli, 'helped out with a dome'. Both were in the grounds of a late eighteenth-century East Anglian mansion inherited by Mr Humphreys from an uncle he had never met. Since Humphreys had spent five years as a government servant, at that date he must have had a public school education, of course enabling him to read Latin inscriptions.

He was shown the temple on his tour of the grounds with the bailiff, who told him that the pile of thick circular blocks on its floor had been removed from the maze. Each had a single letter deeply cut on its upper surface. Humphreys set off towards the maze while the bailiff went to get the key to the gate. When he did not return, Humphreys impatiently kicked at the lock, which fell at his feet. He forced his way through and, evidently because he was a son of the house, he found the centre. There was a stone column with on top of it a globe engraved with outline figures and letters. He thought it was a celestial globe but it was too dark to see properly. When the bailiff, who followed the track Humphreys had beaten out, caught up with him, he explained he had not been able to find the key. Asked if he had any idea why his uncle had kept the place locked, the bailiff knew only that even when Lady

Wardrop, 'a *great* gardener', had applied for permission to see it, she was refused. His uncle had disliked the memory of his grandfather who had the maze laid out. His remains were not included in the family vault, though a tablet was put up to him in the parish church.

James's maze may have been suggested to him by the one at Somerleyton Hall, near Lowestoft, but he transformed it into a very sinister one. He did this first by introducing a late seventeenth-century sermon entitled 'A Parable of this Unhappy Condition', which Humphreys found in the library. In it a man went in to a maze in search of a jewel that would enrich the finder for life. He found there were creatures 'peering and looking at him', and when it got dark he heard a band of them rustling, creaking and whispering. When he paused, so did they. He ran, and sometimes out of breath, lay flat on his face, but his pursuers too paused and he could hear them pant and snuff, causing 'so extream an Horrour of mind' that he tried turning and doubling to throw them off the scent. He was eventually found unconscious outside the maze. The parable lay in the jewel as an emblem of satisfaction with this world's pleasures which, it was unnecessary to explain, turn to dust and ashes.

Humphreys did not take heed of the warning given by the inscription on the gate, and of course neither he nor the head gardener was able to lead the bailiff's wife and daughter to the centre. Humphreys promised to make a plan and then found, now that the brambles and weeds had been cleared, that the globe was not a celestial one. It was encircled by a winged serpent. In the upper hemisphere a large figure with outspread wings was inscribed 'the prince of darkness'. A hatched space denoted 'the shadow of death' and figures resembling patriarchs of evil appeared in the lower hemisphere.

Humphreys was unexpectedly delayed in completing the plan and in the meanwhile had a letter from Lady Wardrop requesting permission to see the maze, soon if possible, as she was shortly going abroad for the winter and wanted to include it in a Book of Mazes she was about to publish. He suggested the following day and finished the plan in the interval. He and Lady Wardrop, 'a stout elderly person, very full of talk', both made a thorough examination of the grounds. She was particularly delighted with the temple, and told him one of her mazes had a track marked out with lettered tiles just like his blocks. Taken in the right order, the letters formed an inscription. She would never forgive him if he injured his maze – almost every day mazes were being grubbed up.

Both went in without hindrance, although Lady Wardrop manifestly did not qualify for entrance. She pointed out a series of little depressions in the ground which she thought marked the places of the lettered blocks, and dated the maze to about 1780. The globe was unique in her experience and she wanted a rubbing, though she trusted Humphreys would not attempt it on her account. 'I shouldn't like to take any liberties here. I have the feeling that it might be resented.' She asked if he hadn't felt that a watch was being kept on them and that if they overstepped the mark in any way, there would be 'well, a pounce'. On the way back to the house she said she wasn't sure that if, after all, she wouldn't forgive him if next spring she found the maze had been grubbed up. He promised to trace a copy of the plan for her that very day. On her way out she told him that it might be worth his while to look at the underside of the stones in the temple.

Humphreys began tracing his plan that evening, when the windows had to be open as it was still and stuffy. He 'had more than one grisly encounter with a bat', or something more considerable. When he compared his tracing with the original, there was a bad confusion at the centre. He carefully followed the last turnings of the path leading without a hitch to the middle space – but there was an ugly black spot 'about the size of a shilling' which resembled a hole, though a very odd hole which seemed to go not only through the page but right through the table too. 'Yes, and through the floor below that, down and still down, even into infinite depths.' From the first it was hateful to him but he had gazed at it some moments before a feeling of anxiety came upon him, 'stronger and stronger – a horror lest something might emerge from it, and a really agonizing conviction that a terror was on its way, from the sight of which he would not be able to escape.' Far down there was a movement upwards, coming nearer and nearer. It was of a blackish grey colour and took shape as 'a *burnt* human face'. With the odious writhings of a wasp creeping out of a rotten apple, there clambered out the appearance of a form, waving black arms prepared to clasp the head bending over them. 'With a convulsion of despair

Humphreys threw himself back, struck his head against a hanging
lamp, and fell.' After a long spell in bed with concussion and shock,
he asked for the globe in the maze to be opened. The doctor eventually told him that it all went to bits with the first blow of the chisel.
'It was half full of stuff like ashes' – the cremated remains of its
creator.

The maze was grubbed up and Lady Wardrop proved right about
the stones in the temple. Thanks to a numeral on each, Humphreys
was able to reconstruct the inscription 'Penetrans ad interiora
mortis.' ('Penetrating to the inner places of death.') One of the
oddest things was the disapperrance of the book containing the
parable.

At a later date than the completion of Castringham Hall, an
Elizabethan country house in Suffolk, the setting of 'The Ash-Tree'
(*Ghost Stories of an Antiquary*, 1904) its squire, after travelling in Italy,
had some indifferent Roman marbles installed about the entrance
hall and gardens and, again, a representation of the Sibyl's temple at
Tivoli erected on the opposite bank of the mere. But the main
feature of the garden was an ash tree close to the wall of the house.
The Hall (suggested probably by a haunted country house James
visited at Nun Monckton, Yorkshire, in 1898) had been completed
in 1690, when a number of trials of witches took place in the district;
its owner, Sir Matthew Fell, Deputy Sheriff, had watched a Mrs
Mothersole from his window on three occasions, gathering twigs
from this ash-tree at full moon. Clad only in her shift she seemed to
be talking to herself while she cut off twigs with a peculiar knife.
Each time Sir Matthew did his best to capture her but she had
always been alarmed by some accidental noise and all he could see
when he got down to the garden was a hare running in the direction
of the village. On the third night he went straight to her house, but
only after battering at her door for a quarter of an hour did she come
out, very cross and apparently very sleepy. Mainly on this evidence,
despite efforts to save her made by several farmers of good standing,
she was found guilty and, with five or six more reputed witches,
was hanged a week after the trial in the presence of the squire.
Whereas the other witches were apathetic or broken down with
misery, Mrs Mothersole's 'poysonous Rage' was described as that
of a 'mad Divell', and she looked at those who laid hands on her with
so dreadful and venomous an aspect that it preyed on their minds.

All she was reputed to have said was, 'There will be guests at the Hall.'

A few weeks later, when Lady Fell was away, the vicar had supper with the squire at the Hall and at full moon both took a turn on the gravelled walk at the back of the house. Sir Matthew wondered what it was that ran up and down the ash. The vicar could have sworn it had more than four legs. Next day Sir Matthew did not appear. When the servants opened his door they found him dead and black. There were no marks of violence, but the window was open. His body was twisted as if he had died in great pain though there was no trace of venom in his evening drink of small ale. The physicians who examined the skin of the breast with a magnifying lens found only a couple of small punctures. They concluded the venom might have been introduced there.

The room in which Sir Matthew had died was not occupied by his son, Sir Matthew; he died a natural death in 1735, but during his reign there was increasing mortality among his cattle and livestock until he shut them up at night, after which it affected wild birds and beasts of the chase. It was his son, Sir Richard, who travelled in Italy and introduced the Italian features to the garden and a pillared portico. He also had a great family pew built out on the north side of the parish church, disturbing several graves, including Mrs Mothersole's, on that unhallowed side of the building. When she was exhumed, though her coffin was sound, there was no trace of body, bones or dust in it.

Sir Richard did not sleep in his grandfather's room until he once had a very bad night caused by a smoking chimney and something rattling the windows. Then he decided he must sleep in another room, facing west so that the sun would not wake him up too early, and also out of the way of the business of the house. When his housekeeper told him that the only room like that in the house was Sir Matthew's West Chamber, he decided to have it. In the afternoon guests arrived. Sir Richard did not open the window that night but was kept awake by noise he thought came from twigs sweeping the glass. However, one of the visitors, the Bishop of Kilmore, pointed out that none of the branches could touch the window except in a gale. They agreed that rats must have come up through the ivy, covering the dust on the sill with lines and marks.

The next night was still and warm, so the window was open. The following morning Sir Richard was found dead and black in bed. As the party of guests and servants gathered under the window they saw a white tom-cat in the lower boughs of the ash crouching and looking down into the hollow of the trunk. As it craned over, a bit of the edge it was standing on broke and it slithered in. There were two or three screams and then 'a slight and muffled noise of some commotion or struggling'. They got a gardener to go up on a ladder with a lantern let down by a rope and saw his face struck 'with an incredulous terror and loathing before he cried out in a dreadful voice and fell back from the ladder'. The lantern fell inside the tree, setting it on fire. First the watchers saw a round body the size of a man's head, covered with fire, which fell back five or six times. Then another leapt into the air and fell on the grass. When the bishop went as near as he dared, he saw that it was the remains of an enormous spider, veinous and seared. As the fire burned lower down, more of the spiders darted out and were killed. When, after a long interval, no more appeared, they found below the tree roots a hollow place where two or three spiders had been smothered by smoke. At the side against the wall was the crouching skeleton of a human being, with the skin dried on its bones and having some remains of black hair. It was pronounced to be undoubtedly the body of a woman dead for a period of fifty years.

No wonder Monty's friends at King's were thrilled by the ghost stories he read them at Christmas; no wonder boys at Eton between 1918 and 1936 prized deeply an invitation to the Lodge.

Who's Who

NIGEL COLBORN writes about horticulture and farming. He is the author of *The Container Garden* (1990) and lives with his wife and children at Careby Manor in Lincolnshire.

BETH CHATTO is the author of several books including *The Dry Garden* (1978), *The Damp Garden* (1982) and *Beth Chatto's Garden Notebook* (1988). Her garden and nursery are at Elmstead Market near Colchester, Essex.

JOHN FRANCIS writes regularly for HORTUS about gardens in fiction. His other subjects have included E. F. Benson, Ronald Firbank, Barbara Pym, Molly Keane and Alice Thomas Ellis.

HEDVIKA FRASER is a translator working in Czechoslovak, Russian and Polish. She participates in botanical tours around the world and tends her orchids in Lincolnshire.

NANCY-MARY GOODALL writes and lectures on many horticultural aspects and is also a garden photographer. She is a regular contributor to HORTUS.

STEPHEN G. HAW has been both a student and a teacher in a Chinese university. His book *The Lilies of China* was published in 1986.

JOHN HUBBARD is a painter and a gardener. His 2-acre hillside garden at Chilcombe, near Bridport, Dorset is occasionally open to the public.

STEPHEN LACEY is the author of *The Startling Jungle* (1986) and *Scent in your Garden* (1991).

ALVILDE LEES-MILNE gardens in the village of Badminton, Gloucestershire. With Rosemary Verey she co-edited *The Englishwoman's Garden* (1980), and its two sequels, *The Englishman's Garden* (1982) and *The New Englishwoman's Garden* (1987).

AUDREY LE LIÈVRE is the author of *Miss Willmott of Warley Place* (1980). Her work for HORTUS includes a valuable series of monographs about tulips, violas and primulas.

HAZEL LE ROUGETEL has written widely about roses. Her two books are *A Heritage of Roses* (1988) and *The Chelsea Gardener*, a biography of Philip Miller, published in 1990.

GILLIAN MAWREY has been Literary Editor of *Commonwealth* and *The European* magazines. She has written for HORTUS about the gardens at Glyndebourne and the Château de Villandry in the Loire Valley.

PAUL MILES is a garden designer whose practice is based in Wood-bridge, Suffolk. He regularly lectures on plants and gardens.

JOHN NEGUS is a freelance writer contributing to a number of British magazines.

CAVAN O'BRIEN is a former National Trust tenant of The Hunting Lodge.

HERMIA OLIVER is the author of *Flaubert and an English Governess* and has written for HORTUS about the gardens in Flaubert's novels and about Colette's gardens and the gardens at Malmaison.

MIRABEL OSLER is the author of *A Gentle Plea for Chaos* (1989) and recently completed a manuscript about contemporary French gardens.

ANNA PAVORD is the Saturday garden columnist of *The Independent* and the presenter of a successful series of garden programmes on British television.

RALEIGH TREVELYAN is a publisher whose own book, *The Golden Oriole* (1987), recalls his five journeys to India.

DAVID SAYERS runs his own travel programme of botanical holidays to many parts of the world and writes in HORTUS often about plants in many countries.

Index

Page numbers in *italic* refer to the illustrations

HORTUS Subscription information

HORTUS is available by post and can be sent to an address anywhere in the world.

Full subscription details available from

HORTUS
The Neuadd
Rhayader
Powys LD6 5HH, Wales

Telephone: Rhayader (0597) 810227; Facsimile: Rhayader (0597) 811386